Devon Jackson has written about a variety of subjects for publications such as *Vanity Fair*, *The New York Times*, *Outside*, *The Village Voice*, and *Rolling Stone*. He can be e-mailed at djsponge@juno.com.

Official Memorandum

Conspiranoia!

The Mother of All Conspiracy Theories

Devon Jackson

A Plume Book

This book was not prepared, approved, licensed, or endorsed by any of the owners of the trademarks or brand names referred to in this book.

PLUME
Published by the Penguin Group
Penguin Putnam Inc., 375 Hudson Street, New York, New York 10014, U.S.A.
Penguin Books Ltd, 27 Wrights Lane, London W8 5TZ, England
Penguin Books Australia Ltd, Ringwood, Victoria, Australia
Penguin Books Canada Ltd, 10 Alcorn Avenue, Toronto, Ontario, Canada M4V 3B2
Penguin Books (N.Z.) Ltd, 182–190 Wairau Road, Auckland 10, New Zealand

Penguin Books Ltd, Registered Offices:
Harmondsworth, Middlesex, England

First published by Plume, a member of Penguin Putnam Inc.

First Plume Printing, January, 2000
10 9 8 7 6 5 4 3 2 1

Ⓟ REGISTERED TRADEMARK—MARCA REGISTRADA

LIBRARY OF CONGRESS CATALOGING-IN-PUBLICATION DATA
Jackson, Devon.
Conspiranoia! : the mother of all conspiracy theories / Devon Jackson.
p.   cm.
ISBN 0-452-28128-8
1. Conspiracies.   I. Title.
HV6275.J33   2000
909—dc21   99-28706
                                                                      CIP

Printed in the United States of America
Set in Mrs. Eaves
Designed by Mark Melnick

Contents

Contents

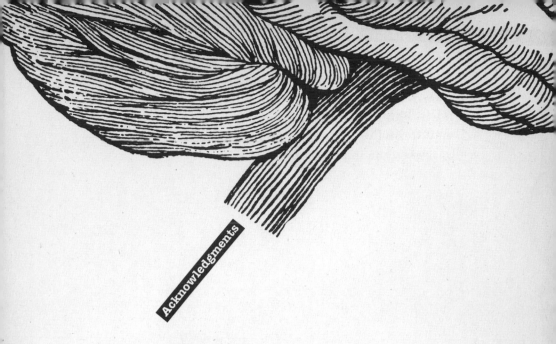

Acknowledgments

I've tried to give credit where credit is due, but because of the unique admixture of this project, because of what has been proven and what has yet to be proven, which is the essence of all conspiracy theories, I decided not to supply *Conspiranoia!* with any sources or references—in the same way, if not for the exact same reasons, E. L. Doctorow or Tom Clancy chose not to provide references or sources for books like *Ragtime* or *The Hunt for Red October*. Still, I must acknowledge and thank three groups of people: my family and friends who stuck with me throughout this whole sick process (Deborah Grossman, Joan McCann, Bonnie and Sy, Marc Maron, Ken Cunningham, Laura LaRosa, John, John, Papa, Kyle, and J⁴); my colleagues and other publishing people who in one way or another had a hand in *Conspiranoia!* (Sally Chew, Abigail Thomas, Daniel Greenberg, Deb Brody, Lisa Kennedy, Andrew Lee, Lisa Chase, Nora Krug, Matt Tyrnauer, Alex Heard, Bill Shapiro, and Stephen Wright); and to the many journalists, writers, and assorted conspiranoiacs who've paved the way and without whose work there would be no *Conspiranoia!* (George Johnson, Jonathan Vankin, Alex Constantine, Kenn Thomas, Jim Keith, Oliver Stone, Ron Rosenbaum, Philip Weiss, Jim Hougan, Christopher Hitchens, Susan Faludi, Michael Moore, John Loftus, Seymour Hersh, Adam Parfrey, Sara

Diamond, Jack Anderson, Martin Lee and Bruce Shlain, James Ridgeway, Neil Postman, Janet Lowe, Jim Martin, Duncan Roads, Al Hidell, Phil Mushnick, and Leslie Savan).

To all those I've left out or forgotten to cite, my bad, although really, it was done to protect the innocent.

Conspiranoia (kən - spir - ə - noí - ə): *n*. The tendency on the part of an individual or group toward rational or irrational, justifiable or excessive suspiciousness and distrustfulness of others based on the belief that others have joined in a secret agreement to commit an unlawful or wrongful act.

The earth is hollow. There's a vast subterranean network of alien government bases underneath the very ground we all walk on. The smallpox and polio vaccines are part of a federal plot to catalog people for future mind-control experiments. There's a 200-mile-per-gallon car out there and a limitless supply of crude oil, but the auto industry and the oil cartels have prevented both from ever reaching consumers. The ink used to print the words you're reading has a top-secret chemical in it that will be used to trace your every movement.

Sound familiar?

When Dostoyevsky wrote about terrible beauty, he may as well have been talking about the pretty scary, scary-pretty relationship between paranoia and conspiracy theories. After all, just because you're paranoid doesn't mean that people aren't out to get you. That's the beauty of paranoia. The scary part about conspiracy theories is that even the most outlandish of scenarios has a wisp of the possible in it somewhere. (John Tesh *must* be an extraterrestrial.)

Who knows just when it was that paranoia took hold of folks (Was it a post—Industrial Revolution development? Did it run rampant in the Roman senate?), or when this or that conspiracy notion really began to seep into our collective unconscious. But by now, before most non-Semitic peoples have met a Jew, before the typical teenager has given up nearly 20 percent of his or her first paycheck to the federal government or can explain the difference between the CIA and the FBI, they've already heard the age-old fancies that the Jews control the media and the banks, the IRS laid claim to all but our souls at birth, and the two intelligence agencies have been and always will be directly or indirectly responsible for any and all of the country's (and the world's) darker deeds—from assassinations and brainwashings to wiretappings and coups d'état and anything and everything in between.

It's an Us versus Them proposition. Or, more to the point, it's *You* versus Them. (It's in your DNA—and, most likely, it's a chromosome implanted in you *by Them*.) And you don't exactly know who *They* are. (What is a Freemason? An Illuminati? Who are the Insiders? What does the Trilateral Commission do?) But They know *you* and *your kind* very, very well.

They. They are the nameless figures in dark suits, the black helicopters buzzing in the night sky. They are the cabals, the corporations, the faceless entities pulling the strings, pulling *your* strings. They want money, power, control—and you. And for every scrap of information you knowingly or unknowingly reveal to Them, in return you're given misinformation, disinformation, no information, or way too much information.

They. They carry out their covert operations in ivory towers and back alleys, in boardrooms and jungles. They wink, they exchange secret handshakes, they wash one another's backs. They love titles with words like *International* and *World* and *Central.* They love words like *synergy* and phrases such as *plausible deniability.*

They want more money, more power, more control—and more information about *you*, more control over *you.*

As Fox Mulder said on *The X-Files*: They prevaricate. They deny. They obfuscate. And always, They leave you one step behind at best. Left in their wake to pick up the pieces, uncover the hidden meanings, follow the trails of paper and blood, map out the genealogies, chart the connections, decipher the symbologies and codes. But where did They all come from? And where are They taking you?

While not the be-all and end all of conspiracy webs, this book should provide you with enough of a historical map to the cover-ups and covert operations—and outline who's who, who's done what, and who's sleeping with whom—for you to finally get a grip on where They came from and where They want to take you.

Here's how to use this book: Each chapter, beginning with the Master Plan, which outlines all the major players (the folks who lie at the bitter root of virtually every other conspiracy theory), opens with a map of sorts, a visual guide that shows just how everyone and everything connects. The book is arranged somewhat chronologically, and the entries in every chapter are organized alphabetically. Each entry is then defined but only the first time it appears: for example, the Nazis, who first show up in "The Master Plan," are defined there and only there. However, each subsequent entry of the Nazis—and they turn up in many other later chapters—is cross-referenced with an appropriate chapter icon that represents other chapters in which the Nazis appear. Also, within each entry are people, groups, or events that appear in boldface type. This means that each word in boldface has its own entry, which can be located by looking in the index. For example, Henry Kissinger's defining entry is in "The Church-22 Conspiracy," and is also highlighted in the definition for the Banco Nazionale del Lavoro in "The Curious George Conspiracy."

So that's how to work the book, now how the book works.

Is it fact? Is it fiction? Creative nonfiction? Rumor and urban myth, or suppressed secrets finally brought to light? It's all of the above and more, because that's how conspiranoiacs work, be they Ralph Nader or the late Mae Brussell (a legend among conspiracists and whose dogged muckraking skills were no less intense than her wonderfully widely cast theories). Most conspiranoiacs often rely, at first (if not entirely) on supposition, on perception. Which is not to say that they're living in a bad dream world and not in reality but that they're willing to follow any and all paper trails, even if those trails lead them into some murky depraved never-neverland behind the looking glass, even if they never produce a smoking gun that vindicates them and their notions of a grim grand scheme.

Conspiranoiacs also tend to work according to the notion of guilt by association: I saw Rudy Giuliani wearing a yarmulke at that columnist's funeral, ergo, Rudy's really a Jew and he's part of the International Zionist Conspiracy. Sometimes these conspiranoiacs' machinations go nowhere or border on the fanciful, to say the least, but every now and then a rumor or an allegation leads to disclosure, to revelation, or to an admission of guilt, of complicity. Still, what makes this phenomenon so fascinating and complicated and insurmountable is that it's not merely a matter of whom to believe, it's a matter of battling the almost innate feeling that what we *perceive* to be true is more true than any stack of so-called facts. As Noam Chomsky, the distinguished MIT academic who is perhaps the most solemn of all conspiranoiacs, said in a 1999 interview in *Speak* magazine, "You have to look at sources with a skeptical eye. . . . If people ask me what they should rely on, my answer always is 'your own intelligence,' and that includes when you're reading what I say. If you rely on what I say, you're in trouble because you're starting with the assumption that somebody's got the truth, and that's not the case." Or, as the nineteenth-century German philosopher Ludwig Feuerbach observed more than a hundred years ago: "The present age . . . prefers the sign to the thing signified, the copy to the original, representation to reality, the appearance to the essence . . . *illusion* only is sacred, *truth* profane."

Still, as *Conspiranoia!* (and any other book about conspiracy theories) demonstrates, there are those who just *believe*. There are many people out there, for example, who, for whatever reason, and despite his being found not guilty, believe that O.J. did it. Or that Tom Cruise is gay. Or that Madonna is the Antichrist. Let 'em protest their innocence, their heterosexuality, their Christliness till they're blue in the face, reality is hardly any match against perception.

So proceed with caution, read at your own risk (especially if you're one of the so-called conspirators herein). Conspiranoia is as much hearsay and conjecture as it is fact. Because that's what conspiranoia is: a kind of gray area between what you *know* is true, what is proveable and documented, and what you *feel* is just as true, if basically *un*proveable and *un*documented.

As Dostoyevsky, a paranoiac among paranoiacs, would probably attest, the world's only as sane or insane as you make it—or as it makes you. And if it gets too overwhelming, too scary, if all this begins to make you feel just a wee bit out of sorts, as if someone's watching you, as if you're not alone, just remember to say to yourself again and again: It's only a theory, it's only a theory, it's only a . . .

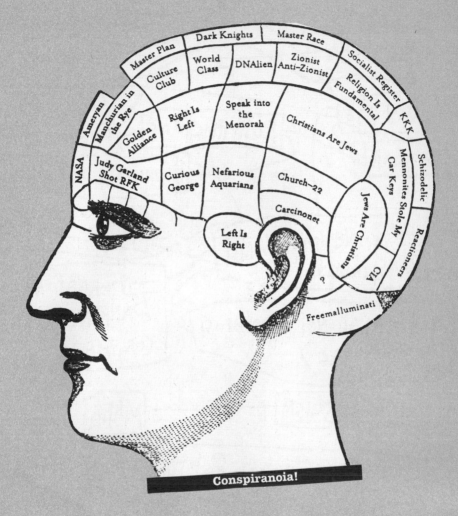

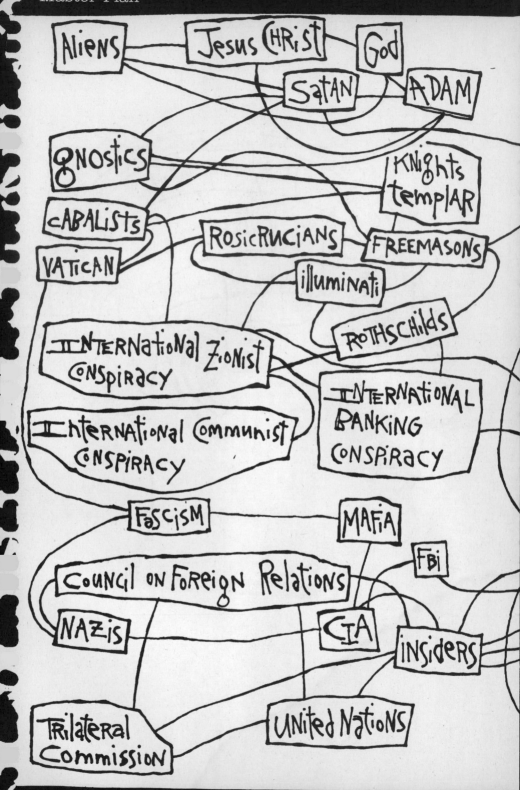

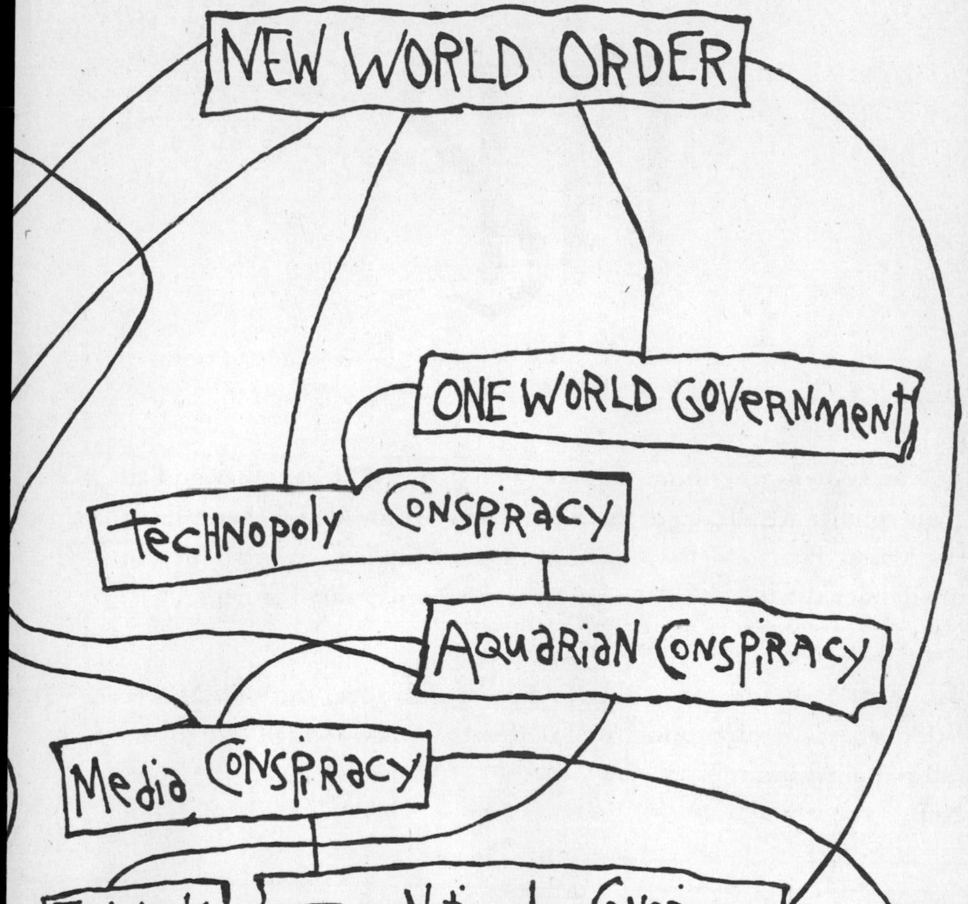
NEW WORLD ORDER
ONE WORLD GOVERNMENT
technopoly CONSPIRACY
AQUARIAN CONSPIRACY
Media CONSPIRACY
TAVISTOCK
TRANSNATIONALS CONSPIRACY
MILITARY-INDUSTRIAL COMPLEX CONSPIRACY
MULTINATIONAL CORPORATIONS CONSPIRACY

♍

Jews and Aliens, the Illuminati and a New World Order, they and all their cohorts are all part of the Plan. Here, arranged alphabetically, is the Master Plan, which works more like a template, an introduction to all other conspiracies, conspirators, and conspiracy theories.

Adam

The First Man and, according to **Freemason** lore, the first Master Builder. Adam succumbed to Lucifer the snake—which led to the fall of humankind.

✗ ❋

Aliens

Also known as little green men, Greys, extraterrestrials, or extraterrestrial biological entities (EBEs), Aliens count as anything not of this Earth. Some say Aliens are the gods and demons who crop up in many of the world's religions and myths; some even think Aliens are **God** and **Satan,** and that both "deities," or "superior beings," visited Earth in otherworldly **UFO** lightships and freely roamed the planet. Others postulate that Aliens may have put us humans here on the big blue planet as part of a research experiment and that each close encounter is but another Alien stopover to check on our progress, to see how well we're adapting to this atmosphere, to all the radiation, et cetera.

✗ ❋ ⚚ ∿ ☉

There is just enough sanity in some of these conspiracy theories to make them almost believable. By and large, however, they are creations of very rich imaginations because we simply can't accept life as it is.

—**Ray Brown, Bowling Green University professor**

Aquarian Conspiracy

Not just the title of **New Age** advocate Marilyn Ferguson's 1980 book (which, according to conspiranoiac writer Dr. John Coleman, was based on a top-secret **Stanford Research Institute—Tavistock-ABC-NBC-CBS-**funded technical paper put together in 1979, and whose authors included B. F. Skinner and Margaret Mead), but a philosophy and a master plan, too: The Aquarian Conspiracy is industry's mystical striving for a unity of politics, economics, and spiritualism that will give rise to a **New World Order** of humans as gods; these Aquarian notions drew heavily from the **Eleusinian** mystery cults, the teachings of **Madame Helena Blavatsky** (and her Theosophical Society), and the **Cabala**—and can be seen today in the writings of Shirley MacLaine, **Deepak Chopra,** and the late French **Jesuit** priest Pierre Teilhard de Chardin.

Cabalists

This Jewish mystical sect, which first popped up in twelfth-century Spain, was reviled by Orthodox rabbis for emphasizing revelation and ecstasy and claiming to possess a hidden knowledge (cabala means "tradition received," the tradition being Moses' esoteric side text to the Old Testament). Cabalists felt they could return to the universe's source of light—i.e., to **God**—by systematically meditating on the names of God and on the twenty-two letters of the Hebrew alphabet. They lifted a good part of their rituals from the **Eleusinians,** and in turn, the Cabalists influenced later mystics like the **Hermetics, Christian Rosencreutz,** the **Rosicrucians,** the Invisible College, and the **Hermetic Order of** the Golden Dawn—all of whom incorporated the Cabala into their teachings. Recently, the Cabala has caught on among Hollywood truth-seekers and trendsetters, attracting Jews and non-Jews alike, from Madonna and Roseanne to Sandra Bernhard, among others. ✗ ✡ ༄

Central Intelligence Agency (CIA)

Also known as the Agency, the Company, and the Cookie Cutter, the CIA was founded by former **OSS** bigwigs **Allen Dulles** and William "Wild Bill" Donovan (along with the help of **Reinhard Gehlen** and other ex-**Nazis**) and okayed by President **Harry Truman** in 1947. Ostensibly set up in order to "gather, evaluate and prepare foreign intelligence for the executive branch," in reality, the Agency began to function as a clandestine operational arm almost immediately. This was possible due to two acts pushed through Congress by Dulles and Wild Bill: The National Security Act of 1947, which stated that the CIA can "perform such other functions and duties related to intelligence as the **National Security Council** may from time to time direct," opened a loophole for the CIA to add bribery, blackmail, propaganda, disinformation, assassination, paramilitary operations, psychological warfare, and an array of other "dirty tricks" to their arsenal. The second act was the 1949 Central Intelligence Agency Act, which expanded the Agency's exemptions from normal congressional review. The CIA maintains innumerable "fronts," or "proprietaries," i.e., fake businesses and corporations (sometimes commercial, sometimes nonprofit) that are ostensibly private but are, in reality, secretly owned and run by the Agency: These are used as covers and headquarters for covert operations, and they occasionally make a tidy profit for the "officers" of the false company. (For instance, the infamous **Air America** commercial airline company that ran drugs from the **Golden Triangle** of southeast Asia during the **Vietnam War** received countless lucrative government contracts.) The Agency also ran many "psychotomimetic" experimental drug programs (and **Mind Control** projects) from the 1940s to the 1970s, in conjunction with the **NIMH,** the **FDA,** and pharmaceutical companies like **Eli Lilly & Co.** and Sandoz—**MK-ULTRA** being the most infamous.

★ ⌂ ✝ ⚐ ☞ ⋙ △ ⬭ ⤳ ⚱ ☺ ▦ ⊕ ☉

Council on Foreign Relations (CFR)

The Manhattan-based foster home for the **Insiders,** this pro-internationalist consortium of oilmen, Wall Street kings, and D.C.'s Beltway bigwigs was founded in 1921. It's also where the **Cold War** became policy. In George Kennan's highly persuasive 1947 *Foreign Affairs* article (a call-to-war piece Kennan wrote under the seductive pseudonym "X"), Kennan thundered, "Let's *contain* **Communism,**" a tack the U.S. government pretty much took, proving the old Beltway wonks right when they say that today's article in *Foreign Affairs* is tomorrow's U.S. foreign policy. Inside the CFR is where the ideas for the **United Nations,** the **World Bank,** and the **International Monetary Fund** were first bandied about. Its current president is former *New York Times* columnist Leslie Gelb, who was an official in the State and Defense departments and who also oversaw the cabal that wrote the **Pentagon Papers.** Some CFR critics say the **Korean War,** the **Vietnam War,** and the civil rights movement were all arranged and approved by the CFR and the Insiders—and that each one has played on a kind of mass reverse psychology: the more societal unrest there is, the more people will turn to its government for control, eventually becoming so desperate for order that they grant their government more and more

CFR Members Past and Present

Roone Arledge, former president of **ABC** News and ABC Sports; **Bill Clinton; George Bush; Jimmy Carter;** former Secretary of State Warren Christopher; **Reverend Jesse Jackson;** Diane Sawyer; ex-Harvard president Nathan Pusey; intellectual Irving Kristol; Mike Ovitz; Farrar, Straus & Giroux editor Elisabeth Sifton; media mogul Larry Tisch (co-CEO of Loew's Inc. theater chains); former **CIA** director **Allen Dulles;** actor Ron Silver; *Primary Colors* author and disgraced political pundit Joe Klein; real estate tycoon and publisher of *U.S. News & World Report* Mort Zuckerman; historian Arthur Schlesinger, and anchormen Tom Brokaw, Dan Rather, and Jim Lehrer.

power over *every* citizen's private life. The CFR also helped set up **GATT** and **NAFTA** and is pushing for the acceptance of the **Multilateral Agreement on Investments.**

✍ ∾ ☺ ⊕

Fascism

✥

A sometimes totalitarian, sometimes authoritarian, and usually always antidemocratic, reactionary political philosophy espousing nationalism and often sympathetic to capitalism.

✳ ♀ ♰ ⛰ ⤳ ♰ ☺

In this industry, people are used to treating Microsoft somewhat like the Mafia.

—**Marc Andreessen of Netscape,** *The New Yorker,* **March 1998**

Federal Bureau of Investigation (FBI)

Government agency created by the **Justice Department** in 1908 to suss out criminals involved in sabotage, conspiracy, and treason. From 1924 to 1972, cross-dressing bureau chief **J. Edgar Hoover** ruled over the Bureau with an iron fist. The FBI is rumored to have been a key player in the 1947 **Roswell Incident**—G-men supposedly took part in the dissection of the one (or two) alleged **Alien** survivor(s) who crashed in the New Mexican desert. Agents also hounded Wilhelm Reich, the mad genius psychoanalyst and agit-prop radical, to insanity and eventually to death. During the late sixties and seventies, its **COINTELPRO** counterintelligence program infiltrated and discredited dissident groups and leaders of the civil rights movement, feminists, and the New Left, plus the Weathermen and the Black Panthers. At one time the Bureau had its own self-formed **KKK** chapter. It's been suggested that cult leader **Jim Jones** got his files on black radicals from the Bureau. Civil rights leader Martin Luther King, Jr., was constantly harrassed by

Hoover and the FBI; when he was killed, the first person to reach him after he'd been fatally shot was not **Freemason Jesse Jackson** but a Bureau man: faux black radical Marrell McCullough, later a **CIA** agent, who, at that time, worked possibly for the FBI and the Memphis police. (At one point, the FBI had offered mob boss **Sam Giancana** one million dollars to knock off King.) Some speculate that the feds and the **Nation of Islam,** in their attacks on **Malcolm X,** may have encouraged his assassination. The FBI has also been fingered as a participant in the assassination of **John F. Kennedy** via their legendary ultrasecret assassination unit, **Division 5,** and threats on Kennedy's life by mob figures like **Carlos Marcello** were basically ignored by the Bureau. **Wackenhut Securities** was founded by ex-G-man George Wackenhut and includes a number of ex-FBI officials on its board. The **Church of Jesus Christ of Latter-Day Saints** has long been a recruiting ground for FBI agents. **The Program,** aka the Plan and the Black Genocide Program, is an alleged FBI/CIA scheme that employs crack, heroin, and **AIDS** to systematically murder inner-city blacks. The FBI is also one of the federal agencies involved in the rumored **National Police Force**—an Orwellian concept only worsened by the FBI's recent disastrous interactions with far-right groups and militia organizations (Ruby Ridge, Waco, etc.). Key FBI informants have included Supreme Court Chief Justice Warren Burger, **Walt Disney,** and Elvis Presley (who, alas, never really got to fink out on any of his rock 'n' roll pals).

✳ ✝ ☞ ♒ △ ✿ ⊕ ☉

Freemasons

The fraternal order of the Free and Accepted Masons, an organization based on "the Fatherhood of God and the brotherhood of man" that practices what writer George Johnson called "morality veiled in allegory and illustrated by symbols." Freemasonry may be the largest worldwide secret society in existence, consisting of approximately 4.8 million members grouped in lodges around the globe; lodges, in turn, overseen by administrative grand lodges. Freemasons claim that they are not a

9

secret society but rather a "society with secrets." Freemasonry is intensely hierarchical, with up to thirty-three degrees. Most Masons, however, never progress beyond the third degree and do not learn the more esoteric secrets of advanced freemasonry. Although the modern form of the order began in 1717 when the first grand lodge was founded in London, the symbols and rites of Freemasonry can be traced back to the guilds of the medieval stonemasons who built Europe's grand cathedrals. Some trace Freemasonry back even further, to architectural fellowships of biblical times that may have been responsible for the building of ancient monuments such as the Egyptian pyramids. Freemasons claim Hiram Abiff, for example, not only as one of their own but as their inspirational martyr-hero: Abiff, a master mason extraordinaire, designed King Solomon's Temple and was ritualistically murdered days before its completion. Medieval Freemasons organized themselves into guilds, and, with their knowledge of ancient architecture, built many of the huge Christian cathedrals. These professional organizations and guilds, originally created to protect trade secrets, evolved during the seventeenth and eighteenth centuries into hierarchical secret societies that used the symbology of architecture and tools to espouse an ethical code. The Freemasons link their history to other semimystical brotherhoods like the **Rosicrucians** and **Illuminati** and have ties to other powerful organizations like the **Vatican** (despite the long-standing animosity the Church has had for Freemasons—go figure). Freemasons were heavily involved in the revolutions of the eighteenth century, and many of them helped lead the Boston Tea Party, the **American Revolution,** and the **French Revolution.** Many groups adopted or were influenced by Masonic rites, organization, and hierarchy, or were even founded by Freemasons, including the **Knights of Columbus,** the Shriners, the U.S. Order of De Molay, the **Knights of Pythias,** the Society of Pythagoras, the **Decembrists,** the **Carbonari,** the **Nation of Islam,** the **Church of Jesus Christ of Latter-Day Saints,** the **Independent Order of B'nai B'rith,** the **Ku Klux Klan,** the **Skull & Bones Society,** and the **Propaganda Due Lodge.** Sixteen presidents of the United States have openly admitted to being Freemasons, many of them Masters of the 33rd degree; many other presidents and leaders may have been Masons but chose not to admit their membership in public, for fear of arousing anti-Masonic sentiments. The Catholic Church has long condemned Freemasonry for being a heretical religion and a secret society. For example, they regard the initiation rite of a Master Mason, which involves a symbolic death and rebirth, as a travesty of **Christ**'s resurrection. But Masons have also had a number of other enemies. Since the early 1800s, they've been feared and persecuted by groups like the Anti-Masonic Party, the Nativists, and the Know-Nothings. In the United States, home to nearly two-thirds of all Masons, a number of Masonic groups have been formed to organize social and charitable activities; among the best known are the fez-bedecked Shriners.

✳ ✡ ⚲ △ ☺

Free to Be Freemasons

Thomas Paine (author of both *The Age of Reason* and *Origins of Freemasonry*); George Washington; James Madison; Ethan Allen; architect Sir Christopher Wren; Frederick the Great of Prussia; Mozart; John Paul Jones; Danton; Robespierre; Paul Revere; Samuel Adams; Marquis de Lafayette; King Edward VII; U.S. presidents **Franklin D. Roosevelt, Harry Truman, Lyndon Johnson, Gerald Ford, Ronald Reagan,** and **George Bush; FBI** head **J. Edgar Hoover; Reverend Jesse Jackson; CIA** founder and director **Allen Dulles;** former CIA director **William Casey;** Supreme Court Chief Justice Earl Warren; Louis Armstrong; Gene Autry; Count William Basie; Irving Berlin; Napoleon; Ernest Borgnine; Eddie Cantor; Casanova; Winston Churchill; Ty Cobb; Nat King Cole; Jack Dempsey; Sir Arthur Conan Doyle; W. E. B. Du Bois; Duke Ellington; Douglas Fairbanks; W. C. Fields; Clark Gable; George Gershwin; Reverend Billy Graham; Oliver Hardy; Jesse Helms; Bob Hope; Harry Houdini; Burl Ives; Al Jolson; Jack Kemp; Rudyard Kipling; Louis B. Mayer; Tom Mix; Audie Murphy; Arnold Palmer; Alexander Pushkin; Sugar Ray Robinson; Roy Rogers; Will Rogers; Peter Sellers; William Shakespeare; Red Skelton; John Philip Sousa; Jonathan Swift; Danny Thomas; Strom Thurmond; John Wayne; Oscar Wilde; William Wyler; and Darryl Zanuck.

Gnostics

Followers of Gnosticism (circa A.D. 250) believed that each person had the power to realize her own salvation through mystical exploration. (**Freemasons** say the Gnostics followed the teachings of the **Eleusinians.**) Although not strictly worshipers of the Devil, they admired **Satan** for his knowledge-giving role as the snake in **God**'s Garden of Eden. Centuries later, groups like the **Cathars** held on to the Gnostic belief that divinity dwells within everyone—the foundation of the **New Age** movement.

✕ ⸸ ∾

> Conspiracy theories are as old as history.
>
> —Stephen Ambrose, *The New York Times Book Review* (1992)

God

According to the **Freemasons,** God is the Great Architect of the universe. According to others, though, God is but an **Alien,** or an Alien spawn, and other likely Aliens (or fellow Alien-Human half-breeds) are his rival, **Satan,** and God's erstwhile son, **Jesus Christ.** According to author Zecharia Sitchin, God and the Devil represent two dichotomous camps of godly and demonic Aliens. God razed the Tower of Babel and commissioned Enoch to dig a cavern deep in the Earth and fill it with His secrets, secrets that King Solomon attempted to uncover by building the Temple of Solomon (with its sacred floor plan), secrets the Freemasons have forever been in search of.

✕ ✳ ⸸ ☉

Illuminati

This freethinking, secret sect of secular humanists, sometimes called "the bearers of the light," was founded in Bavaria on May 1, 1776, by rebellious university professor Adam Weishaupt, who'd studied under the **Jesuits.** Originally known as the Order of Perfectibilists, the Illuminati were created to oppose the power of the

Church and the state, and their ultimate goal was the development of an egalitarian society. A "cult of reason" whose members progressed along a hierarchy of "lesser Mysteries and Greater Mysteries," the group was officially disbanded in 1787, after Duke Carl Theodore's royal decree: "If you recruit, you die." From that point on, practitioners and seekers were driven underground, their obscurity fueling all future Illuminati-based conspiracy theories. The Devil himself could be considered the first Illuminati, since one of **Satan**'s nicknames is the Angel of Light (Illumination). The Illuminati were influenced by the mysticism of the East, transmitted via the Sufis and the **Alumbrados** (aka the Illumined Ones of Spain). The Illuminati held out the promise of attaining an ancient secret knowledge, and for that the Vatican has often lumped them in with the **Rosicrucians** and other heretical secret societies. (Ironically, many suspect that Ignatius Loyola and the **Jesuits** were members of the Alumbrados and, later on, of the Illuminati.) **Freemasons** trace their history back to the Illuminati, and as a more mysterious and possibly nonexistent group (some wonder if there even was an Adam Weishaupt), the Illuminati are often tied to and blamed for plots that the Freemasons were involved in, including the **French Revolution,** the **American Revolution,** the Russian revolution, **Communism** in general, and the **New World Order.** The symbol of the Illuminati is the eye in the pyramid, which was placed on the one-dollar bill by **Franklin Delano Roosevelt.**
✳ ✡

Our secret association works in a way that nothing can withstand, and man shall soon be free and happy.

—**Adam Weishaupt, founder of the Illuminati**

Insiders

These influential **International Bankers,** industrialists, CEOs, and academics, and families like the **Du Pont**s, **Mellons,** and **Rockefellers** use their power to alter fiscal policies and control politics. They attend the same schools, vacation at the same exclusive resorts, and network not only in think tanks and secret conferences but in the back rooms of places like the **Council on Foreign Relations,** the **Trilateral Commission,** and the **Ford** and **Rockefeller Foundations.** In the words of John Birch Society founder Robert Welch, an Insider is "consciously a member of an international Master Conspiracy of long standing." It is said that in order to strengthen the power of the federal government over its citizens and ensure huge profits, Insiders engineered the **Vietnam War** and then kept it going to protect their interests—after getting rid of President **Kennedy,** who had threatened to pull out of the war.

International Banking Conspiracy

Intent on shaping foreign and domestic policy, usurious International Bankers like J. P. **Morgan** and John D. **Rockefeller** encourage movements and systems (i.e., the **New Deal** or the **Federal Reserve**) that force governments to borrow from them, sticking those nations with eternal debt. Worse, they sometimes create wars for profit. Some credit **Nimrod,** ruler of ancient Babylon, with inventing banking. The first international banking empire, however, was created by the **Knights Templar,** with the profits won from their exploits during the Crusades. Martin Luther's sixteenth-century Protestant Reformation was largely funded by the emerging merchant and banking classes of Germany who sought to wrest financial control of Europe from the papacy. Jews moved into banking in medieval times because the Christians, due to a biblical ban on usury, could not loan money at interest. This led to a so-called worldwide cabal of Jewish usurers, eventually culminating in the **Rothschild** dynasty. In the early years of the United States, the eastern banking elite managed to temporarily open up the First and Second Banks of the United States. The First Bank was founded by **Freemason** Alexander Hamilton in 1791 and was the first privately owned institution authorized to print national currency, only to be closed down by the Federalists in 1811 (who complained that it too closely allied the government with the country's cliquish commercial and moneyed interests). The Second Bank opened in 1816, but it, too, was suspected of swelling only the pockets of the eastern upper class and International Bankers, so Freemason Andrew Jackson vetoed the bank in 1836. By the late nineteenth century the International Bankers included the Warburgs, the Kuhns, and the Loebs, and gentiles like the Rockefellers, the Morgans, and the Carnegies. Paranoiacs like the Populists were beginning to catch on to the Bankers' ways, however, and soon spread the notion that the little guys were getting screwed over by these Wall Street tycoons. The **Panic of 1907,** for instance, was an economic crisis set off by a cartel of International Bankers in order to make the U.S. government indebted to them. In 1914, Europe was goaded into the Great War **(WWI)** by the International Bankers, who wanted to create profits and economic chaos in order to gain further power. In 1929, the **International Zionist Conspiracy** and the International Bankers teamed up to create Black Friday, the worst stock market crash in history, as part of a Grand Plan for a **One World Government** domination. This, in turn, led to the **Great Depression,** which forced citizens into an even greater reliance on government aid. **World War II** was instigated by Jewish bankers and **Communists** who wanted to create profits by bringing the United States out of its depression. After WWII, in order to rebuild their economies, the world's governments came to depend more and more on the International Bankers. As late as 1991, international banks like the **BCCI** and the **BNL** laundered money and provided financing for drugs-and-arms deals (like the **Iran-Contra** affair) for dictators like **Saddam Hussein** and for **Terrorist** organizations like Italy's **P2.** Banking consortiums like the Lippo Group, a mysterious six-billion-dollar banking, insurance, and real-estate web, have recently come under public scrutiny for trying to manipulate politicians like **Bill Clinton.** Major institutions like the **World Bank** (a gigantic D.C.-based international repo man) and the **International Monetary Fund** bully third world nations into weakness, population control, and dependency on International Bankers and their developed-nations overlords. **Alan Greenspan,** the Federal Reserve Board chairman, has been accused of creating recessions not to stimulate the economy and help small businesses but to keep his International Banker buddies (who pay him enormous sums as a consultant and to whitewash their reputations) from going bankrupt. Nowadays, the International Banking Conspiracy is a driving force behind the **New World Order** and its economic, profiteering aspect,

15

and International Bankers seed and charter other power-wielding groups such as the **Insiders,** the **Bilderbergers,** the **Council on Foreign Relations,** and the **Trilateral Commission,** all of which are rife with International Banker conspirators such as European megabank Deutsche Bank and Japanese powerhouses like Sumitomo Bank and Mitsubishi Bank.

✘ ✡ ★ ✍ 〰 ✐ ∞ 〜 ⚲ ⊕ ✓

International Communist Conspiracy

Waning twentieth-century fear of a Red Planet, i.e., that the godless advocates of the elimination of private property will win out over democracy and capitalism. The International Communist conspirators include the Communist regimes of Lenin (initiated in the **Bolshevik** revolution), Stalin, Mao Tse-tung, Fidel **Castro,** and the Communist puppet states that the United States fought in the **Korean** and **Vietnam Wars. Communism** also spawned a number of related ideologies, like **Anarchism** and **Socialism.** Labor unions are chockfull of Communist sympathizers, as were the civil rights movement and **Terrorist** groups like the Weathermen and the Black Panthers.

✳ ✡ ✍ △ 〜 ☺ ☼ ✓

International Zionist Conspiracy

✡

This anti-Semitic movement was first propagated in 1905 in czarist Russia with the news of the First International Zionist Conference, which had been held in Basel, Switzerland, by Theodore Herzl, and bolstered several years later with the publication of *The Protocols of the Elders of Zion.* Jewish conspiracy history, however, started much earlier, going back to the mystical **Cabalists** and medieval usurers, who became Europe's premier moneylenders due to a biblical ban on usury for Christians. Around 1798, the anti-Semitic French priest, Abbé Barruel, popularized the myth that during the Middle Ages a secret cabal of wealthy Jewish conspirators, the Secret Council of Rabbis, had holed up in Spain, plotting to take over Christianity and all European governments. No wonder then that by the mid-1800s— right around the height of the **Rothschild** Jewish banking dynasty, whose members seemed to be meddling in all sorts of international affairs—people began to conflate the International Zionist Conspiracy with the **International Banking Conspiracy.** In the minds of some, bankers=Jews. When Czar Alexander II of Russia was assassinated in 1881, the Russian government blamed Jewish conspirators. The stock market crash of 1929 and the subsequent **Great Depression** have also been dumped on **Illuminati** Jews and other International Bankers, who made a lot of money by loaning relief funds to President **Roosevelt.** Likewise, **World War II** was blamed on Jewish bankers who ostensibly wanted to make profits by bringing the United States out of the depression. The graduated income tax, the **Internal Revenue Service,** and the **Federal Reserve** are all parts of what some anti-Semites call the **Zionist Occupied Government,** which controls the government and sucks money out of the American middle class and puts it into the coffers of International Zionist Bankers.

✘ ✳ ✿ ✍ ∽ ▦ ⊕

Jesus Christ

The Son of **God.** According to some, Jesus is a genetically engineered **Alien-Human Hybrid** (a product of the Virgin Mary's artificial **Alien** insemination). After his execution by the Romans, the religion of Christianity sprung up around his (peculiarly socialist) teachings, although it incorporated many elements of paganism and **Mithraism.** The **Priory of Sion,** a French organization that may just be an elaborate hoax, claims to have been created about nine hundred years ago to protect the **Merovingian** bloodlines (whose kings claimed to be direct descendants of King Solomon and Jesus). The **Knights Templar** claimed to have a container of his blood, the Holy Grail. **Freemasons** link Christ to the Masonically designed Temple of Solomon.

✘ ✳ ↷ ⚕ ☉

If the chronology of the third chapter of Genesis is correct, conspiracy was the first spontaneous activity in which any creatures participated after the Creation, antedating even sex, which does not make an appearance till Chapter IV.

—Robert Wernick, *Smithsonian* (1994)

Knights Templar

Chivalrous order of righteous ex-sinners named after the Temple of Solomon (later, the **Freemasons'** key symbol) who solidified as a group in 1118 under the leadership of Frankish knight Hugh de Payens. Papally exempted from the authority of secular rulers, these warrior monks participated in several Crusades (and fought alongside Richard the Lionhearted), policed the Holy Land route, guarded the **Pope,** consorted with the **Assassins,** and used their Crusades profits to create one of the first banking and real estate empires. Forming a church within the Church, the Templars devoted themselves to the Virgin Mary and swore to "consecrate their swords and their lives to the defense of the mysteries of the Christian Church." They used ruthless loansharking and landlord tactics to extract money from people and countries throughout medieval Europe. Although said to have been the possessors of the Holy Grail (the container that held **Christ**'s blood), they were expulsed by the **Vatican** in 1291 and virtually exterminated by King Philip IV of France in 1307. Philip, it turned out, had borrowed large sums from the Templars to wage war and install a French puppet in the papacy, Pope Clement V, but he needed more money and sought to confiscate all of the Templars' holdings. So Philip accused the Templars of homosexuality (kissing the mouth, navel, and anus of an initiator was part of one Knights Templar rite), heresy (spitting on the cross was part of another rite), and worshiping Baphomet—an occult idol sometimes represented by a wooden phallus, other times just a jeweled skull without the body. Between 1307 and 1314, most of the order was tortured and executed. In 1314, seven years after his arrest on Friday the thirteenth, October 1307, the last of the Knights Templar's grand masters, Jacques De Molay, was burned at the stake. Some Templars later found safety under the protection of the Freemason king of Scotland, Robert the Bruce (Mel Gibson's betrayer in *Braveheart*). The Templars are thought to have received the secrets of the **Cathars** before that group was wiped out by the Vatican in the thirteenth century, and Italian fantasy author Umberto Eco, in his 1989 book *Foucault's Pendulum,* spread the story that renegade members of the Knights Templar went on to form the **Rosicrucians.**

✘ ✳ ⚲ ↪

Mafia

Aka the Mob, this worldwide network of criminals got its start among the Carbonari in seventeenth-century Sicily and later took hold among certain Italian-Americans in the United States. The Mafia specializes in organizing illegal activities like gambling, prostitution, drugs, and murder, and its members have used their muscle to influence politicians, merchants, religious leaders, and anyone else who might be of use to them.

✳ ⛰ ⋙ △ ✏ ☺ ▨

> The CIA and Outfit had become so intertwined that to say there had been a conspiracy between the two overlooked the mere fact that they had become—for all practical purposes—one.
>
> —Sam Giancana and Chuck Giancana, *Double Cross: The Explosive, Inside Story of the Mobster Who Controlled America* (1992)

Media Conspiracy

Fueled by unregulated mergers and a lack of government and public antitrust activism, media monopolies continue to expand. Television, newspapers, radio, the Internet, movies, music, magazines, video, advertising, and sports—all are owned and ruled by a handful of infotainment megacorporations (Disney, Fox, Microsoft, Nike, and precious few other corporations), which are ruled by a handful of megalomaniacal CEOs (Michael Eisner, Rupert Murdoch, Bill Gates, Phil Knight, and one hundred or so other white guys).

✡ ⋙ △ ⌇ ✿

Military-Industrial Complex Conspiracy

A supply-and-resupply marriage of the Pentagon and its corporate manufacturers. Since WWII, the U.S. defense industry (Lockheed-Martin, General Motors, and Westinghouse, among many others) has worked intimately with the defense department to create a booming secret economy in which a surplus of weapons and $800 ashtrays are continuously available to our military (and to our enemies' militaries).

★ ♱ △ ▯ ☺ ✿ ▨

19

Multinational Corporations Conspiracy

A postwar phenomenon, the Multinationals are those Fortune 500 megaconglomerates whose CEOs wield as much power as any president or prime minister. According to rumor, the Multinationals may have had a hand in arranging for President **Kennedy**'s death, because, shortly before his murder, JFK apparently had vowed to tone down U.S. involvement in the **Vietnam War,** meaning that the Multinationals and the corporations of the **Military-Industrial Complex** might never have been able to reap the war's ongoing financial benefits. But, really, the Multinationals don't care who's in power, whether they're left, right, **Fascist,** queer, black, or dull as a butterknife, just so long as they have free access to more consumers who'll buy up products that the Media conspirators tell them they have to have; why, the Multinationals are fine with whatever social, political, or religious system a country prefers.

✝ △ ⊕

> People don't want to be informed; they only want the illusion of being informed.
>
> —**Roger Ailes (chairman of Rupert Murdoch's Fox News, former executive producer of Rush Limbaugh's TV talk show, and onetime imagemaker and political consultant to Reagan, Bush, Nixon, and Rudy Giuliani),** *New York* **magazine, 1997**

Nazis

Also known as National Socialism, an extreme nationalistic and militaristic party founded in Germany in 1918. The Nazis were refashioned by **Adolf Hitler** and his henchmen into one of the largest, most feared and destructive cults in history. Influenced by the pro-Aryan beliefs of groups like the **Thule Society** and the **Order of New Templars,** and vindicated by conspiracy-pushing works like *The Protocols of the Elders of Zion,* they regarded Jews and other ethnic minorities as subhuman. Using the racially suspect theories of **Eugenics** as a somewhat scientific basis for their racialist aims of "furthering the master race," they sought to wipe out all other races except their own. These "racial hygiene" ideas were vali-

dated (for them) by the work of people like onetime Nazi and otherwise respected ethnologist (and postwar Nobel Prize winner) Konrad Lorenz, who believed that genetics determined one's behavior and that society should aim for the "elimination of morally inferior human beings." Jews, Gypsies, homosexuals, and other "subhumans" were herded into concentration camps and most were "eliminated" with poisonous gases such as cyanide and Zyklon-B. Some believe that the Nazis were working on a final secret weapon at the end of the war: a flying saucer developed with **Alien** help. After the Nazis were defeated, certain prominent and important ones escaped prosecution with the help of Nazi sympathizer and collaborator **Allen Dulles** and the **OSS**'s Project **Paperclip.** (The **Red Cross** also helped out with the Nazis' exfiltration, as did the **Vatican.**) Among the Nazis the United States funneled out of harm's way were V-2 rocket scientist **Wernher von Braun** (and one hundred or so other top Nazi engineers), **Otto Skorzeny,** and **Klaus Barbie.** Money stolen by the Nazis from deported and murdered Jews was laundered by Swiss banks like the **Bank for International Settlements,** and was first used to fund the German war effort and later bankrolled the Nazis' escape from Europe. On the other side of the Iron Curtain, the **KGB** conducted its own recruitment program, smuggling out and hiring Nazi experts to develop the MiG fighter jet and help set up their future **Biochemical Warfare** network, the **Biopreparat,** among other things. The Nazis have inspired countless other **Fascists** and racists, among them the Neo-Nazis, the Order, the "Christ Militant" Silver Shirts, the **Liberty Lobby,** the **World Anti-Communist League** (where many former Nazis hung out), the **American Nazi Party,** and the **Aryan Nations.**
★ ✝ ⛪ 🐖 ⚱ ☼

New World Order (NWO)

The Masonic "Novus Ordo Seclorum" and one of **Freemason George Bush**'s favorite phrases during his presidency, the NWO (now also the slogan of World Championship Wrestling) offers a kind of Orwellian view of the future in which **Communists** and International Bankers (aka Jews) work together to form a One World **Socialist** Government. The NWO is currently nearing reality under the protection of free-trade agreements like **NAFTA** and **GATT,** political and economic mergers like the EEC and **NATO,** and military operations such as the **Gulf War.** The **Peace Corps** is a training ground for future New World Order drones; the **IMF** and the **World Bank,** along with clueless well-meaning organizations like the Audubon Society and Zero Population Growth and diseases like **AIDS** and other plagues keep the population at a manageable number and eliminate those who are undesirable; and militarily, those unmarked black choppers and the imminent **National Police Force** keep unruly citizens in check. In the late eighties, the NWO's plan for a government-controlled United States was audaciously revealed on the back of a box of Kix, the children's breakfast cereal.

✳ ✍ ∾ ☺ ⊕

One World Government Conspiracy

The paranoid belief that the world is ruled by a cabal of elderly white guys, or, that the United States in particular is soon to fall under the control of the **UN** and its Establishment bosses—a consortium of **Insiders, International Banking Conspirators, International Communist Conspirators, International Zionist Conspirators,** British royalty, and many more), all of whom will stop at nothing short of global totalitarianism. Originally born out of the paranoia among the established governments and religions of the eighteenth century, which feared immigrants, Communism, et cetera, this notion has gained in popularity, particularly among those in the Militia Movement and among leftists, both groups seeing each and every "world" or "international" move as but one more step toward a faceless global society ruled over by a handful of greedy businessmen.

✡ ✍ ∾ ⊕

Rosicrucians

Nicknamed "the Invisibles," this early-1600s quasi-theological society of chosen individuals fancied alchemy and occult symbology (e.g., the rosy cross, the swastika, and the pyramid). The Rosicrucians strove for a hidden half-mystical, half-scientific wisdom gained through esoteric study and intense contemplation and derived mainly from the teachings of apocryphal German mystic **Christian Rosencreutz.** Italian author Umberto Eco says the Rosicrucians were founded by a group of renegade **Knights Templar** who had survived the extermination of their order in the fourteenth century. Others trace the Rosicrucians' roots back to Eastern mystics such as the **Alumbrados,** Jewish **Cabalists,** and the **Hermetic** magicians and alchemists. The Rosicrucian philosophy, that the divine lies somewhere in all humans, can be traced back to the **Gnostics.** In any case, Rosicrucian philosophy influenced a number of seventeenth-century scientific thinkers, among them Francis Bacon and members of the **Royal Society,** such as Isaac Newton. The **Freemasons** also trace their roots to the Rosicrucians. The Vatican, never particularly happy with their claims of a secret knowledge, lumped the Rosicrucians in with other revelation-seeking heretics, such as the **Illuminati,** and denounced Rosicrucian groups like the Invisible College for "tempting Catholics to renounce their faith." By the late eighteenth century, vaguely Rosicrucian hybrids such as the **Sublime Perfect Masters** (an Italian revolutionary group) and the **Order of the Brotherhood of Asia** had appeared. Prominent Rosicrucians have included Charlemagne, the Three Magi, Dante, Paracelsus, Sir Christopher Wren, **Benjamin Franklin,** Thomas Jefferson, and Claude Debussy.

✖ ✳ ⚹

The Rothschilds

International Bankers extraordinaire and consummate **Insiders.** The Rothschilds' banking dynasty was founded in the nineteenth century by Jewish financier Mayer Amschel Rothschild (1744–1812), a onetime coin dealer from the Jewish ghettos of Frankfurt, Germany. Possessors of the world's oldest and last family-owned investment bank, the Rothschilds followed in the footsteps of previous Jewish moneylenders, a tradition that goes back to the medieval usurers. After making huge profits on the Napoleonic Wars by backing England, Mayer installed his five banker sons into Europe's cultural epicenters: Frankfurt, Vienna, London, Naples, and Paris. This ensured him of a virtual hundred-year family stranglehold on European economics and politics. The family financed various European kingdoms and railway systems, helped in the British acquisition of the Suez Canal, and in 1868 acquired the prized Château Lafite winery in Bordeaux,

France. The Rothschilds invested in **Cecil Rhodes**'s De Beers diamond mines and helped incorporate Israel. They also financed the Civil War, in an effort to force the United States into their debt. Rather than knuckling under to another Rothschild loan, though, **Abraham Lincoln** instead printed more currency to pay off the Union's war debts to the Rothschilds—and was fatally shot shortly afterward. Via two of their family representatives in New York, **J. P. Morgan** Co. and Kuhn, Loeb & Co., the Rothschilds pushed the Federal Reserve Act through Congress and purchased controlling stock in the **Federal Reserve** Bank of New York, establishing a private piggybank for themselves and other International Bankers. Since then, they've been blamed for most of the wars and economic disasters that have befallen the United States and the world, mostly because they're Jewish.

✡ ★ ✍ ⌇

Satan

The Devil. Beelzebub. The Dark Angel goes by many different names and is thought by some to have been spawned by **Aliens.**

✖ ⌇

Tavistock Institute

Affectionately referred to as the "Freud Hilton," this London, England, Institute for Human Relations was founded in 1946 and is renowned among psychologists and psychiatrists as a kind of think tank for mental-health practitioners. Critics, however, say it was actually founded much earlier, about 1921, by the same folks—those pesky meddling **Insiders**—who created the **Council for Foreign Relations,** and that, since its formal creation, British intelligence **(MI6)** and **Masonic** members of the establishment have used Tavistock as a tool for securing the **New World Order**—the evidence being Tavistock's financial support from groups like the **Ford** and **Rockefeller Foundations, RAND,** and the **World Health Organization.**

↬ ⌇ ▩ ⊕

Technopoly Conspiracy

Technopoly represents a modern-day spin on the Synarchie, Frenchman Jean Coutrot's 1930s secret society whose goal was a faceless bureaucracy based on hierarchy and specialization of function. Today's Synarchie is an information age of faceless computocracies and microserfs run by **Bill Gates** and a few other Synarchical megalomaniacs and builders of the information technology, smart weapons technology, and the **Internet.** Technopoly, in the words of social critic Neil Postman from his book *Technopoly,* is when "culture seeks its authorization in technology, finds its satisfactions in technology, and takes its orders from technology. . . . This requires the development of a new kind of social order . . . those who feel most comfortable in Technopoly are those who are convinced that technical progress is humanity's supreme achievement and the instrument by which our most profound dilemmas may be solved."

〰 ✿ ⊕

Transnational Corporations Conspiracy

The notion that certain megacorporations' economic power and political influence are so deep in certain countries' socioeconomic systems that those countries might someday name themselves after their primary employer-exploiter (i.e., Argentina may someday be called **ITT**tina or Vietnam may soon end up as **Nike**nam). Scoff not, ye free-market Noam Chomsky naysayers, if the fine print of the **Multilateral Agreement on Investment** goes through, that's exactly what could happen.

✝ ✿ ⊕

Trilateral Commission

In 1973, **Insider David Rockefeller** asked **Zbigniew Brzezinski,** erstwhile national security advisor to **Richard Nixon,** to put together an organization of the top political and business leaders from around the world. The result? The TC, which today persists as an elitist, worldwide **Establishment** organization of "concerned" corporate leaders formed under the guise of fostering international relations and encourag-

TC Attendees

Former L.A. mayor Tom Bradley, **George Bush, IBM** CEO Louis Gerstner, *Washington Post* chairman Katharine Graham, **Time-Warner** CEO Gerald Levin, Sony chairman Akio Morita, and columnist George Will.

ing the trilateral economic linkage among Japan, Europe, and North America. In actuality, their goal is to rule the world—just listen to the late senator Barry Goldwater. In his book *With No Apologies,* he called the commission "David Rockefeller's newest international cabal" and said, "It is intended to be the vehicle for **Multinational** consolidation of the commercial and banking interests by seizing control of the political government of the United States."

✍ ✀ ☺ ⊕

United Nations (UN)

A world congress founded in 1945. The UN's headquarters in New York City was built on land donated by the **Rockefellers.** Proud sponsors of the coming **New World Order** and its **One World Government.**

✡ ✍ ✀ ⊕

It's great to be back from vacation. . . . It's much more fun to be at work here, blocking reform, flying my black helicopters, imposing global taxes.

—**Boutros Boutros-Ghali,**
former United Nations Secretary-General (1996); after the United
States vetoed a second term for Boutros-Ghali, he laid part of the blame
for his ouster on the black helicopters

Vatican

The headquarters for the pope and the Roman Catholic Church and an independent sovereign state (in a triangular section of Rome). Its financial subsidiary, Vatican Inc., is a tax-exempt entity. The Catholic Church staunchly opposes abortion, birth control, and homosexuality and has long railed against the evils of **Freemasonry** and **Communism** while remaining more than warm toward **Nazis** and **Fascists** (after **WWII,** the Vatican willingly exfiltrated large numbers of Nazis and fascists out of Europe and into the safer climes of Latin America and the Middle East, via its infamous Ratlines). Marco Politi and Watergate reporter Carl Bernstein, in their 1996 book, *His Holiness: John Paul II and the Hidden History of Our*

Time, argued that there existed a "Holy Alliance" between Pope John Paul II and the **Reagan** administration, a conspiracy that brought down the USSR. Elders of the Catholic Church modeled much of the power structure of their organization after that of the Babylonian priests. Some say that the Vatican has a list of all Protestants inside its walls, names being kept in a gigantic computer that the Catholic Church keeps updated in preparation for a future inquisition.

✗ ✳ ⅋ 🏯 ⚱ ☺ ☉

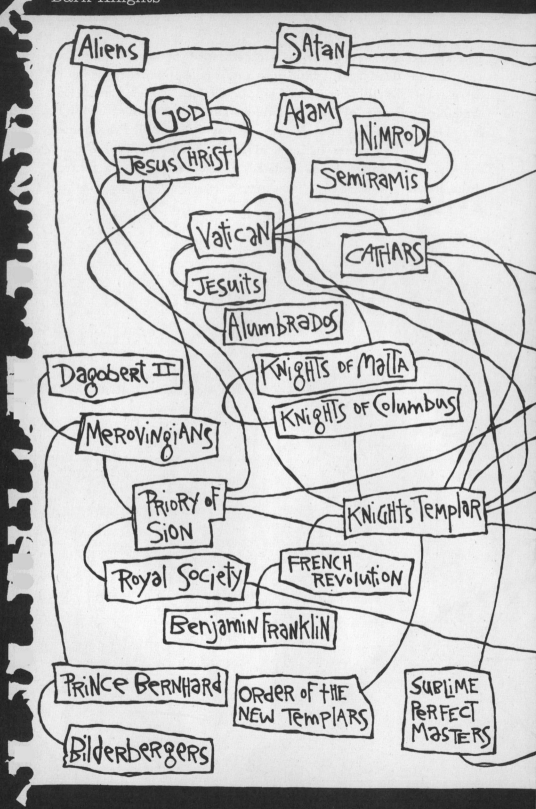

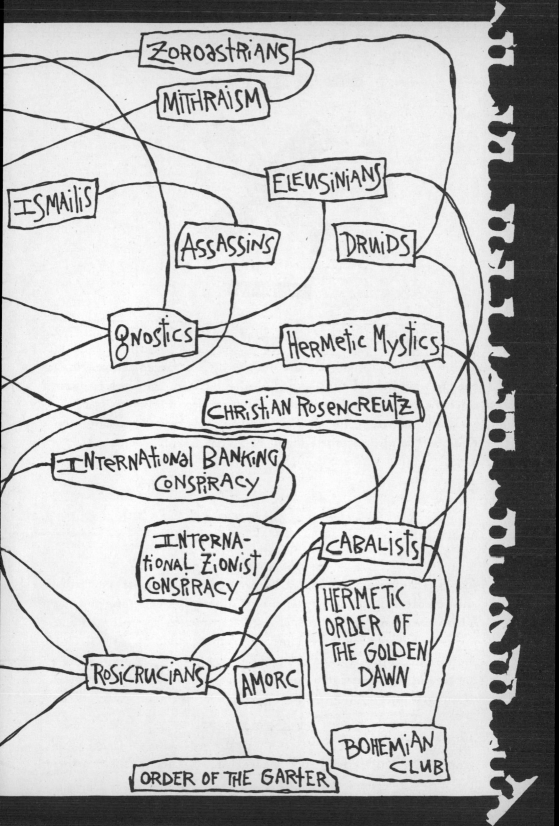

Conspiracy

✛

Going way back to before there was the light of organized religion, back to when the Aliens spawned God and Satan, the Dark Knights trace the evolution of the mystery cults and pagan religions and how these all gave rise to the Church and Europe's courtly warriors, the Knights Templar and the Knights of Malta.

Adam

♍ ✳

Aliens

♍ ✳ ↑ ♒ ☉

Alumbrados

Aka the Enlightened, or the Illuminated Ones, these sixteenth- and seventeenth-century forerunners of the **Rosicrucians** and the **Illuminati** originated in Spain and aspired to a "union of the mind with their master." They were condemned in an edict of the Grand Inquisition of 1623 as heretics of the Church. St. Ignatius and his **Jesuits** have long been accused of secretly belonging to this group.

AMORC

This San Jose—based Ancient Mystical Order Rosae Crucis was founded in the United States by adman H. Spencer Lewis in 1915.

America's only "official" **Rosicrucian** organization, AMORC seeks to merge science with religion and pursues alchemical studies and the occult. AMORC turned up in the odd scrawlings of **Sirhan Sirhan,** the lone gunman assassin of **Bobby Kennedy.**
❧

> The government of this country has not only to deal with governments, kings, and ministers but also with secret societies, elements which must be taken into account which at the last moment can bring all our plans to nought, which have agents everywhere, who incite assassinations and can if necessary lead a massacre.
>
> —Benjamin Disraeli, 1856

Assassins

These "masters of quiet death," aka the Hashishim, and not to be confused with the Jewish Hasidim, were organized by the Persian Shiite Muslim Hasan-i-Sabbah and were originally called the Order of the Devoted. They combined **Mind Control** and hash highs to turn murder into an art form (and their forte). During the Crusades, they crossed paths (and exchanged tips) with the **Knights**

Masonic Symbology

The chisel represents education; the gavel or hammer, conscience; the twenty-four-inch ruler, the day. The square (morality), level (equality), and plumb (rectitude) are used together to "build spiritual walls." The pencil and compass are a reminder of the Great Architect who designed the universe according to a harmonic plan. (**Adam** was **God**'s Master Builder, and as His first Mason, he passed his knowledge on to other Ancient Masons of biblical times, such as Cush, who built the Tower of Babel.) The letter *G* inside a triangle is a version of the ancient tetragrammation of the Hebrew letter Yod in a triangle.

Templar and even helped Richard the Lionhearted on occasion. Their symbol, a red cross on a white background, is identical to the Templars'.

Bilderbergers

Held every year since 1954, when it was founded in Oosterbeek, Holland's Bilderberg Hotel, by Prince Bernhard of the Netherlands and Joseph Retinger, a 33rd-degree **Freemason** and **Jesuit** priest, this highly secretive three-day gathering of Europe and America's most influential politicos and wealthiest business leaders (not all of whom are Jewish, by any means) consists of networking and meetings on how to run the world better and make even more money doing so, i.e., make it even more conducive to free-market capitalism. No conclusions from the meetings are ever published or announced, and critics claim the group manipulates global finances and establishes rigid and binding international monetary rates. The idea of the European Common Market was nurtured at the Bilderberg, as was **GATT,** and at the 1972 gathering, attendees hand-picked **Jimmy Carter** as the 1976 presidential candidate and even supplied him with the list of names of people who would fill his cabinet. The Bilderbergers have a huge crossover of membership with other global power councils, such as the **Center for Strategic and International Studies (CSIS)** and the **Trilateral Commis-**

Bilderbergers

George Soros, **David Rockefeller,** the queens of the Netherlands and Spain, U.S. Secretary of Defense William Perry, former **Clinton** adviser George Stephanopoulos, former U.S. senator Sam Nunn, **William F. Buckley,** Lloyd Bentsen, **Henry Kissinger, World Bank** president James Wolfensohn, former National Urban League president Vernon Jordan, **Jimmy Carter,** former West German chancellor Helmut Kohl, former British prime minister Lord Hume, and the editors and publishers of *Fortune, Forbes, Newsweek, The Economist, Le Monde, Die Ziet, **Time, The Washington Post,*** and ***The New York Times.***

sion—in fact, the idea of a Trilateral Commission was first proposed by Bilderberger leader **David Rockefeller** at one of the group's annual meetings.

✍ 🌐

Bohemian Club

A males-only invitation-only secret society formed in 1872 by five *San Francisco Examiner* journalists on the premise of promoting good fellowship. Deemed by *Newsweek* as "the world's most prestigious summer camp," the club holds an annual two-week-long July retreat in Bohemia Grove, California, a vast forested area near San Francisco. During this time, local legend has it that attendees such as Merv Griffin, **Henry Kissinger,** and **George Bush** parade naked through the rolling hills and wrestle with each other—and sometimes get around to determining the course of the world. It was here that the **Manhattan Project** was thought up and where attendees selected **Dwight Eisenhower** as the Republicans' 1952 presidential candidate. Intensely private and awash in **Druidic** rituals, some conspiranoiacs claim that some Bohos participate in **Cabalistic** rituals, too, and that it has a Leather Room and a Necrophilia Room. Every Republican president since Herbert Hoover has belonged to the club.

🏕 〰 ☺

Boho Attendees and Invitees

Jack London, Newt Gingrich, Walter Cronkite, Stephen **Bechtel,** George Schultz, **Joseph Coors,** Caspar Weinberger, Merv Griffin, **William F. Buckley, George Bush, Gerald Ford, Henry Kissinger, Manhattan Project** physicist and "father of the hydrogen bomb" Edward Teller, **William Randolph Hearst, Grateful Dead** guitarist Bob Weir, Herman Wouk, Ambrose Bierce, Mark Twain, Dan Rowan, Dick Martin, Charlton Heston, Bob Hope, Bing Crosby, **David Rockefeller,** and Art Linkletter.

Cabalists

✡ ∽∽

Cathars

Southern French group who were deemed heretics for their refusal to acknowledge the Catholic Church and so were wiped out by the **Vatican** in the thirteenth century for their **Gnostic**-like belief that a bit of the divine rested in everyone. Before being phased out entirely, the Cathars (the "pure ones" in Greek) supposedly passed on their secrets to the **Knights Templar**.

Dagobert II

A seventh-century French king (maybe mythical) of **Merovingian** descent murdered by Assassins sent by the pope. Some claim Dagobert (and the Merovingians, or "long-haired ones") was actually a descendant of a union between either **Jesus** and **Aliens** from the planet Sirius or Jesus and Mary Magdalene.

⊙

Druids

An ancient Celtic priesthood of sun worshipers, magicians, and wizards, the Druids' rites are very similar to those of the solar-gazing **Zoroastrians**.

✳

> The distinguishing thing about the paranoid style is not that its exponents see conspiracies or plots here and there in history, but that they regard a "vast" or "gigantic" conspiracy as *the motive force* in historical events. History *is* a conspiracy.
>
> —Richard Hofstadter,
> *The Paranoid Style in American Politics and Other Essays* (1967)

Eleusinians

A Greek, sixth-century B.C., pagan mystery cult that styled themselves after Persephone, the goddess of vegetation. As an annual rite, the Eleusinians toured underworld caverns, hoping to be symbolically reborn into light. In *The Road to Eleusis*, authors Gordon Wasson, Carl Ruck, and Albert Hofmann (the chemist who discovered **LSD**) posited that, during the hallucinogenic orgiastic rites known as the Eleusinian Mysteries, followers supped of the holy *kakeon*, a drink topped off with ergot, the fungus from which LSD is made.

✳ 〰〰 〰

Benjamin Franklin

Legendary essayist, scientist, statesman, diplomat, philosopher, and ladies' man, and dubbed by his fellow Masonic chums as the "Pythagoras of the New World," Franklin (1706–1790) was an influential Worshipful Master in both Europe and America—where he was an instrumental figure in the **American Revolution** and during the early days of the new U.S. government. A card-carrying regular at London's sex-goth **Hell Fire Club,** Franklin initiated Voltaire into **Freemasonry** at Paris's Masonic Lodge of Nine Sisters, where the ideology behind the **French Revolution** was developed.

✳

French Revolution

The overthrow of the French monarchy and ancién régime, inspired and led by **Freemasons** and the **Illuminati**. The revolution may have also been instigated in part by the **Knights Templars'** esoteric "Grades of Vengeance" ritual (a vigilante-style call to action), in retaliation against the French monarchy, who had banned their order and executed Templar leader Jacques De Molay centuries earlier. Among the Illuminati clubs that participated in the revolt: the Sophisters of Impiety, the Sophisters of Rebellion, and the Sophisters of Impiety and Anarchy. In the 1790s, anti-Illuminati Frenchman and lapsed Freemason Abbé Barruel accused the three groups of conspiring to overthrow *all* monarchies and *all* property. The French Revolution spawned a number of ideological trends, including **Terrorism** (whose adherents took a cue from the horrific and morale-quashing Reign of Terror) and **Socialism** (whose advocates admired the active roles given to workers and the lower classes). Many other secret clubs, such as the

Sublime Perfect Masters, also arose out of the messy chaos of the revolution.

✳

Gnostics

♍ ⚹ ♒

God

♍ ✳ ⚱ ☉

Hermetic Mystics

☿

Medieval practitioners of the ways of Hermes Trismegistus (aka the Thrice Greatest Hermes), known among ancient Greeks as the androgynous god Hermes and to the Egyptians as Thoth. The Hermetics' "devilish arts" included the practice of magic, the **Cabala,** astrology, alchemy, and occult wisdom and their Hermetic lore influenced **Christian Rosencreutz,** the Invisible College, and the **Rosicrucians,** among others.

Hermetic Order of the Golden Dawn

A men's and women's secret society founded in 1887 (or 1881) by London coroner Dr. William Wynn Westcott. The Golden Dawn rooted their teachings in the **Hermetic Mystics** and the **Cabala** and studied magic (whereas the Theosophical Society did not—W. B. Yeats joined the Dawn for just this reason after being kicked out of the society for "magical practices"). **Aleister Crowley** was also a member until they kicked him out, too (Al had too much sex on the brain, even for the Dawn). The group's themes and symbology can be found in the works of James Joyce, Ezra Pound, and T. S. Eliot— and today's tarot deck owes its existence to the one created by the Dawn.

International Banking Conspiracy

♍ ✿ ★ ✍ 〰〰 ⌔ ∝ ♒ ⚱ ⊕

International Zionist Conspiracy

♍ ❋ ✡ ✍ ∽ ▦ ⊕

Ismailis

This unorthodox eighth-century splinter group of Shiite Muslims, also known as the Seveners, claim to be descendants of Muhammad. The infamous **Assassins** belonged to this sect, whose modern-day spiritual leader is the Aga Khan, an **International Banker** extraordinaire.

Jesuits

♇

Roman Catholic order, devoted to missionary and educational work, founded in 1540 by St. Ignatius of Loyola. The Jesuits, also known as the Society of Jesus, sometimes worked as the pope's special agents (really, as the **Vatican**'s shock troops), toiling to counter the Protestant Reformation. In the eighteenth century, the order's Black Popes, a cabal of superdedicated Jesuit generals, carried out the Vatican's dirty work (knocking off Europe's anti-Catholic kings and queens) and were accused of plotting to kill William of Orange, Henry III, Henry IV, and Elizabeth I. The Jesuits were the confessors of European royalty and also went undercover in Protestant countries in order to clandestinely spread Catholicism. St. Ignatius and his Jesuits have long been accused of secretly belonging to the **Alumbrados,** the mystical group condemned by the Church in 1623. Later on the Jesuits were suspected of consorting with the **Illuminati.** Some suspect the Jesuits pressured Karl **Marx** to push the idea of an egalitarian godless society in his *Communist Manifesto*.

❋ ⚥

Jesus Christ

♍ ❋ ∽ ⚰ ⊙

Knights Templar

♍ ❋ ⚥ ∽

Knights of Columbus

This **Masonic**-style lodge for American Roman Catholic men was founded in Connecticut in 1882 to protect the interests of

37

the **Vatican**. They're responsible for Columbus Day, in honor of Christopher Columbus, genocidal discoverer of the New World. ✳

Knights of Malta

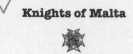

A Catholic order of various holy military fraternities formed in the 1100s during the Crusades, these knights settled in Malta in 1530 (a U.S. branch opened in 1926). The knights have about ten thousand members, half of whom belong to a scary subgroup of European nobility known as the Black Families.
🏛 ⚱ ☺

Merovingians

A thought-for-dead Frankish dynasty that lasted from the fifth to the eighth centuries. One bizarre theory has it that the Merovingians descended from a Bible-time union of **Aliens** from Sirius (the Dog Star) and ancient Israel's Tribe of Benjamin (or maybe it was a union of Sirians and **Jesus**? or was it Mary Magdalene and Aliens?). The Merovingians, however, did not die out in 751 with the murder of **Dagobert II**, no sir. **Bilderbergers** founder **Prince Bernhard** is a Merovingian, as is Otto von Hapsburg, who is also a Bilderberger and **Knight of Malta**.
⊙

Mithraism

An offshoot of **Zoroastrianism** based on the worship of the god Mithra (Old Persian for "friend"), the god of light and the sun. This ancient cult of fifth-century B.C. Aryans (in what is now Iran)

Notable Knights of Malta

Former CIA director **William Casey, John McCloy, Licio Gelli, Reinhard Gehlen,** Alexander Haig, former West German chancellor Konrad Adenauer, Princess Grace Kelly, former CIA director William Colby, **Ronald Reagan,** Lee Iacocca, Otto von Hapsburg, Francis Cardinal Spellman, and Clare Boothe **Luce.**

practiced the standard sacramental forms of most mystery cults: baptism and the sacred banquet (involving the ritual slaying of a bull).

Nimrod

The son of Cush and grandson of Noah, Nimrod is a legendary biblical figure, described as the first powerful king on earth who ruled Assyria and Babylonia (Genesis 10:8–12, Micah 5:6). In addition to being a king, Nimrod was a "mighty hunter before the lord" as well as a stonemason and is said by **Freemasons** to have built Nineveh and Babylon. Nimrod is also said to have married his mother, **Semiramis,** and is credited by some as the inventor of banking. Late in life he returned to the mystery cult religions and quested for a kind of **New Age** self-deification.

Order of the Garter

A secret-society spin-off of the **Rosicrucians** founded in 1348 by King Edward III of England and dedicated to the Virgin Mary. Garter meetings took place in a special room in Windsor Castle around a table just like the mythical one used by King Arthur and his knights. The order's motto: Evil be to he who evil thinks. Charles II was a Garter, as was Dr. John Dee (1527–1608), Queen Elizabeth I's confidant. The order actively encouraged Martin Luther and his Protestant Reformation—since it weakened the political power of the Vatican, the order's enemy and the enemy of **Freemasonry,** the **Knights Templar,** and the **Cathars.** Lately, the order has served as Queen Elizabeth II's elite of the elite cadre.

Order of the New Templars

Aka Ordo Novi Templi, this German secret society was founded in 1871 by the extreme **Fascist** Lanz von Liebenfels and later served as a front for the **Nazis.** The mystical group's magazine, *Ostra,* depicted Teutonic Aryan gods battling bestial subhumans. The young **Adolf Hitler** was a devoted reader.

Everywhere do I perceive a certain conspiracy of rich men seeking their own advantage under that name and pretext of the commonwealth.

—Sir Thomas More (1478–1535)

Prince Bernhard

An international businessman, supposed descendant of the **Merovingians,** leader of the Black Families of Europe, and co-founder of the **Bilderbergers,** Bernhard, born in 1911, was the nephew of Leopold IV, the last reigning prince of the German state of Lippe. In the early days of the Third Reich, Bernhard was a member of the **Hitler** Youth Movement, and as a young man he worked for **I.G. Farben.** After his wife was crowned queen of the Netherlands in 1948, Bernhard became increasingly involved in international business matters, working with the **Royal Dutch** Petroleum Company (Shell Oil) and other **Multinationals.** In 1952, Bernhard was approached by Joseph H. Retinger about bringing together **NATO** leaders and various international financiers for informal and unofficial meetings to discuss the problems facing the capitalist West. As a result, two years later Bernhard called the first meeting of the Bilderbergers and served as its chairman. The Bilderbergers have met every year since then. In 1976, Bernhard resigned in disgrace from all of his businesses after it was disclosed that **Lockheed** had paid him millions to convince the Dutch to buy its Starfighter warplanes and other aircraft. In 1980, Bernhard's daughter, Princess Beatrix, ascended the throne of the Netherlands. ✝

Priory of Sion

A **Gnostic**-style order, aka the Prieuré de Sion, the Priory of Sion was originally created to preserve the **Merovingian** bloodline (whose kings claimed to be direct descendants of King Solomon and **Jesus**). Established in 1099 on Mount Zion, just outside Jerusalem, this guiding force for **Freemasonry** and the **Knights Templar** included such members as Leonardo Da Vinci, Isaac Newton, Joan of Arc, Claude Debussy, and Jean Cocteau.

❋

✓ Christian Rosencreutz

Supposed German mystic of the 1400s (some question whether Rosencreutz ever even existed) whose three alchemical tracts (*Fama Fraternatis of the Meritorious Order of the Rosy Cross*, *Confessio Fraternatis Rosae Crucis*, and *Chemical Wedding of Christian Rosencreutz*, which weren't published until 1614–1616) proclaimed that all previously unknowable secrets were accessible via study and contemplation. Rosencreutz inspired the works of the Invisible College and the **Rosicrucians** and has been the forefather of sorts to all **Illuminati** and **Freemasons**. ❊

✓ Rosicrucians

♍ ❊ ⚸

✓ Royal Society

Founded by **Freemasons** and **Rosicrucians** in 1660, the society's mission was to reform science, religion, and art. The society structured itself after the medieval **Hermetic-Cabalist** brotherhood, the Invisible College. Its presidents included Samuel Pepys and **Priory of Sion** Grand Master Isaac Newton.

✓ Satan

♍ ∽

✓ Semiramis

Aka Ishtar, Minerva, and Diana, Semiramis was an Assyrian queen who cofounded Babylon with and married her son, **Nimrod**. Elevated to goddesshood, Semiramis's followers adhere to her **New Age** credo: "You shall be as gods." She also inspired numerous mystery cults—all of which emphasized sensual fulfillment and personal godhood. ∽

✓ Sublime Perfect Masters

An **Anarchistic**, secret revolutionary French Masonic lodge patterned after the **Illuminati**, the Cathars, and the **Rosicrucians**. This pan-European secret society, based in Italy, was founded in the early 1800s, in the aftermath of the **French Revolution**, by Filippo Buonarotti, a **Freemason**,

Italian nobleman, and coconspirator of **Conspiracy of Equals** leader François-Noël Babeuf's. The Masters opposed Napoleon and sought to do away with private ownership.
❋

Vatican

♍ ❋ ⚷ ⛰ ⚒ ☺ ☉

Zoroastrians

Sixth-century B.C. Persian worshipers of the light god Mazda. Their philosophy depicted a cosmic eternal struggle between the forces of light and dark.
⚷

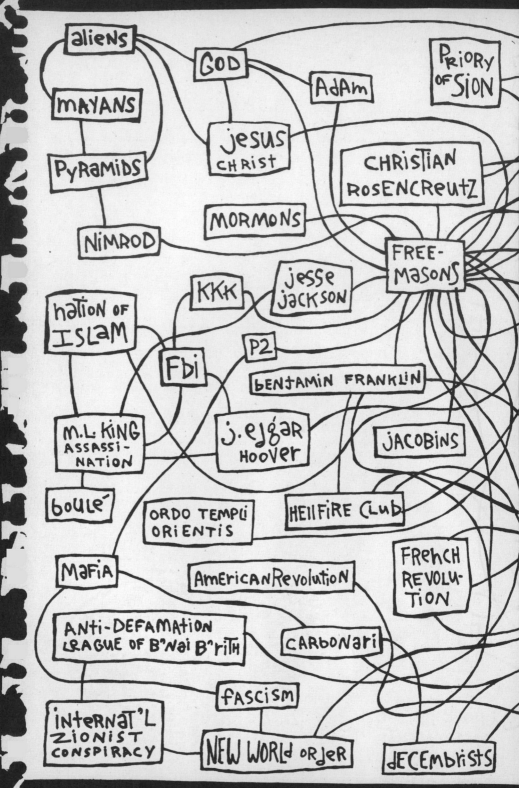

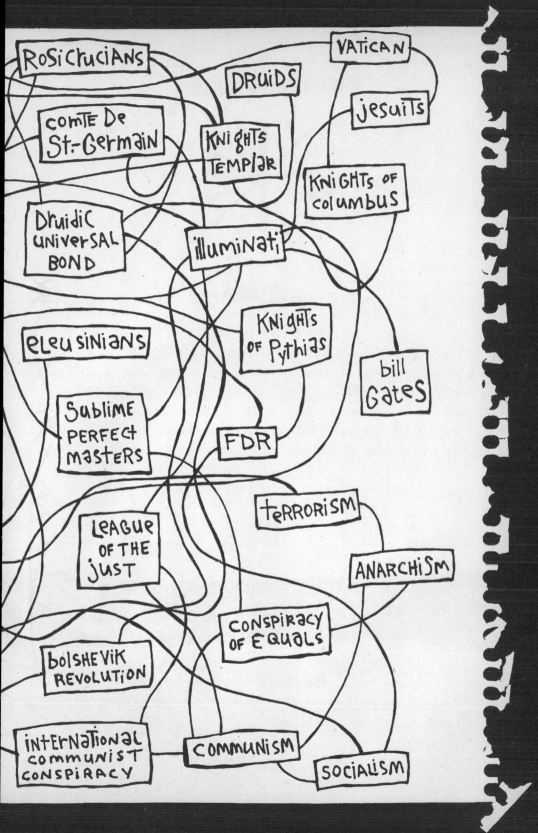

Conspiracy

A one-two sucker punch of Freemasons and the Illuminati, who together comprise both the wicked roots and the evil twin towers of all medieval and modern-day conspiracy theories. Aside from the Jews, these two groups seem to have had their hidden hands in anything and everything, from **Terrorism** and the Mormons to the Nation of Islam and the rise of Bill Gates and Microsoft.

Adam

♍ ✖

Aliens

♍ ✖ ⚶ ∾ ☉

I've heard the truth. Now what I want are the answers.

—**Agent Scully to Agent Mulder,** *The X-Files*

American Revolution

A Masonic-inspired uprising of the thirteen colonies against British rule.

Anarchism

Personified by Russian anarchist philosopher and **Freemason Mikhail Bakunin** (1814–1876), the Anarchists' primary international objective was the overthrow of all governments and social institutions, and considered violence an acceptable and sometimes even necessary means to achieving their goals.

Anti-Defamation League of B'nai B'rith (ADL)

The B'nai B'rith's anti-anti-Semite watchdog committee, suspected by some as being part of a British intelligence operation. Founded in the United States by **MI6,** some say, and run for a time by U.S. representative Saul Steinberg (a rumored business partner of the **Rothschilds**). Its sister organization, the Independent Order of B'nai B'rith, which means Brotherhood of the Covenant, is an assimilationist Jewish pride lodge that was founded in 1843 in a New York City restaurant by immigrant **Freemason** Jews who wanted to become good Americans (its members included Eddie Cantor and Leon Trotsky).

Bolshevism

An early-twentieth-century Russian outgrowth of **Marxism,** this national secret society, led by **V. I. Lenin,** advocated a dictatorship of the proletariat via an immediate and violent revolution, which the Bolsheviks later carried out. Some Russians think that the Bolsheviks, who may have been financed by German aristocrats and Jewish bankers like the **Rothschilds** and Warburgs, were, in actuality, the Okhrana—the czar's secret police.

The Boulé

A black men's elite secret society founded in 1904 as the black Greek fraternity Sigma Pi Phi. Modeled after the "talented tenth" theory once espoused and later renounced by Boulé member W. E. B. Du Bois, the Boulé adopted most of the rites and brotherly notions found in **Freemasonry**. Non-Boulé blacks have often blamed the Boulé as part of a conspiracy to keep other blacks—especially poor blacks—down. Its members have included Vernon Jordan, Martin Luther King, Jr., and almost every black mayor in America.

Carbonari

The "charcoal-burners," a heavily **Masonic** anti-**Vatican** secret lodge of early-nineteenth-century Italy (and throughout Europe) led by Giuseppe Garibaldi and initially founded by Pierre Joseph Briot in opposition to Napoleon's presence in Italy (though others claim the group originated in Scotland, during the reign of **Freemason**-friendly Robert the Bruce). Often pictured with a cross and an ax, some charcoal-burners were later incorporated into the Sicilian **Mafia**. Their revolutionary tactics in Italy inspired the **Decembrists** to undertake a similar revolution in Russia.

Communism

Based on the principles laid out by Karl Marx and Friedrich Engels in the *Communist Manifesto* (1848), Communism is a yet-unrealized political system in which there is neither a state nor a class nor a common ownership of land. Nonetheless, Communist countries include(d) the USSR, Cuba, and China.
✡ ✍

Comte de Saint-Germain

Once mentor to future **Freemason** traitor, Count Cagliostro, the comte was a mystery man of eighteenth-century Europe: a spy, an **Illuminati**, a **Rosicrucian,** and an alchemist. The comte also experimented in Tantric sex magick, studied the occult (with Tibetan adepts), worked as an agent of the French royal family, and plotted to overthrow Russian czar Peter the Great. And still he had the time to found two secret societies: the Asiatic Brethren and the Knights of the Light. Or maybe he had all that time because he was indeed an immortal vampire, as some said, who'd been alive since the 1500s.
ƒ

Conspiracy of Equals

Radical pre-**Anarchist** François-Noël Babeuf's failed revolutionary group who instigated a bloody uprising in 1796 France. The Equals fought on behalf of the sans culottes, the radical lower-class republicans who were "without breeches." Babeuf was in cahoots with Italian **Freemason** Filippo Buonarotti, who started his own postrevolutionary secret society, the **Sublime Perfect Masters**. Babeuf and his Equals' aims also rubbed off on Louis-Auguste Blanqui, who came up with the catchy slogan "the dictatorship of the proletariat," which was later adopted and popularized by **Marxists** and **Communists**.

Decembrists

Striving for a more liberal society, these **Carbonari**-inspired former Society of Pythagoras fanciers of **Masonic** lodges and symbolism revolted against the repressive Czar Nicholas I on December 14, 1825. Though their coup attempt failed miserably, their revolutionary spirit and goals were later taken up by the **Bolsheviks**.

Druidic Universal Bond

A neo-Druidic society founded in 1717. The Bond's members included **Hell Fire Club** founder Sir Francis Dashwood. As a group, they hoped to revive the Celtic religion. Their chief Druid was the mystical poet William Blake (who was also a **Rosicrucian**).

Druids

✖

Eleusinians

✖ 〰 ∞

Fascism

♏ ⚔ ✝ ⛰ ☞ ⚱ ☺

FBI

♏ ✝ ☞ 〰 △ ☼ ⊕ ☉

Benjamin Franklin

✖

49

Freemasons

♍ ✡ ☥ △ ☺

French Revolution

✖

Bill Gates

Megalomaniacal software-computer control-freak geek-tycoon, co-founder, and CEO of Microsoft, whose allegedly predatory and monopolistic business practices have made him the richest nerd in the world and landed Microsoft in various antitrust suits. (Microsoft controls nearly 80 percent of the world's PCs and is a sponsor-investor of the **MIT Media Lab**, among many, many other technocracy-friendly endeavors.) Gates is now also suspected of being the modern-day incarnation of **Illuminati** founder Adam Weishaupt. After all, Bill Gates, goes the theory, is the name of a magical character in the **Aleister Crowley** book *Moonchild,* and German Illuminati members address one another by the abbreviated form B (for Bavarian) Ill(uminati), or just plain Bill for short; and "Gates" is but an acronym of the Germanic spelling of the American Illuminatis' lodge, the Geheime Amerikanische Tochtergenossenschaft der Erleuchteten Seher.

✿ ▦ ⊕

> Everybody in the communications business is paranoid of Microsoft—including me.
>
> —**Rupert Murdoch, chairman and CEO of News Corporation**

The Killing of the King

Part of the **Freemasons'** three-step method of how to achieve world domination and bring about the **New World Order,** the Killing of the King was achieved in 1963 with the assassination of **John F. Kennedy** (head of Camelot), who was killed in Dallas, which is located at 33 degrees latitude, and along the Trinity River near a triple underpass. There are thirty-three degrees of Freemasonry, and **Christ** died at age thirty-three. In 1977, Elvis Presley, the King, died in Memphis, Tennessee—nine years after the assassination of **Martin Luther King, Jr.,** in the same city.

God

♍ ✖ ⚷ ☉

Hell Fire Club

The popular name for London's notoriously libidinous eighteenth-century Masonic den of iniquity, where many prominent **Freemasons** (like **Benjamin Franklin**) sated their most demented of carnal lusts. In public, these Hell Fire Masons preferred the more chaste name, the Friars of St. Francis of Wycombe. In private, they engaged in quasi-**Satanic** acts and practiced the **Eleusinian** mysteries.

J. Edgar Hoover

A conspiranoiac nonpareil, this **Freemason** and cross-dressing head of the **FBI** (1924–1972) consorted with racists and bigots; persecuted Communists, liberals, and other "agitators"; and maintained an Orwellian "Security Index," an official laundry list of people to be locked away in the event of a "national security emergency." Using wiretaps and surveillance, Hoover maintained a vicious vendetta against **Malcolm X** and the Reverend **Martin Luther King, Jr.**, going so far as to try to smear King's reputation with "revelations" about his homosexuality and adulterous affairs. Hoover may have been trying to preempt attempts by others to out him by first getting whatever dirt he could muster on everyone else—tapping phone lines, bugging offices and tryst spots, and secretly filming and photographing any act that might be construed as adulterous, illicit, or just embarrassing. For example, Hoover claimed to have had pictures and tapes of **John F. Kennedy** and **Marilyn Monroe**; Kennedy and gangster moll Judith Exner; **Robert Kennedy** and Marilyn Monroe; John F. Kennedy and movie star Angie Dickinson; Martin Luther King, Jr., and various unnamed liaisons; and **Richard Nixon** and a Hong Kong travel guide named Marianna Liu (though

Liu, who later relocated to Tricky Dick's hometown, denies there was any affair). He also collected fabricated "homosexual" stories about many people, such as King, and even collected ammunition for another supposed gay frame-up, this one involving Nixon aides H. R. Haldeman, John Ehrlichman, and Dwight Chapin in a ménage à trois. He loathed the Kennedy brothers for their numerous sexual liaisons and was friendly with other Kennedy haters like Nixon and Texas oilman **Clint Murchison.** He did, however, work closely with Robert Kennedy in going after the Mob, despite his public proclamations that the **Mafia** did not exist.

△

Illuminati

♍ ✡

International Communist Conspiracy

♍ ✡ ✍ △ 〰 ☺ ✿

International Zionist Conspiracy

♍ ✖ ✡ ✍ 〰 ▦ ⊕

Reverend Jesse Jackson

A **Freemason** and a member of the **Council on Foreign Relations,** Jesse Jackson is a southern minister and a former presidential candidate and was influential in the civil rights movement. Politically ambitious, Jackson happened to be present at the assassination of **Martin Luther King, Jr.,** in 1968 and was one of the first people to reach King's side as he lay dying.

△

Jacobins

Radical French sect of the revolutionary era who sought to represent the commoners and limit the powers of the monarchy, the aristocracy, and the church. Inspired by the philosophy of the Masonic Club Breton (the late-eighteenth-century clubhouse formed by French **Freemasons**), and led by Danton and Robespierre, the Jacobins instigated the Reign of Terror—in which thousands of Parisians were beheaded—and the **American Revolution.** Thomas Jefferson was later branded a Jacobin by anti-Mason Jedediah Morse.

✗ ↑

> Because it is sometimes so unbelievable, the truth often escapes being known.
>
> —**Heraclitus**

Jesus Christ

♍ ✗ ⊶ ⚰ ☉

Martin Luther King, Jr., Assassination

The minister and black leader of the sixties' civil rights movement, King was relentlessly harassed by **FBI** director **J. Edgar Hoover,** who amassed false documents that purported to show that King was having affairs with both women and men. On April 4, 1968, King was murdered by "lone gunman" **James Earl Ray** in Memphis, Tennessee. However, King's widow and sons, Martin III and Dexter, think that **Lyndon Johnson** may have had a hand in their father's murder and none believe that Ray acted alone (if at all). Aside from what Ray and **Jules Kimble** say (that there was a King assassination team, which included Ray, Kimble, and seven **CIA** men—three of them disguised as Memphis police—and a mysterious figure whom both Ray and Kimble called "Raoul"), Memphis police were scarcer than ever that day (despite numerous threats on King's life), and the first person at King's side was **U.S. Army** spy Marrell McCullough and the second was the ever-ambitious **Jesse Jackson,** a **Freemason** but not a fellow **Boulé** brother of King's. Plus, **Mafia** boss

53

Sam Giancana claimed he turned down a joint CIA-FBI offer of one million dollars to kill King.

☞ △

Knights of Columbus

✖

Knights of Pythias

Freemason-influenced American fraternal order born during the Civil War in Washington, D.C. The Pythians sought to embody a spirit of friendship as deep as that between the mythical Damon and Pythias. Their most famous member was **Franklin Delano Roosevelt.**

Knights Templar

♍ ✖ ⚱ ᴄᴐ

Ku Klux Klan (KKK)

Creeps in white sheets famous for lynchings, bad genes, and unmagical wizards. Also known as "the Invisible Empire," the KKK is easily America's most famous white-supremacist hate group. Dating back to the southern **Masonic** chivalric order founded in 1866 in Pulaski, Tennessee, the Knights of the Ku Klux Klan hoped to evoke the chivalry of **Templarism** and adopted many Masonic symbols (as well as their argot and rituals), and based their fraternity of hatred on the concept behind the Greek word *kuklos,* meaning "circle." The Militia Movement is rife with Klansmen and Klan-connected figures: **Christian Identity** minister Connie Lynch and **Aryan Nations** founder Richard Butler hobnobbed with them, Tom Metzger was a KKK Grand Dragon before founding the White Aryan Resistance (WAR), and many Klansmen belong to the latter-day **Populist Party,** which sponsored former national director of the Knights of the KKK David Duke for president in 1988.

△ ⚑

League of the Just

Aka the League of Just Men, this radical, mid-nineteenth-century **Illuminati**-influenced secret society was formed by French insurrectionist and workers' advocate Louis-Auguste Blanqui. The league commissioned Karl **Marx** and Friedrich Engels to write the *Communist Manifesto*.

Mafia

꿰 🏛 〰 △ ✏ 😊 🔳

Mormons (Church of Jesus Christ of Latter-Day Saints)

Founded in the 1840s by longtime **Freemasons** Joseph Smith and Brigham Young, the church is now run out of Salt Lake City by an inner cabal called the Council of Twelve. Characterized by tithing and intense proselytizing (via their famous "missions" to other countries), they stress the importance of procreation and revelation (Smith received directions to the long-buried *Book of Mormon* tablets from an "angel," whom some theorize was an **Alien**). The church has long been a favorite recruiting ground of the **FBI** and the **CIA** (Mormons adhere rather strictly to a life of no alcohol, no caffeine, and no drugs, and have the reputation for being notoriously well mannered and assiduous followers of the company line). Late in the sad, sordid life of billionaire **Howard Hughes**, five Mormon male nurses rarely let anyone from the outside world get anywhere near their barely preserved but dying sugar daddy. In 1970, his five Mormon attendants spirited Hughes off to the Bahamas in a weird

Interesting, I Didn't Know Rabbi Weitzmann Was a Mormon

The **Mormons** run one of the world's largest and most controversial databases, into which they've been assiduously adding the names of as many of the world's people as they can, as part of what they claim is a good-faith effort to rechristen anyone and everyone—dead and alive, Mormon and non-Mormon—an honorary Mormon. This tends to get them into trouble, as it did in the mideighties, when Jewish groups found out that the Mormons had gotten hold of a list of Jewish victims of the **Holocaust** and were adding them to their New Mormons list.

power grab for the Old Man that came to be known as the Thanksgiving Coup. Led by Hughes's Mormon personal assistant, Bill Gay, the coup permanently cut longtime Hughes aide **Robert Maheu** out of the tycoon's life and also fueled rumors that the old bastard had actually died but the Mormons had set up an elaborate ruse of Hughes still being alive—not only to enrich their own pockets but to transfer the Old Man's wealth and assets to Mormon HQ back in Salt Lake City.

Nation of Islam

☪

A quasi-religious U.S. black nationalist organization founded in the 1930s by ex-con Wallace Fard, aka Walli Farrad and Farrad Mohammed (reportedly an initiate **Freemason**), and solidified as a Muslim outfit by Fard's protégé, the legendary onetime Georgia migrant worker Elijah Poole, later Elijah Muhammad (a member of the High Degree Prince Hall Freemason group). Poole-Muhammad claimed that blacks were actually a race of beings from the moon and there's a **UFO** mother ship orbiting the Earth, which will soon wipe out the world's whites and rescue all the blacks. The NOI is now led by alleged anti-Semite and UFO contactee **Louis Farrakhan.**
△ ☉

New World Order

♍ ✍ ∾ ☺ 🌐

Nimrod

✖ ✡ ∾

Ordo Templi Orientis

Seminal occult order founded between 1895 and 1900 by two German **Freemasons**, the OTO drew heavily on the traditions and rites of the **Knights Templar** and engaged in Tantric sex magick. **Aleister Crowley** joined the OTO in 1912 (after being kicked out of the **Hermetic Order of the Golden Dawn**) and quickly rose to top-dog position as Outer Head. **Charles Manson** belonged to OTO—although not to one recognized by most other Templi folks.
ᵔᴗ

Priory of Sion

✖

Propaganda Due Lodge (P2)

A **Fascist**, anti-Communist **Terrorist** network and **Freemason** lodge founded in 1966 by Italian Mason, **Knight of Malta,** and **Mafia** consort **Licio Gelli.** In the late 1980s, P2, whose American members included **William Casey,** allegedly assassinated Italian prime minister Aldo Moro (guilty of tolerating Commies). The lodge also had ties to the **Vatican Bank** and may have been involved in the mysterious death of Pope John Paul I (who'd threatened to fumigate the **Vatican** of its P2 and Masonic elements). They also infiltrated the **Banco Nazionale del Lavoro** (BNL) via its Atlanta, Georgia, branch and, perhaps with help from **Henry Kissinger,** expedited loans to one of the bank's clients, **Saddam Hussein.** Many of P2's leaders and members were regulars at the **World Anti-Communist League,** a sort of Fascist-Terrorist United Nations.

🏛 ☺ 🔲

Franklin Delano Roosevelt (FDR)

The U.S. president from 1933 to 1945, FDR was also an **Illuminatus,** a **Freemason,** a Shriner, and a **Knight of Pythias.** FDR put the Masonic pyramid-and-the-eye insignia on our one-dollar bill. He was also a good friend of Sosthenes Behn, the **Nazi** collaborator and owner of the enormous **Multinational ITT.** To bolster the economy after the stock market crash of 1929, Roosevelt was forced to borrow huge sums of money from **Illuminati** Jews like the **Rothschilds.** In 1933, he used this money to launch the New Deal, **a Socialist** program of relief, recovery, and reform intended to solve the economic and social problems created by the **Great Depression.** FDR survived the 1933 plot to overthrow him (the **Capitol Hill Coup**).

✍ ✝

Christian Rosencreutz

❋

Rosicrucians

♏ ✖ ♐

57

Socialism

The transitional stage (between capitalism and **Communism**) of no private property and state-owned and state-controlled means of production.

✡ ✍ ∾

Sublime Perfect Masters

✖

Terrorism

Etymologically rooted in the **French Revolution**'s Reign of Terror, modern-day terrorism involves covert warfare or violence against selected targets or random targets—the goal being the creation of a state of fear.

★ ⛰ ☺

Vatican

♍ ✖ ⚐ ⛰ ⚑ ☺ ☉

Official Memorandum

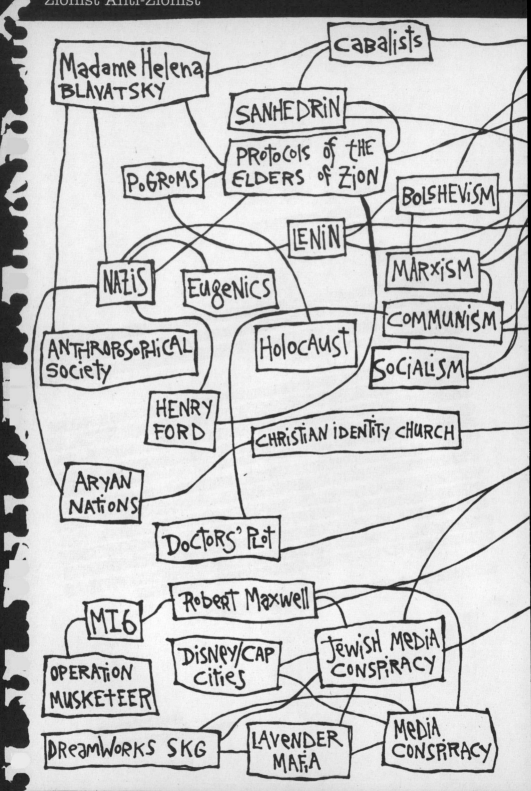

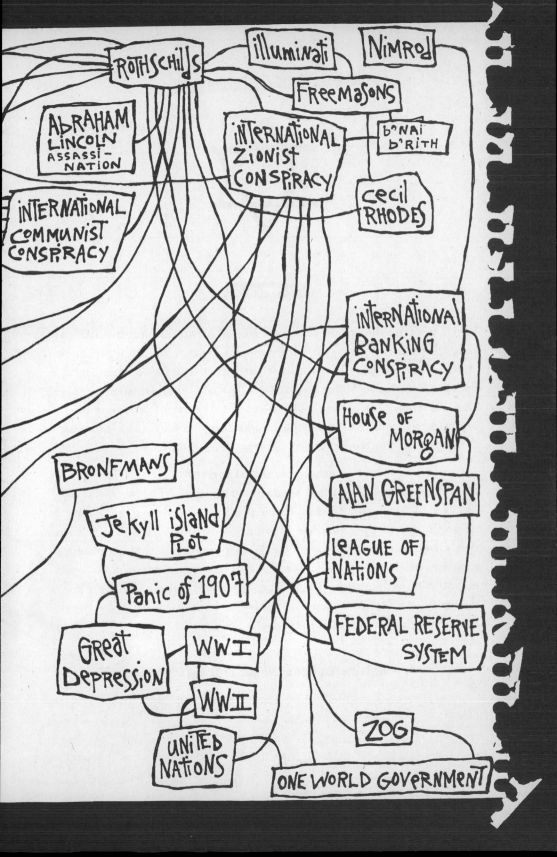

Conspiracy

While it's true that some Jews have played a role in Communism or have indeed run some of Hollywood's studios or managed their share of the world's financial institutions, they've also been blasted by anti-Semites as being responsible for *all* things sinister—a position the anti-Zionists then use to justify all sorts of far worse deeds enacted by themselves against Jews, like the pogroms, the Holocaust, the denial of the Holocaust, et cetera.

Anthroposophical Society

Shortly after breaking from **Madame Blavatsky**'s Theosophical Society in 1909, occult teacher Rudolph Steiner (1861–1925), a kind of godfather to the **New Age** movement of today, in 1923 formed this **Christ**-centered East-meets-West philosophy that espoused a new spiritualism via radical art, architecture, medicine, and art education (with philosophical and ritualistic echoes of the **Freemasons** and **Rosicrucians**). Steiner eventually settled in Basel, Switzerland, and founded his famous Steiner Schools.

Anti-Defamation League of B'nai B'rith

✓ Aryan Nations

Richard Butler's white-supremacist Idaho-headquartered Church of Jesus-Christ Christian (one of several hundred churches affiliated with "Identity," a pseudo-theological hate movement). Founded in the mid-1970s, Aryan Nations is a hybrid of Neo-**Nazism** and Christian Identity, the identity part being that Anglo-Saxons, not Jews, are the biblical "chosen people," nonwhites are "mud people" (on the level of animals), and Jews are the "children of **Satan**." Before founding AN, Butler served as pastor of Gerald Swift's **Christian Identity Church,** where he hooked up with future Posse Comitatus honcho, William Gale.

†

✓ Madame Helena Blavatsky

An aristocratic Russian émigré who founded the **Theosophical Society** in New York City in 1875. Theosophy, to which even the great Mahatma Gandhi was drawn, blended **Cabalism, Hermetic** lore, and the mysteries of Isis, and ostensibly promoted universal brotherhood through the study of all great religions, philosophies, and sciences and through the investigation of the unexplained laws of nature and the psychic powers of human beings. Blavatsky (1831–1891) was also a spiritualist, an astrologist, and a hash addict—and something of a bigot. Her Theosophical Publishing Society published tracts popularizing an image of Jews as secret con-

✓ The Date of Martyrdom

The significance of April 19 among members of the Militia and the extreme right builds and builds upon itself. April 19, 1775: Battle of Lexington opens the American Revolution. April 19, 1993: Siege of Waco, Texas, Branch Davidians compound ends. April 19, 1993: The false date of issue for Oklahoma City bomber Timothy McVeigh's fake South Dakota driver's license. April 19, 1995: Date of execution of Richard Wayne Snell, member of the Covenant, the Sword and the Arm of the Lord, for the murder of a Jewish businessman and a black police officer, and also date of the Oklahoma City bombing.

spirators and demonic abusers of black magic. In her Tibetan travels she supposedly met up with the mythical adepts of the Great White Brotherhood and supped tea with the indefatigable **Comte de Saint-Germain.** Studied by **Aleister Crowley,** Blavatsky continues to be esteemed today among certain **New Agers** for her quest for Eastern-based spiritual enlightenment.

ꭍ ⌖ ꮗ

Bolshevism

❋

The Bronfmans

During Prohibition, Sam and Harry Bronfman allegedly got their liquor from Chicago's Black Hand **Mafia** and bootlegged the illicit booze for Meyer Lansky, Lucky Luciano, and Bugsy Siegel. After Prohibition, the Bronfmans went on to solidify Seagram's as North America's largest liquor company. Scion Edgar Jr., son of Ed Sr., has since branched out with the family business (after taking over from his father as CEO in 1994), risking the family fortune by selling off their stake in **Du Pont** and buying up film and music companies like so much candy: Ed Jr. now owns **MCA**/Universal and Polygram, and has a distribution deal with **DreamWorks SKG** and a 15 percent share in **Time Warner.** His buddies include **Lavender Mafia** man David Geffen, and he and Ed Sr., as president of the World Jewish Congress, led the campaign to force Swiss banks to compensate **Holocaust** victims.

△ ⌖ ▦

Cabalists

✖ ꮗ

Christian Identity Church

Associated with the **Populist Party,** the **Aryan Nations,** and the Church of **Jesus Christ** Christian and an offshoot of the Jew-friendly (yes, Jew-friendly) **New Right Fundamentalists,** these white supremacist extremists claim that white Christians (whom they call the thirteenth tribe of the Manasseh) are the true Israelites, the true inheritors of the earth, not the Jews of the Old Testament (and everyone else, well, they're just "mud people"). In the 1960s, Christian Identity minister Connie Lynch hobnobbed with both the

United Klans of America and the Minutemen, Robert DePugh's paramilitary anti-Commie ring. CI members Charles Barbee and Robert Berry were for a time suspected of having been involved in the 1996 Atlanta Olympics bombing (although they were never charged).

✡ ✝

> Often, the less likely it seems, the more we are attracted, as though we liked it that *non sequiturs* are basically always *sequiturs*.
>
> —Richard Ford, *The New York Times Magazine*, September 1998

✓Communism

※ ✍

✓Disney/Cap Cities

Disney was founded in 1923 by animation pioneer Walt Disney, a longtime snitch for **J. Edgar Hoover** (he happily informed on liberals, **Communists**, and agitators of any stripe) and an avid Fundamentalist. In 1948, eccentric Texas billionaire **Howard Hughes** (via his RKO studios) floated Walt a cool $1 million interest-free loan. Now a global infotainment monolith, Disney's rodent-based empire has grown substantially since Michael Eisner (a Jew) took over in 1984 and since its 1995 takeover of Cap Cities/**ABC**. Derisively referred to by some of its own employees as Mauschwitz, Disney's media reach extends to Mammoth Records,

ESPN, Hyperion Books, EuroDisney, Major League Baseball's California Angels, *Los Angeles* magazine, **ABC**-TV, and the National Hockey League's Mighty Ducks, not to mention film and TV studios (Buena Vista, Miramax) and the Disneyfication of New York City's Times Square.

The Doctors' Plot

Near the end of his totalitarian reign (and near the end of his mind), in January 1953 the ever-paranoid Soviet leader Joseph Stalin concocted the idea that a cabal of Jewish doctors, in conjunction with Israel and NATO countries, were plotting his death and the murders of other prominent **Communists**.

DreamWorks SKG

Entertainment company formed in 1994 by film and music moguls Steven Spielberg, Jeffrey Katzenberg, and David Geffen—all three Jews, and Geffen, who's at least out about his homosexuality and is the most prominent member of the **Lavender Mafia**. (Paul Allen, **Bill Gates**'s former partner and Microsoft cofounder, is DreamWorks's largest shareholder).

Eugenics

The use of selective mating to weed out the "flaws" among certain groups within the human species, eugenics was first raised by British psychiatrist Francis Galton (Charles **Darwin**'s cousin) as a means of uplifting society, a notion embraced by many British leftists of the 1930s, who thought of the average Brits as "sub-men." (Even great thinkers such as Bertrand Russell suggested the use of state-issued "procreation tickets," so as not to dilute the elite's high-IQ DNA with plebeian muck.) The **Nazis** adopted eugenics and applied it to their "racial cleansing" programs; in the United States, in the 1920s, eugenics found support at the Carnegie Foundation and in projects like the **Tuskegee Syphilis Study**. In 1925, the **Rockefellers** wrote over $2 million in checks to Germany's Kaiser Wilhelm Institute, some of which went to the institute's Department of Anthropology, Eugenics, and Human Heredity. Later, in **WWII**, body parts of concentration-camp victims were shipped to the institute for study—and also at the institute were psychiatrists Ernst Rudin and Franz Kallmann. Both men escaped the Nuremberg trials, and despite Kallmann's work with the Nazis' despicable T4 unit, for instance, where scientists murdered nearly 200,000 mentally ill persons, they were later moved stateside, where Kallmann, who was half Jewish, later helped found the American Society of Human Genetics—the organization that helped set up the **Human Genome Project.**

ꝭ ᷡ ☼

> This act establishes the most gigantic trust on earth. . . . When the President signs this act, the invisible government by the money power, proven to exist by the Money Trust Investigation, will be legalized. . . . The new law will create inflation whenever the trusts want inflation.
>
> —**Charles A. Lindbergh, Sr., U.S. congressman, on the passage of the Federal Reserve Act, 1913**

Federal Reserve System

The central banking system of the United States since 1913. Nicknamed the Fed, it is comprised of twelve privately controlled central district banks that are supervised by a board of governors in Washington, D.C. All national banks must belong to the Federal Reserve System, and many state banks belong voluntarily. The system has a variety of major functions that many of its critics do not believe should be performed by privately controlled entities: to hold the deposits of America's commercial banks, to control the issuance of coins and paper currency, to regulate the practices of its member banks, and to serve as the basic controller of credit in the U.S. economy (and, in so doing, to determine the money supply and interest rates for borrowing). The 1913 Federal Reserve Act, which outlined the way the system would work, was drafted at the supersecret **Jekyll Island** Conference in 1910. (In 1996, the World Jewish Congress, under the leadership of Edgar **Bronfman,** Jr., cited declassified U.S. documents indicating that six tons of **Nazi** gold are currently held by the Federal Reserve and the Bank of England.) The Fed operates independently of and unaccountable to both the president and Congress, leading some to believe that the Fed is nothing more than the personal piggybank of the **International Bankers** and/or the **International Zionists,** who use the system to create recessions and depressions to their own advantage. Along with the graduated income tax and the **Internal Revenue Service,** which act as collection agents, the Federal Reserve forms what some anti-Semites call the **Zionist Occupied Government.** The current head of the Fed is **Trilateralist Alan Greenspan,** who was formerly employed at **Morgan** Guaranty.

♍ ✍ ⊕

Henry Ford

This Michigan-based auto tycoon was a spiritual forefather to many a race baiter and bigot. Ford, a raging anti-Semite, popularized the **International Jewish Conspiracy** myth and championed *The Protocols of the Elders of Zion* as gospel. A **Freemason,** he also helped to finance the National Socialists (the future **Nazis**) of Germany, and was the only American favorably cited in **Hitler**'s *Mein Kampf*. Hitler reportedly said, ". . . we look to Heinrich Ford as the leader of the growing **Fascist** movement in America."

★

> This movement among the Jews is not new. From the days of Spartacus-Weishaupt, to those of Karl Marx, and down to Trotsky (Russia), Bela Kun (Hungary), Rosa Luxemburg (Germany), and Emma Goldman (United States), this worldwide conspiracy for the overthrow of civilisation and for the reconstitution of society on the basis of arrested development and envious malevolence and impossible equality has been steadily growing. It has been the mainspring of every subversive movement during the nineteenth century.
>
> —Winston Churchill, 1920

Freemasons

♍ ✳ 🕯 △ ☺

Great Depression

A **Rothschild**-orchestrated economic crisis of the 1930s that forced U.S. citizens into a greater reliance on government aid. In turn, **Illuminati** Jews and **International Bankers,** who were already bankrolling the government, reaped ever-increasing interest payments.

Alan Greenspan

A **Trilateralist,** Greenspan earned the nickname Dr. Pain because of his willingness, as chairman of the **Federal Reserve,** to create recessions (in attempting to stimulate the economy by lowering interest rates—ostensibly to help out the little people, i.e., consumers and small businesses, but really a tactic to try to prevent his **International Banker** allies from going bankrupt). When not serving as Fed chairman or as presidential economic adviser, Greenspan likes to shill for various banks. In the mideighties, for instance, he earned huge sums (as a paid consultant) from crooked bankers such as **Charles Keating** (whose Lincoln Savings & Loan thrift led to the **S&L Debacle**) in return for offering up glowing reports about Lincoln to the government.

Holocaust

Among the hardcore of anti-Semite revanchist revisionist claims is the idea that the **Nazis'** systematic extermination of up to 10 million Jews, Gypsies, homosexuals, political prisoners (particularly Poles and Russians), and the mentally and physically handicapped was a) an overinflated number, b) a hoax, or c) a **Zionist** plot to extract reparations from Germany in order to finance the state of Israel.
ƒ ★ ⬧ ✦

House of Morgan

The empire of John Pierpont Morgan and Sons, the American family of financiers, investment bankers, and industrialists. John P. Morgan (1837–1913) was an **International Banker** extraordinaire, creating U.S. Steel, the world's first billion-dollar corporation. In 1933 (during the 1867–1943 tenure of his son, J. P. Morgan, Jr.), three high-level House of Morgan executives were involved in the preempted **Capitol Hill Coup** to overthrow Franklin Delano Roosevelt. The **American Legion,** another group implicated in the coup, was founded just after WWI by

69

House of Morgan director Grayson Murphy. The House of Morgan also had ties to the **Rothschild** banking empire and to the **Nazis' J. Henry Schröder Banking Corporation**. The Morgan banking dynasty was also responsible for the rise of **General Electric**.

✍ 🏛

✓ Illuminati

♍ ✳

✓ International Banking Conspiracy

♍ ✘ ★ ✍ 〰 ✎ ☞ ∾ ⚱ ⊕

✓ International Communist Conspiracy

♍ ✳ ✍ △ ∾ ☺ ✿

✓ International Zionist Conspiracy

♍ ✘ ✳ ✍ ∾ ▨ ⊕

The Jekyll Island Plot

It was here at this Georgia retreat in 1910 that the idea, nay, the actual formation, of a central U.S. bank (what later became the **Federal Reserve**) was drawn up—in the wake of the **Panic of 1907**. Sworn to secrecy by all those who attended, among whom were **International Bankers** Paul Warburg (the Jewish financier who later confessed to being there and to what transpired), J. P. **Morgan**'s right-hand man Benjamin Strong, and gentile **Insider** and Rhode Island senator Nelson Aldrich (grandfather of **Nelson Rockefeller**).

✍

✓ Jewish Media Conspiracy

This popular offshoot of the **Zionist** and media conspiracy theories posits that Jews control most, if not all, of the major media. Prominent Jews in the media business include Michael Eisner of **Disney**; publishing magnate **Si Newhouse**; the triumvirate that founded **DreamWorks SKG**, filmmaker Steven Spielberg, former Disney executive Jeffrey Katzenberg, and bisexual music mogul and EST grad David Geffen; the owners of *The New York Times* and *The Washington Post*; Gerald Levin, the head of **Time Warner**; the founding Warner brothers, Sam, Jack, Harry, and Albert; other early Hollywood moguls like Darryl Zanuck and Samuel Goldwyn; **Lew**

Wasserman, a former president of **MCA** and **Reagan**'s Hollywood agent; and on and on.

Lavender Mafia

The paranoid right's *Spy*-magazine-driven notions that Hollywood (and the Media) is pretty much a Queer Nation, controlled by (mainly male and mainly Jewish) homosexuals like the openly bisexual mogul David Geffen (the G in **DreamWorks SKG**) and Jann Wenner (the recently divorced founder and publisher of *Rolling Stone* and *US*), and that most heterosexuals can't (and won't) ever get a fair shake, since gays only promote (or hire) other gays.

League of Nations

The first step toward a **One World Government,** the league was set up after **WWI** by U.S. president Woodrow Wilson at the behest of the British-influenced **Round Table** and a cadre of U.S. aristocrats who called themselves the Inquiry. The league, along with **International Bankers** and **International Zionists,** set off the stock market crash of 1929 and the subsequent **Great Depression** as part of a Grand Plan for a One World Government dominated by the United States and Great Britain.

Vladimir Lenin

Leader of the **Bolshevik** revolution and advocate of **Marxism** and **Communism,** Lenin purportedly received $5 million in gold from German-Jewish financier Max Warburg (as a promise not to wreak Commie chaos in Germany). Founder of the **KGB.**

Abraham Lincoln Assassination

While watching the comedy *Our American Cousin* at Ford's Theatre in Washington, D.C., on April 14, 1865, five days after Robert E. Lee's surrender at Appomattox, Lincoln was shot and killed by disgruntled thespian and southern sympathizer

71

John Wilkes Booth. Postwar tension was used as the reason for his murder, but others have always wondered if maybe it was Honest Abe's decision to print his own currency to pay off the Union's war debts—rather than knuckling under to another prohibitive **Rothschild** loan—that led to his assassination.

✓ **Marxism**

The political and economic theory of Karl Marx (a German Jew and Socialist writer) on which **Communism** is based and which served as inspiration for the **Bolshevik** revolution (and many other twentieth-century revolutions). Marx and Engels's *Communist Manifesto* reads like a conspiracy blueprint, arguing for, among other things, 1) a one-world godless society, 2) a graduated income tax, and 3) a centralization of credit in a national bank.

✍ ☺

✓ **Robert Maxwell**

Distant relative of concentration-camp survivor (and Nobel laureate) Elie Wiesel, Maxwell (1923–1992), like Wiesel a Jew, was born Lev Hoch in rural Czechoslovakia, lost most of his family in the **Holocaust,** and joined the French and then the British to fight the **Nazis.** After the war, he founded Pergamon Press with **MI6** agent **Count Frederick Vanden Heuvel.** Initially a publishing-front company, Maxwell turned it into a media empire. Before MI6 ruined his credit and brought down his business (leading to his "sui-

✓ **That Would Be John Fitzgerald . . . Lincoln?**

The names **Lincoln** and **Kennedy** both have seven letters.

The names of their assassins **Lee Harvey Oswald** and John Wilkes Booth both have fifteen letters.

Their respective successor vice presidents: Lincoln's successor, Andrew Johnson, was born in 1808; Kennedy's, **Lyndon Baines Johnson,** was born in 1908.

Lincoln's secretary's name at the time of his assassination was Kennedy, and Kennedy's secretary's name was Lincoln.

Both Lincoln and Kennedy were involved in messy wars, and both supported the rights of blacks.

cide"), Maxwell, a **Zionist** at heart, in 1948 rescued the aborning state of Israel from certain annihilation by secretly arming the new nation against the attacking Egyptians. Pergamon also sold a bastardized version of the **PROMIS** software and in the 1970s and 1980s Maxwell teamed up with Japanese **Fascist Ryoichi Sasakawa.**
꠸

Media Conspiracy

⑫ ⋙ △ ∽ ✸

MI6

Those clever Brits. Deliberately, the great minds there at England's secret intelligence agency dispatched to D.C. MI6 agents they knew were gay, in the hopes of compromising suspected American homosexuals like **J. Edgar Hoover**—leading to the likelihood that the infamous smoking-gun photo of Hoover in drag may indeed have been taken by one of Hoover's MI6 flings. The MI6 then lent the picture to the **CIA** to keep the head G-man and his boys in check. MI6 also worked with the **Vatican** in moving **Nazi** loot out of Germany and away from the Soviet Union.
✐ ∽ ꠸

Nazis

⑫ ★ ✝ ⛰ 🐾 ⚱ ✸

Nimrod

✖ ✺ ∽

One World Government

⑫ ✍ ∽ ⊕

Operation Musketeer

Code name for the 1956 deal set up by the French and the British, whereby in order to ensure a smooth flow of oil to the West, and by the West (via Western-owned oil companies like British Petroleum and Gulf Oil), Israel was pressured into attacking Egypt (and its anti-West leader, Gamal Abdel Nasser) so that the French and the British would then intervene and take the Suez Canal by force (and oust Nasser to boot). Worse, true to their anti-Semite bones, the British and the French let the Egyptians and the Syrians know beforehand to expect a **Zionist** invasion.

73

Panic of 1907

An economic crisis set off by the collapse of New York's esteemed Knickerbocker Trust Company, contributed to by J. P. **Morgan** and a cartel of **International Bankers,** back then known as the Money Trust. Morgan dumped a huge load of securities on to the stock market and their prices plummeted. Morgan and his cronies did so in order to indebt the U.S. government to them and to frighten the average citizen into demanding a new system of banking—the **Federal Reserve.**

Pogroms

This organized massacre of Russian Jews ran off and on from the 1850s through the 1920s—triggered by the assassination of Czar Alexander II in 1881, for which the government tacitly blamed the Jews, and so, rarely intervened in any pogrom attacks. The Czarists also claimed that the pogroms were justified because of the **International Zionist Conspiracy,** as revealed in *The Protocols of the Elders of Zion.*

The Protocols of the Elders of Zion

Concocted in Paris in 1905 by **Madame Blavatsky** follower Yuliana Glinka and other Russian émigrés, this publication claimed to be a firsthand report of the (actual) First Zionist Congress in Basel, Switzerland, in 1897, which was held by Theodor Herzl—when, in fact, nine-tenths of the book was faked and probably orchestrated by the Paris chief of the Okhrana (the czar's secret police). Nonetheless, the *Protocols* promoted the idea of an **International Zionist Conspiracy** and propagated the myth that every one hundred years, a sneaky group of old Jewish guys known only as the Elders (the heads of the twelve tribes of Israel) gather in a Jewish cemetery in Prague and map out the next one-hundred-year course for gentile enslavement and a **One World Government.**

There has come up in recent years . . . something called a conspiracy psychology. . . . We are on the road to a paranoid explanation of things.

—Henry Steele Commager, U.S. historian (1967)

Cecil Rhodes

A brutal nineteenth-century British colonialist-financier (1853–1902), Rhodes helped establish British rule in South Africa. After making a financial killing from the diamond fields at Kimberley (1871–1888), he formed the De Beers Mining Company and eventually controlled 90 percent of the world's diamond production. (The De Beers cartel now controls 80 percent of the world's diamond market and shamelessly exploited South Africa's apartheid-era poor blacks to work in their deleterious mines.) By the end of the century, Rhodes's company controlled Northern and Southern Rhodesia (named, of course, after him)—the former is now Zambia and the latter, once Rhodesia, is now Zimbabwe. Rhodes lent his name and bequeathed part of his fortune to the Oxford University Rhodes Scholarships. A longtime **Freemason,** the **Round Tables** were his idea and apartheid came about in no small way thanks to Rhodes.

Rothschilds

♍ ★ ✍ ∾

The Sanhedrin

A cabal of occultish Jewish rabbis who last met in A.D. 66 but whose legacy was resuscitated by Napoleon in 1807, when the Little General assembled France's most important Jews in Paris and termed the meeting the Great Sanhedrin. Napoleon was hoping that these Jewish businessmen would back him and his campaigns.

Socialism

❋ ✍ ∾

United Nations

♍ ✍ ∾ ⊕

World War I

The Great War of 1914 to 1918. A result of Europe's having been goaded into conflict by the **International Bankers** (like the **Rothschilds**), who wanted to create profits and economic chaos to gain further power.

Practically all the ruses and stratagems of war are variations or developments of a few simple tricks that have been practiced by man on man since man was first hunted by man. . . . The elementary principle of all deception is to attract the enemy's attention to what you wish him to see, and to distract his attention from what you do not wish him to see.

—Gen. Sir Archibald Wavell,
memorandum to the British Chiefs of Staff, 1940

World War II

The second World War (1939–1945). Instigated, some claim, by Jewish bankers and **Communists** who wanted to create profits by bringing the United States out of its **Depression**.

Zionist Occupied Government (ZOG)

ZOG, an acronym frequently used by members of the U.S. Militia Movement and other anti-Semites, refers to governments in which Jews have become "diabolically entrenched." The components of the ZOG include the **Federal Reserve System,** which acts as the **International Zionists'** piggybank and allows them to create recessions and depressions whenever it's to their advantage; the **Internal Revenue Service,** a glorified collection agent for the Federal Reserve that may actually be a private Jewish-run corporation; and the graduated income tax, designed to suck the middle class dry, making them, and the U.S. government, easy prey for the plans of the **International Bankers** and International Zionists. The idea of ZOG also extends to the myth of a Zionist-ruled **One World Government**—or, Zoglandia.

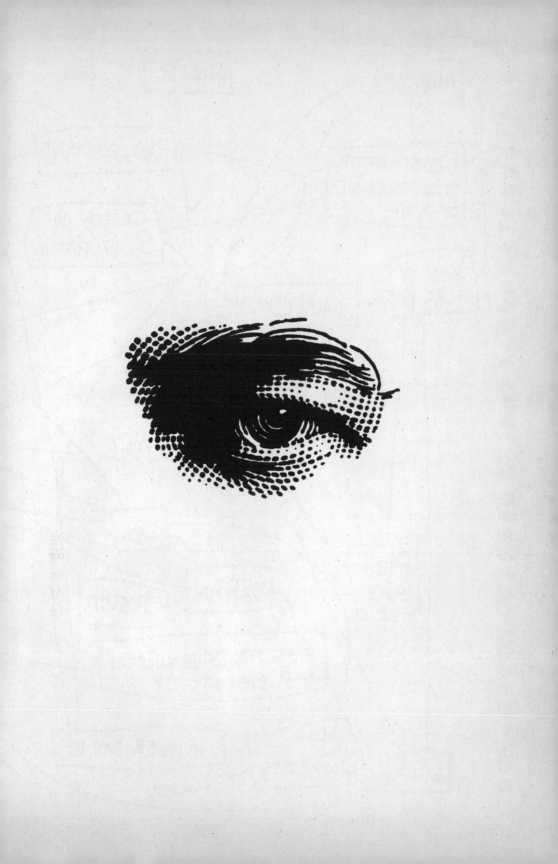

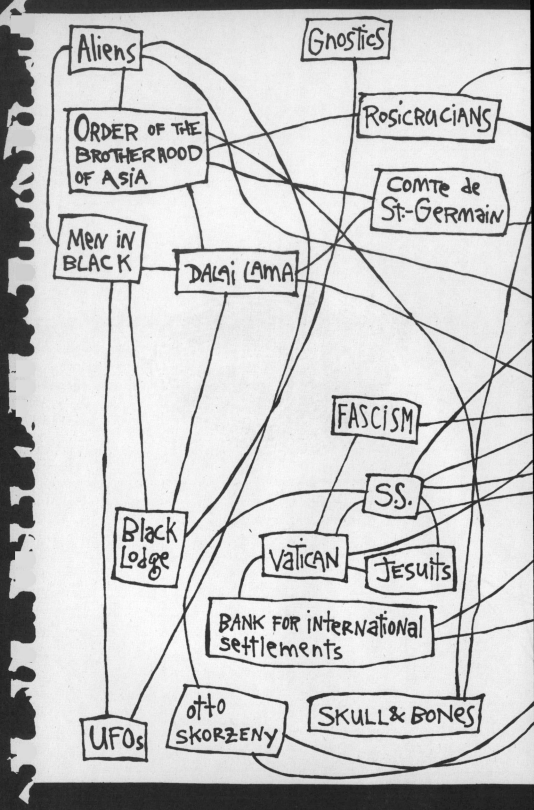

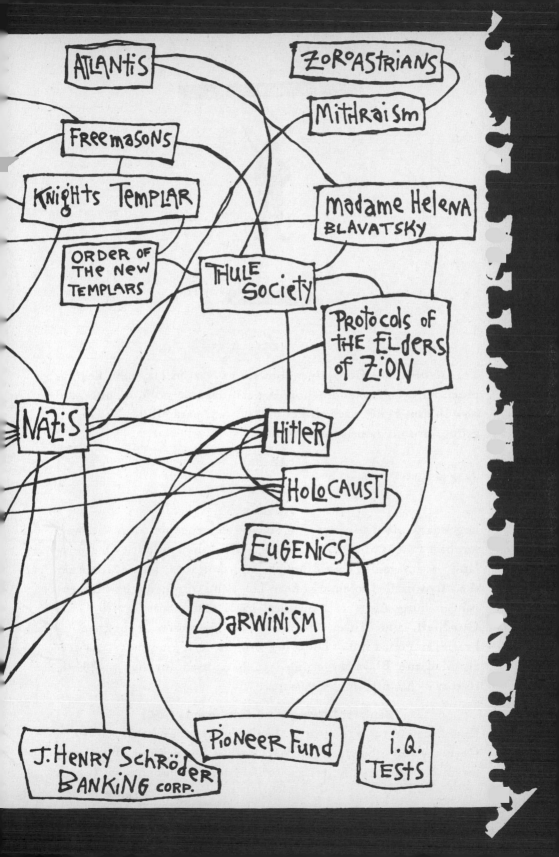

The Master Race Conspiracy shows how Nazism may have been as much an occult phenomenon as a military or political one—and how Nazism's philosophy lives on in postwar paramilitary and occult groups, from satanists to the Militia.

Aliens

♍ ✖ ✳ ∾ ☉

Atlantis

Legendary underseas utopia of aquatic superpeople from way, way, way back (about 60,000 years back). When their Atlantic Ocean island was ravaged by an earthquake and sank into the sea, some say the survivors fled to an area near Tibet and founded a new subterranean burg—Agarthi, a mythical town that, according to **G. I. Gurdjieff,** and **Hitler**'s mentor Karl Haushofer, contained libraries crammed full of books detailing esoteric knowledge, materials **Madame Blavatsky** claimed to have used for her prophetic history of Atlantis, *The Secret Doctrine*.

Bank for International Settlements (BIS)

Established in 1930 to assist in the payments of reparations owed by Germany and other losers of **WWI**, by the beginning of **WWII** this Swedish, **Nazi,** and American-run thirteen-member cabal (which now includes **Federal Reserve** chairman **Alan Greenspan**) used its Basel, Switzerland, headquarters to funnel Nazi money (stolen from Jews) to fund Germany's war effort and keep the **Holocaust** in high gear. After the war, the BIS transferred the **Nazis'** money to Argentina (and other Latin American countries) via the **Vatican.**

★ 🏛 〰 🌐

Black Lodge

According to **Gnostic UFO**logist Allen Greenfield, these occult shock troops operate in a universe not unlike the good-versus-bad mythology of *Star Wars*: As adepts of the dark side of black magick, the Black Lodge aims to retard human progress and enslave the planet, and they carry out their program via such dark occult leagues as the **Thule Society,** the **Church of Satan,** and the **Temple of Set.** Even the mysterious **Men in Black** may be Black Lodge representatives, given that they may be from the Nation of the Third Eye (i.e., Tibet, home of possible Third Eye leader the **Dalai Lama**).

⊙

Madame Helena Blavatsky

✡ ➤ 〰

Comte de Saint-Germain

❋

Dalai Lama

⊕

The exiled spiritual leader of Tibet (location of the mythical city Shambhala, which is the secret HQ of occult adepts known as the Great White Brotherhood—or the Secret Chiefs, or the Hidden Masters). In the 1960s, the **CIA** agreed to train some of the Dalai Lama's troops (and other Tibetan exiles) in the hopes that he and his boys might one day retake their sacred homeland from the evil Chinese **Communists** who've occupied it since they invaded it in 1945. In 1997, three members of the Dalai Lama's inner circle were ritualistically murdered by unknown assailants, and in 1998, the Dalai Lama discouraged fellow Buddhists from worshiping Dorje Shugden, a protector deity of the Geluk sect (to which the Dalai Lama himself once belonged). The Dalai

Lama called Shugden an "evil spirit." His Holiness has also come out in support of India's thermonuclear bomb tests and accepted about 170 million yen from Japan's **Aum Shinrikyo** cult—prior to their attack on the Tokyo subway system, he even met with the cult's leader, Shoko Asahara. Much to Richard Gere's chagrin, the Dalai Lama recently passed over the *American Gigolo* star (who is a longtime Buddhist and one of the Dalai Lama's most devoted spokespeople) for public honors, instead reaching out to *Hard to Kill* action figure (and professed spook) Steven Seagal and declaring him a "tulku"—a reincarnated lama.

✝ ➣ ⌇ ☉

Darwinism

The central theory of British naturalist Charles Darwin (1809–1882), namely, that species evolve through a process of "natural selection," i.e., well-adapted individuals have a greater chance of surviving, reproducing, and passing on their genes to their offspring than poorly adapted individuals. This led to his theory of evolution, which holds that all living species have evolved from preexisting forms—a concept long denied and contested by Fundamentalists. Others see Darwinism as a Jewish-**Freemason**-spawned ideology that posits humans as animalistic consumers of products made by shysters who control the world's economy, ironically, a notion that's often used *against* the Jews as justification to eliminate them. That **Eugenics** evolved out of Darwinism is no surprise.

✿

Eugenics

✡ ⌇ ✿

Fascism

♍ ❋ ✝ ⛪ ➣ ⚔ ☺

Freemasons

♍ ❋ ✡ △ ☺

Gnostics

♍ ✖ ⌇

Adolf Hitler

An Austrian-born draft dodger, failed housepainter, and watercolorist, and the führer and cult leader of **Nazi** Germany from 1934 to 1945. Hitler had his soft head massaged by occultists from the left and right (though mostly from the extreme right—and anti-Semitic and nationalistic). The two who most thoroughly worked him over were Dietrich Eckart and Karl Haushofer, the latter a onetime Munich university professor (where his assistant was Rudolph Hess, future deputy führer) who felt the Aryan race originated near Tibet, which is where, in 1908, Haushofer met up with the legendary Russian mystic **George Ivanovich Gurdjieff.** Eckart, a leader of the messianic anti-Semitic **Thule Society,** saw in Hitler a man the Thulists had always desired: a despotic leader who would reclaim the world from subhumans like the Jews for the Aryans (the Thules). Hitler nearly accomplished this by carrying out the **Holocaust.**
★ ✝ ▓

The Nazis acted as though the world were dominated by the Jews and needed a counterconspiracy to defend itself.

—**Hannah Arendt,** *The Origins of Totalitarianism* **(1951)**

Holocaust

✡ ★ ✝ ✡

IQ Tests

These biased standardized exams supposedly measure one's intelligence quotient (much like the SAT and ACT supposedly measure one's scholastic aptitude). Nobel laureate William

Shockley caused a huge stir at one point when he offered to pay blacks $1,000 for every point below 100 on their IQ score—if they'd have themselves sterilized. IQ tests are one of the sticking points for bell-curve racists and **Eugenics** proponents (like the **Pioneer Fund**) who honestly believe that whites are intellectually superior to blacks.

J. Henry Schröder Banking Corporation

Founded in the nineteenth century, this vast international network of banks and holding companies has had ties to the **CIA,** the **Federal Reserve,** the **Nazis,** the **Rothschilds,** and the **Rockefellers.** Between 1915 and 1918, its institutions gave money to the German government through the Belgium Relief Commission (which dissuaded Germany from seeking a peaceful end to **WWI** in 1916). Later, Schröder helped finance **Hitler** in 1933, procured an ownership interest in the Federal Reserve Bank of New York, backed the U.S. presidential campaign of Herbert Hoover, placed members on the boards of all German subsidiaries of **ITT,** and financed the **United Fruit Company.** In the 1980s, Schröder placed two major executives (Caspar Weinberger and George Schultz) from its subsidiary firm, **Bechtel** Corporation, in the cabinet of the **Reagan** administration. ★ †

Jesuits

✗ ❋

Knights Templar

♍ ✗ ❋ ∽

Men in Black

Mysterious tall male figures who favor black suits, black Cadillacs, and black choppers (and often black sunglasses), and who often appear out of nowhere at **UFO** sightings—purportedly to intimidate UFO witnesses. Some speculate they're **CIA** or air force investigators—or **NASA** strongmen out to scare off **Aliens.** Others believe they're the so-called custodians of the **Brotherhood of the Snake,** or, given their Asian features and their Eye in the Triangle insignia, perhaps they're **Nazi**-ish Tibetan henchmen. Yet another theory has them as agents of the **Vatican,** offshoots of a 1693 Roman Catholic cabal known as the Knights of the Apocalypse who trolled the earth with the mission to knock off the Antichrist.

Mithraism

Nazis

Order of the Brotherhood of Asia

A rogue **Rosicrucian**-style lodge of late-eighteenth-century Germany, these occult-loving cellar dwellers corrupted Buddhism by affixing a swastika, their adopted symbol, onto the Buddha's belly. They also summoned up "spirit guides" (i.e., **Aliens**) during their initiation ceremonies.

Order of the New Templars

Pioneer Fund

Established in 1937 by textile millionaire Wycliffe Preston Draper, this "race betterment" **Eugenics** research institute seeks to prove blacks inferior to whites and to disprove the Holocaust: The fund shelled out nearly 200 grand to Nobel laureate physicist William Shockley for his notion that whites have higher **IQs** than blacks;

The Seventy-two

The first Jew assassinated by the **Nazis,** on June 24, 1922, was the German minister of affairs. His last words, in response to the question "Who shot you?" were, "The seventy-two who control the world." There were seventy-two members in the "superior college" of the **Order of the Brotherhood of Asia,** the mystical lodge that used the swastika as their symbol. Isis, the ancient Egyptian goddess-queen of birth, rebirth, and fertility, became renowned for having resurrected her consort, Osiris, whose twin brother, Set, plotted with seventy-two conspirators to kill him, which they did—cutting him into pieces.

they were acknowledged by the authors of *The Bell Curve*, the 1994 book that also argued there's a fifteen-point difference in IQs between the races; and Roger Pearson, publisher and former editor of the Pioneer-funded *Mankind Quarterly*, has worked closely with Holocaust denier Willis Carto, organizer of the pro-**Nazi** anti-Semitic **Liberty Lobby**. (Pearson also served on the editorial boards of the **Heritage Foundation** and the **American Security Council** and boasted that he once hid **Nazi** doctor Josef Mengele.)

✝ ⚕

The Protocols of the Elders of Zion

✡

♍ ✖ ✳

Rosicrucians

Schutzstaffel (SS)

Hitler's elite corps of personal bodyguards, a **Templar**-style **Jesuitic** occult order of **Terrorists** dreamed up in 1925 by Heinrich Himmler (whom Hitler referred to as "my Ignatius"). Aka the Order of the Death's Head or the Black Shirts, the SS came complete with mystical rites, rankings by degrees, and incantations. From 1939 to 1945, the SS ran the concentration camps and controlled the Gestapo and all other elements of the German Central Security Office (RSHA), which also included the Einsatzgruppen, the "special action squads" that carried out the mass executions of Jews and other "undesirables" (aka the **Holocaust**).

★

Otto Skorzeny

Also known as "Scarface" and dubbed "**Hitler**'s favorite commando," after the war this **SS** officer helped relocate many fellow **Nazis** (with the **CIA**'s assistance) to South and Central America, where they helped set up death squads, and Mexico, Indonesia, and the Middle East. In 1956, Skorzeny aided Egyptian hardliner Gamal Abdel Nasser in his bid for the presidency of Egypt, then trained Palestinian **Terrorists** like Yasir Arafat (Skorzeny also trained **Muammar Qaddafi** of Libya). He later helped ignite the Suez

Canal crisis. With the support of the CIA, Skorzeny also founded and led the Paladins, a sadistic unit of ex-Nazis who trained many other terrorist groups.

★ ⚑

Skull & Bones

Founded at Yale University in 1833 (and modeled on the **Illuminati**), this **Masonic**-style secret society is an offshoot of Chapter 322, a two-hundred-year-old German secret society. Known among its members as the Order (and long ago referred to as "the brotherhood of death"), it is a senior-year group to which only fifteen new members are selected to join each year, and it is extremely hush-hush and bizarrely ritualistic. Its alumni gather annually on Deer Island in the St. Lawrence River, and its members include **George Bush** and his son George W., the **Rockefellers**, Richard Gelb, John Kerry, **William F. Buckley,** William Taft, Averell Harriman, McGeorge Bundy, **Henry Luce,** and David Boren.

〰 ☺

Thule Society

Messianic 1918 secret German sect of ex–**New Templars,** the Thulists styled themselves as **Aryans** after the Fall and regarded Jews as subhumans. They based their beliefs on a **Madame Blavatsky**–inspired variation of the **Atlantis** myth, wherein Thule, a burgeoning nation of überbeings, vanished in a fateful flood 850,000 years ago as a punishment for the Thuleans/Atlanteans having mated with beings who were beneath them. Impatient to correct their past fatal interbreeding, and eager for übermenschdom once more, they figured the subhumans of their time were the Jews and concluded that by eradicating them they'd be redressing past mistakes. The Thuleans were also possessed of a messianic craving for a despotic leader, so they latched on to **Adolf Hitler.** Early on the society was led by Dietrich Eckart and Baron Rudolf von Sebottendorf, an occult enthusiast and racist who'd fallen under the ways of Sufi mysticism and **Freemasonry.** Sebottendorf was arrested by the Gestapo in 1934 and committed suicide in 1945. The society published and distributed *Protocols*, and among its other members was Bram Stoker, author of *Dracula* and a profound anti-Semite.

✓
UFOs

♓

Unidentified Flying Objects. They're usually shaped like saucers, cigars, or Frisbees and have been around since before **Adam,** but the first modern-day sighting of an otherworldly spaceship was in 1947: first in **Maury Island,** Washington, and then days later in **Roswell,** New Mexico. Since then, UFOs have been spotted all over the world and probably carry **Aliens.**
☺ ☉

✓
Vatican

♍ ✖ ☀ ⛪ ✝ ☺ ☉

✓
Zoroastrians

✖

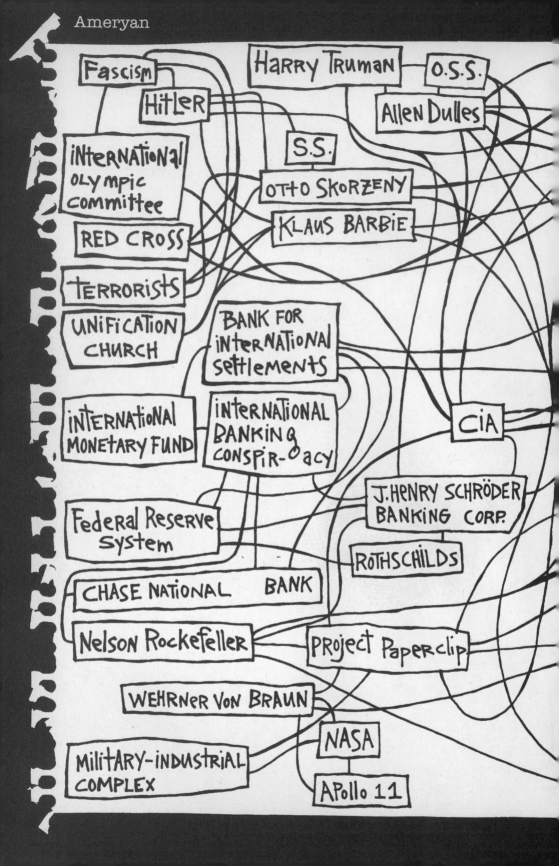

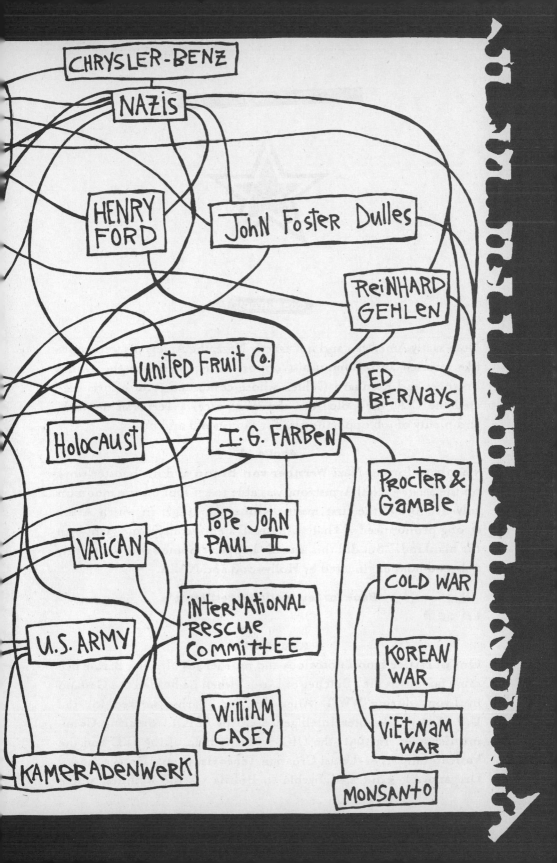

Conspiracy

Not exactly American and not exactly Nazi, the Ameryans were more like staunch anti-Communist opportunists, men like the Dulles brothers and Reinhard Gehlen whose combined joint efforts created the CIA, the Cold War, the space race, a Terrorist network, and plenty of job opportunities for fascists old and new.

Apollo 11

Thanks to former **Nazi Wernher von Braun** and his booster work on the *Saturn 5*, Neil Armstrong was able to set foot on the moon on July 20, 1969 (the first manned lunar landing), in which Armstrong pronounced: "That's one small step for man, one giant leap for mankind." But did this actually happen? Some say it was merely a shrewd hoax engineered by Hollywood and **NASA**.

Bank for International Settlements

✝ ⛰ ∾ ⊕

Klaus Barbie

One of **Hitler's** most notorious and murderous officers, Barbie became famous as the "Butcher of Lyons" when he headed the Gestapo in Lyons during **WWII**. After the war, Barbie worked for the **U.S. Army's** Counter Intelligence Corps (CIC), torturing **Communist** spies. In 1951, the CIC, with the help of the **IRC** and the **Vatican** (and its ex-Ustasi Croatian **Terrorist** priest, Dr. Krunoslav Draganovic), exfiltrated Barbie to Bolivia via the Ratlines, where

Barbie settled in as part of Latin America's **Kameradenwerk** web of repatriated **Nazis.** In Bolivia, he was welcomed by military dictator General Hugo Banzer Suarez, assumed the name Klaus Altman, and pretended to be a businessman. In reality, Barbie continued to work with the United States and formed an elite death squad set up to decimate any and all left-wing groups and Communists. Throughout the 1970s, Barbie and his death squad, with the aid of Barbie's CIA intermediary, Thomas Ward, an official with the **Unification Church's** Causa International, helped the **CIA** support the political ambitions of Bolivia's "cocaine general," Luiz Garcia Meza. In 1987, Barbie was convicted of crimes against humanity by a French court and sentenced to life in prison, where he died in 1991.

✝

Edward Bernays

In 1928, this nephew of Sigmund Freud wrote *Propaganda,* a succinct outline for all prospective spin doctors, covert operations specialists, and Madison Avenue ad executives. Often called the father of public relations, Bernays flakked for such firms as Lucky Strike cigarettes, the **United Fruit Company,** and **Procter & Gamble** (the company with the rumored 666 mark of the beast trademark on the boxes of Crest toothpaste and other P&G products). When Jacobo Arbenz Guzmán was elected president of Guatemala in 1950 and began confiscating United Fruit's landholdings, Bernays helped the **CIA** place agents in Guatemala, agents who successfully waged a disinformation-and-discredit campaign that paved the way for an eventual CIA-engineered overthrow of Arbenz Guzmán. A close friend of H. G. Wells, Bernays studied the sci-fi writer's novels for various **Mind Control** techniques. Future **Nazi** Joseph Goebbels studied Bernays's work and writings assiduously—applying the Bernays philosophy all too well.

The conscious and intelligent manipulation of organized habits and opinions of the masses is an important element in a democratic society. Those who manipulate this unseen mechanism of society constitute an invisible government which is the true ruling power in our country. . . . We are governed, our minds are moulded, our tastes formed, our ideas suggested, largely by men we have never heard of. . . . We are dominated by a relatively small number of persons. . . . It is they who pull the wires which control the public mind, and who harness old social forces and contrive new ways to bind and guide the world.

—Edward Bernays, *Propaganda* (1928)

Wernher von Braun

An **SS** major and rocket scientist, von Braun was part of the elite group of **Nazi** scientists working on Germany's most secret weapons, including the V-2 "vengeance" rockets that were used in long-range bombings of London at the end of the war. In 1945, after surrendering to **Clay Shaw,** von Braun and other Nazi engineers were brought stateside via Project **Paperclip** to continue their research. At **NASA,** von Braun modified his V-2, helping develop the *Saturn I* and *Saturn IB* rocket systems, which carried U.S. astronauts to the moon (for the supposed **Apollo** moon landings).

William Casey

A bit of everything, Casey was a member of Italy's Fascist **P2** lodge and the **Council on Foreign Relations,** a **Knight of Malta** and a **Freemason,** a member of the **Skull & Bones** and the **Secret Team,** and, as former **CIA** director, co-orchestrator of the **October Surprise.** He was also once **George Bush's** business partner and **Wackenhut Securities's** legal counsel. As director of the **International Red Cross** just after **WWII,** Casey helped smuggle **Nazis** out of Europe. In 1954, **Resorts International's** first owners, Thomas Dewey and Lowell Thomas, founded, along with future CIA director William Casey, Capital Cities Communications, the eventual owner of the **ABC** television network. Casey also oversaw the **Iran-Contra** operations on the CIA side (coordinating the logistics of the project with **Oliver North** at the NSC). He died of brain cancer in 1987. 🏨 ✎ ☺ ▦

Chase National Bank/Chase Manhattan Bank

David Rockefeller's financial institution (of which he was chairman). **Henry Kissinger** once oversaw its International Advisory

Committee, and after **WWII**, the **Bank for International Settlements**' Thomas McKittrick became the head of this Rockefeller-founded New York financial institution.

Daimler-Benz

Formerly Chrysler, the American automobile manufacturer, and Daimler-Benz, Germany's premier car maker since 1926, the two merged in 1998 to the tune of $40 billion. Daimler-Benz made the revered Mercedes-Benz line of autos (**Hitler**'s official parade vehicle) before branching out into robotics, aviation, and communications to become Germany's largest industrial company. Until its merger, 14 percent of Daimler-Benz was owned by Kuwait. In post-war Germany, the firm was resuscitated into the black by investor and **Nazi** war criminal Friedrich Flick, who had been convicted in the Nuremberg trials for crimes against humanity (for having used slave labor). Several years ago Daimler-Benz's joint-venture deal between its recent acquisition of Messerschmidt-Bolkow-blohm GmbH, builder of the Third Reich's fearsome Messerschmidt planes, and Mitsubishi, the maker of Japan's **WWII** Zero fighter jets, made more than a few people nervous.

CIA

Cold War

Essentially masterminded and prolonged by **Hitler**'s former **Nazi** intelligence chief **Reinhard Gehlen** and by future **CIA** director **Allen Dulles,** this post-**WWII** struggle between the United States (and its allies) and the USSR and other **Communist** countries grew out of a mutual paranoia between the two ideologies of West and East: The West feared that the Soviets would try to communize western Europe and the rest of the world and vice versa. Gehlen and his Org (a group of spies largely comprised of ex-Nazis) exacerbated both sides' fears of the other with their disinformational intelligence reports. U.S. Cold War policy was largely hatched by the **Council on Foreign Relations** and

lasted from 1945 until the mideighties (the Cold War also led to the formation of the **National Security Council**).
✍ 🏛

Allen Dulles

A **Freemason**, a member of **Skull & Bones**, a partner in New York's Nazi-sympathetic Sullivan & Cromwell law firm, a shareholder, along with his brother **John Foster Dulles** in the **United Fruit Company,** and the second in command of the **OSS**, under William "Wild Bill" Donovan, before cofounding the **CIA** with **Nazi** pal **Reinhard Gehlen**. A buddy of various and sundry Nazis, Dulles had once met **Hitler** personally, and after the war he employed and relocated thousands of former **SS** men under Project Paperclip. As CIA director, he approved the agency's **MK-ULTRA Mind Control** drug program, and as a member of the **Council on Foreign Relations** and of the small, secret group of postwar "players" called the Inquiry, in the 1950s he pushed through the notion that **Multinationals** were so critical to U.S. foreign policy that they should not be subject to any domestic laws. To that end, he nurtured the Nazi-friendly multinational **ITT** back into business and helped broker the postwar German-American business alliance, which involved Germans and/or German businesses that had either been Nazis or had done business with or for the Nazis during **WWII**. In 1961, however, JFK fired Dulles as CIA chief, promising to "splinter the CIA into a thousand pieces and scatter it to the winds." Despite the appearance of a probable conflict of interest, Dulles was brought in as a member of the **Warren Commission.** Dulles was also good friends with many of the heads of the media empires that ran the CIA's **Mighty Wurlitzer** campaign, such as William Paley of **CBS**, Arthur Sulzberger of *The New York Times,* and **Henry Luce** of **Time-Life**. He advised many companies that did business with the Third Reich and also sat on the board of the **J. Henry Schröder Banking Corporation.** He approved the overthrow of Jacobo Arbenz Guzmán's democratically elected Guatemalan government (Arbenz Guzmán's give-the-land-back-to-the-people platform conflicted with Dulles's United Fruit Company investments).
✝ 🏛 🕵 △

It is only by eliminating the lower members [of the human race] that a higher average is maintained.

—John Foster Dulles, date unknown

John Foster Dulles

Older brother of **CIA** cofounder **Allen Dulles,** John was Sullivan & Cromwell's most prominent attorney in the 1920s and 1930s and later a member of the **Rockefeller Foundation.** His specialty was international law and finance and he had many corporate clients with ties to **Nazi** Germany (including **I.G. Farben**). A virulent anti-Communist, he was apparently untroubled by Nazism and often addressed his 1933–1934 cables to German clients with "Heil **Hitler.**" Like his brother, he gave legal advice to the Hitler-helpful **J. Henry Schröder Banking Corporation.** He was also a major shareholder of and attorney for the **United Fruit Company,** which owned most of Guatemala at one point. In 1945, Dulles was part of the U.S. delegation to the San Francisco Conference, which founded the **United Nations,** and he later served as one of the U.S. representatives to the UN. From 1953 to 1959, he was **Eisenhower's** secretary of state, where his rabid anti-Soviet stance basically led to the **Cold War** and the United States's longstanding policy of containment—a cause, in itself, of the **Korean War** and the **Vietnam War.**
✝ ⛰

Fascism

♏ ❋ 🕯 ✝ ⛰ ∞ ⚰ 😌

Federal Reserve System

♏ ✡ ✍ ⊕

Henry Ford

✡

Reinhard Gehlen

Distinguished **Knight of Malta** and chief of **Nazi** counterintelligence on the Eastern Front during **World War II.** At the end of the war, Gehlen charmed **OSS** operative **Allen Dulles,**

97

and in the Nazi-friendly American and his irrational anti-Communist views Gehlen saw not only his survival but his soulmate and meal ticket: Using old, bad, and weak information (and misinformation) that he and his Org had gathered on the Rooskies during WWII, Gehlen told Dulles that in return for freedom and a job he'd happily dig up whatever dirt he could on the USSR and **Communists** everywhere (and if there was no real dirt, he'd just as happily lie and give Dulles fake dirt). So with Dulles's help (and the **CIA**'s), Gehlen settled down in West Germany, where he put his old Org buddies to work in his very own newly created intelligence agency, West Germany's BND. Subsequently, Gehlen and Dulles promoted the **Cold War.** After retiring from spying in 1968, Gehlen moved to a Bavarian chalet that was given to him as a gift by Allen Dulles. In 1969, he began working on classified projects for the U.S. Department of Defense with a California-based high-tech firm.

✝

Adolf Hitler

⚐ ✝ ▨

Holocaust

✡ ⚐ ⚑ ☼

I.G. Farben

A huge **Nazi** Germany chemical cartel, Intersen Gemeinschaft Farben manufactured Zyklon-B (the lethal gas used in the concentration camps and for the **Holocaust**) and employed Auschwitz as an on-site factory (one of Farben's cyanide salesmen, according to conspiranoiac Jack Chick, was none other than future **Pope John Paul II**). Its scientists also invented **Malathion,** the deadly gas later used to spray urban Southern California. **Rockefeller**'s Standard Oil provided Farben with its crucial synthetic rubber patents, and American automobile tycoon Henry Ford merged his motor-company assets to Farben's in 1928. In 1939, Farben received vast amounts of experience and technology from **Dow** and Alcoa. It manufactured sarin and Soman, a fluorinated (**Fluoride**-based) nerve gas. After **WWII,** the company signed deals with **Nestlé,** Bayer, and **Procter & Gamble.** In 1967, Farben, according to conspiranoiac author Alex Constantine, teamed up with **Monsanto** to develop **Biochemical Warfare** agents.

✿

International Banking Conspiracy

♍ ✖ ✡ ✍ 〰 ⬭ ☞ ∾ ⚲ ⊕

International Monetary Fund (IMF)

Originally conceived at the **Council on Foreign Relations** and sub-sequently established on December 27, 1945, as a financial agency of the **United Nations** (to promote international monetary coopera-tion and ensure the stability of currency exchanges), the IMF, head-quartered in Washington, D.C., has 170 members (drawn primarily from nations friendly to **NATO**). Often referred to as the "world's loan sharks" and accused of being the U.S. Treasury Department's lapdog, in the 1980s the IMF became a significant leader to many troubled third world economies, which led critics on the right to claim that it was an agent of international **Socialism,** while critics on the left claimed the austere conditions of its lending policies strained internal political stability in the third world and amounted to a new form of colonialism. Sweden's Per Jacobsson, formerly of the **Bank for International Settlements,** went on to become head of the IMF. Currently, its top two officials, Michel Camdessus and Stanley Fischer, both served as chief economist of the **World Bank.** In tan-dem with the World Bank, the IMF often seems to blackmail its lender countries into devaluing their currencies, implementing IMF-World-Bank-approved population-control programs, and privatizing their industries (to maximize exploitation by **Trans-nationals,** thus pressuring the cash-starved countries into making it a higher priority to please Western-based exporters than to try to house and feed their own people).

∾ ⊕

International Olympic Committee (IOC)

⊙⊙⊙⊙⊙

The controlling organization of the Olympics and arbiter of the world's most famous and lucrative athletic events, the IOC has had many disreputable members. **Nazi** sympathizer,

32nd-degree **Freemason** and Chicago millionaire Avery Brundage served as its president from 1952 to 1972 before handing over his sullied seat atop the 106-member IOC group to the equally unguent Juan Antonio Samaranch, a former Spanish **Fascist** and Francisco Franco loyalist. In the 1980s, Samaranch and Adidas founder Horst "the Fixer" Dassler, in true Olympic spirit, pimped the five rings to whichever sponsors paid them the most. (**NBC, Daimler-Benz,** Visa, Coca-Cola) via International Sport and Leisure, Dassler's Lucerne, Switzerland—based marketing company—and until recently it never seemed to matter to anyone at the IOC that NBC, Visa, and Coca-Cola have had employees who also happened to be IOC board members. Samaranch's key aide is the former Korean CIA operative Kim Un Yong, who was also the right-hand man to KCIA founder **Kim Jong-Pil.** Another IOC member (since 1974) is Rio de Janeiro industrialist and president of FIFA (the international soccer federation) João Havelange, reputed to have been involved in the international-arms trade and allegedly a supporter of Argentina's notorious totalitarian regime of 1976 to 1983. The IOC again disgraced itself in 1999 when its longtime practice of bribe taking and strongarming prospective host cities came to light after investigations exposed its wrongdoings in Salt Lake City and Sydney, leading to the resignations of a dozen or so IOC members.

✝ 🏠

International Rescue Committee (IRC)

This seemingly do-gooder organization, based in New York, seeks to relocate and/or aid persons within and outside their strife-ridden countries. In the late 1940s, it was headed up by future **CIA** director **William Casey,** who used the IRC to recruit **Fascist** "freedom fighters" to the United States (most of whom were ex-**Nazis** and Croatian Ustasi types).

🏠

J. Henry Schröder Banking Corporation

♟ ✝

Kameradenwerk

After being ferreted out of post-**WWII** Europe via the **Allen Dulles–Gehlen** Org–**CIA**–**Red Cross**–**Vatican** Ratlines, most of the exfiltrated **Nazis** and Croatian **Fascists** settled in Latin America, where the financial proceeds from Operation Bernhard (and the added political and financial support of **Nelson Rockefeller**) were used to set up a staunch anti-Communist Nazi-Croatian network—or the Kameradenwerk: **Klaus Barbie** decamped in Bolivia; Josef Mengele, Auschwitz's "Angel of Death," landed in Paraguay with Ustasi mass murderer Ante Pavelic; Walter Rauff, overseer of the SS mobile gas chambers, moved to Chile; and **Otto "Scarface" Skorzeny,** Hans-Ulrich Rudel, and Heinrich Muller set up shop in Argentina.
ᴀⴼ

Korean War

From 1950 to 1953, North Korea (aided by the USSR and **Communist** China) and South Korea (aided by U.S.-dominated **United Nations** forces) fought an inconclusive war that galvanized **Cold War** feelings throughout the West and helped fuel **McCarthy**ism in the United States. But really, the Korean War, like the **Vietnam War,** was arranged and approved by the **Council on Foreign Relations** and the **Insiders.** Just across the border in Chinese Manchuria, the Communists were perfecting their brainwashing and **Mind Control** techniques on prisoners of war from the West. These techniques came from **Nazi** scientist-torturers, who had been absorbed into the **KGB** after **WWII**, and were furthered in the hopes of developing a team of brainwashed Soviet agents (Manchurian candidates) who would return to the West and spread chaos.
◿ 🐦

Military-Industrial Complex

♍ ✝ △ ⚲ 😊 ⚙ 🔲

Monsanto

The United States's third-largest chemical company (behind **Dow** and **Du Pont**), this St. Louis–based giant is now deeply involved in biotechnology and genetic engineering. Monsanto is the manufacturer of both **Dioxin** and **NutraSweet** (as well as

Equal), and the firm's R&D unit introduced its first biotech product in 1994, the Posilac bovine somatotropine (BST), a controversial growth hormone used to increase milk yields in cows. According to conspiranoiac journalist Alex Constantine, in 1967 Monsanto teamed up with the German company **I.G. Farben** in the formation of the Kansas City, Missouri–based Chemagrow Corporation, a front for a joint research project involving ex-**Nazi** scientists and American specialists from the **U.S. Army** Chemical Corps to develop **Biochemical Warfare** agents. In 1985, the company absorbed G.D. Searle, producer of Aspartame, which Monsanto later dubbed NutraSweet. (Until 1985, Searle, incidentally, was under the direction of William L. Searle, a Harvard man who in the 1950s was an officer in the Army Chemical Corps—at a time when the division was testing out **LSD** on soldiers and other "volunteers" for the **CIA**.) One of Monsanto's former directors was William Ruckelshaus, who once served as **Nixon**'s acting director of the FBI (during the agency's **COINTELPRO** years). Also on Monsanto's board was former CIA director Stansfield Turner.

✿

The Revolving Door

While **Monsanto** worked on the development of the new growth hormone Posilac, the company's trade name for bovine somatotropine (BST), the biotech giant's former lab supervisor moved over to the **Food and Drug Administration** to head up the division involved in the technical review of Posilac. Two other FDA officials who had previously been involved with Monsanto (though only tangentially) also took part in the review of Posilac. Although all three FDA officials were later cleared of any conflict of interest questions by the Government Accounting Office (and Monsanto itself was never accused of any wrongdoing), one of the U.S. representatives who called for an investigation into the FDA's seemingly quick approval of the hormone (the FDA had okayed Posilac in 1993, despite BST milk not having been properly tested on humans before its approval) said that the GAO report showed that the "FDA allowed corporate influence to run rampant" in its review of Posilac.

National Aeronautics and Space Administration (NASA)

U.S. government agency responsible for the development of advanced aviation and space technology for both military and nonmilitary purposes. Throughout its history, NASA has been motivated by fears that the United States was technologically inferior to its rival nations (particularly the USSR). Formed in 1951 as NACA (the National Advisory Committee on Aeronautics) amid concern that America was falling behind post-WWII Europe in the area of aeronautical engineering, NACA became NASA in 1958. By then NASA had absorbed many ex-**Nazi** scientists (via **Project Paperclip**), men who'd designed long-range missiles and rocket engines for **Hitler** (the two most prominent being V-2 rocket inventor **Wernher von Braun,** who later helped design the *Apollo 11* spacecraft that landed on the moon, and the evil Dr. Hubertus Strughold, who, despite his inhuman experiments on Dachau concentration-camp prisoners, was welcomed by the United States, and after his retirement he was hailed by NASA as the "father of space medicine." With the help of their ex-Nazis, NASA eventually surpassed the Soviets and developed the Apollo rocket program and then, with varying degrees of success, the Viking, Gemini, Mercury, and Space Shuttle programs. Nonetheless, some accuse NASA of all sorts of chicanery. First, NASA faked the *Apollo* moon landings (as in the 1977 film *Capricorn One*). Second, NASA has concealed life on Mars (for who knows how long) and are the prime perpetrators behind **Moongate.** Third, NASA's been in cahoots with **Aliens, Radio Shack,** and the **American Dental Association,** using our **Mercury Fillings** to communicate with the mother ship up there in the heavens and screening all that personal information Radio Shack gleans from its boob customers for potential lunar-base construction workers. Last but not least (and probably not last either), NASA and the Jet Propulsion Lab faked that **Pathfinder** landing on Mars.
✿ ☉

No objective correlative existed to prove it had not been an event staged in a television studio—the greatest con of the century. . . . Indeed, conceive of the genius of such a conspiracy. It would take men mightier, more trustworthy and more resourceful than anything in this century or the ones before.

—**Norman Mailer,** *Life,* **November 1969**

Nazis

ᛘ ✝ 🏛 🐟 ⚱ ☼

Office of Strategic Services (OSS)

American intelligence agency (1942–1945) set up to gather information and sabotage enemy countries during **WWII**. It was headed by future **CIA** director William "Wild Bill" Donovan and his second in command was **Allen Dulles** (another future CIA chief). The OSS aided ex-**Nazi Reinhard Gehlen** in setting up the Org and also helped **Otto Skorzeny** relocate his fellow Nazis in Central and South America. During the war, the OSS cooperated with the **Mafia,** notably when the Allies enlisted gangster Lucky Luciano to persuade New York's Italian-American stevedores not to sabotage Allied ships when they docked in New York.

🐟

Paperclip

The post-**WWII** smuggling operation of **Nazi** scientists and engineers to the West (to work on missiles, rockets, and other high-tech projects) orchestrated by future **CIA** director, **Hitler** buddy, and unabashed Nazi enthusiast **Allen Dulles,** with the assistance of **Reinhard Gehlen.** Paperclip also involved the cooperation of the **Red Cross** (which issued fake passports) and the **Vatican** (which harbored many a Nazi and then helped smuggle them out of Europe), plus **Nelson Rockefeller** (who helped squirrel away the necessary finances the Nazis would need in places like Latin America). Paperclip became the lifeblood of the West's **Military-Industrial Complex,** proving essential to successes like the V-2 rocket (masterminded by ex-Nazis **Wernher von Braun**) and the **Apollo** missions.

🐟 ☼

Pope John Paul II

His Holiness, the current CEO of the **Vatican.** According to conspiranoiac bigot Jack Chick, in the early 1940s Karol Josef Wojtyla worked for the **I.G. Farben** chemical company as a salesman in Poland (and later at Auschwitz), selling cyanide gas to the **Nazis,** who used it to exterminate Jews and other groups in their concentration camps. As the war progressed and it became increasingly clear that the Nazis would lose, Wojtyla, fearing for his life, joined an underground branch of the Catholic Church, says conspiranoia author Dr. Alan Cantwell. (Although none of the above has ever been close to being verified.) He was ordained a priest in 1946, became Poland's youngest bishop in 1958, and was made a cardinal in 1967. While in his native Poland, claims Cantwell, he befriended **Holocaust** escapee **Wolf Szmuness,** the future epidemiologist. In 1978, after a thirty-day reign, Pope Paul I was assassinated and Wojtyla assumed the papacy as Pope John Paul II. Unlike his unlucky predecessor, he is anti-choice and anti-Communist and has reaffirmed the Church's hard-line position against birth control and homosexuality. In the late 1980s, Pope JP II granted former **Vatican Bank** president Paul "the Gorilla" Marcinkus sanctuary inside the Vatican—despite Marcinkus having been implicated in various illicit **P2-Mafia** money deals. According to the book *His Holiness*—coauthored by Watergate reporter Carl Bernstein—the pope and the **Reagan** administration (via Reagan's **Knight of Malta** D.C.-Vatican liaison William Wilson) reached a near agreement regarding Central America, particularly Nicaragua and El Salvador. The pope would chastise, perhaps even excommunicate, Central and South America's politically active liberation theologists. In return, the United States would help the Church drive **Communist** General Wojciech Jaruzelski and his Soviet-backed bosses out of Poland, the pope's beloved homeland.

✝ ✡

Procter & Gamble

The world's largest consumer-products company, based in Cincinnati. In 1955, P&G introduced Crest, the first toothpaste to contain **Fluoride.** Since the midseventies, the company has been besieged by rumors (later spread by **Amway**) that some of its executives are **Satanists** and that its moon-and-stars logo (which it no longer uses) contained the numbers 666 (the mark of the beast). P&G's latest anti-satanic lawsuit against Amway was dismissed in 1999.

✡

Red Cross

During **WWII,** the Red Cross's International Rescue Division couriered intelligence for the **Nazis,** and after WWII, under the direction of the **OSS,** issued fake ID cards to Nazis so that they could

Mark of the Beast

Given that the mark of the beast is 666 (Revelations 13:16–17), and given that it's written in the Bible that the apocalypse is near when 666 shows up on people's right hands or foreheads, no wonder Apocalypse Now is forever around the bend. The **World Bank**'s computer code is 666. Upon the reopening of the Suez Canal in 1975, Egyptian president Anwar Sadat sailed through on a warship emblazoned with 666 on its bow. Six years later, on October 6, 1981, Sadat was gunned down by six assassins. According to the numerology of the **Cabala, Jesus Christ,** the perfect man, adds up to 777, so 666 equals the value of Jesus Christ's name minus his unity (number value: 111), leaving his evil twin, the Antichrist. Some speculate that Lucent Technologies, AT&T's new name for their Bell Labs subsidiary, might be an acronym for Lucifer's Enterprise—and don't laugh, the name of Lucent's network operating system is Inferno and Lucent has an office at 666 Fifth Avenue in New York City—the Devil's playground.

move internationally through the refugee camps and escape prosecution for war crimes. The postwar head of the international committee was French ex-SS man and Klaus Barbie liaison, Andre François-Poncet, who also served in Charles de Gaulle's administration along with other Nazi collaborators.

Nelson Rockefeller

A key heir to the immense Rockefeller fortune, Nelson (1908–1979) was one of the most powerful men in the country, holding down board of director memberships with Exxon, Mobil, Eastern Airlines, **Chase Manhattan Bank,** and Met Life. Before and during **WWII,** Rockefeller's Standard (Oil) of New Jersey continued to fuel the **Nazi** war machine (Standard was also still in partnership with **I.G. Farben**). Meanwhile, the ambitious Nelson used his appointment as head of the Office of Inter-American Affairs (President **Franklin D. Roosevelt** had given him the post) to monopolize the Latin American markets (and economies and each country's leaders as well). His buddy **John Foster Dulles** was a trustee of the **Rockefeller Foundation.** Rocky was also partners then with the Nazis' **J. Henry Schröder Banking Corporation.** More pro-money than pro-Nazi, and certainly no Zionist, in 1947 Rockefeller caved in to David Ben-Gurion and the Zionists' push for the creation of the state of Israel. In return for the Jews not publicizing Rocky's business relationships with the Nazis, his postwar help in relocating ex-Nazis in Latin America, and his help in smuggling Nazi war criminals and their **Vatican** cash to Argentina, Rocky guaranteed the Jews that Latin America would vote for Israel statehood in the days-away **UN** vote. *Violà!* On November 29, 1947, every one of Rockefeller's Latin American contingency voted for Israel (or abstained). In 1958, he began his first of four terms as the governor of New York and was later widely criticized for his role in the Attica prison riot. Although President **Nixon** loathed him, Rockefeller was appointed vice president by President **Gerald R. Ford.** He served as vice president from 1974 to 1977, during which time he chaired an investigatory commission on the **CIA.** Rockefeller died while allegedly having sex on his office desk.

✝ ⚏

Rothschilds

♍ ✡ ✍ ∽

Schutzstaffel (SS)

⚔

Otto Skorzeny

⚔ ⛰

Terrorism

✳ ⛰ ☺

Harry Truman

The thirty-third president of the United States (1945–1953), Truman succeeded his **Masonic** brother, **Franklin Delano Roosevelt,** as president. (Early in his political career, in order to secure victory in a Missouri judgeship contest, Give-'em-hell Harry joined the **KKK** to ensure their support.) He approved the creation of the **CIA** (ostensibly to continue the work of the **OSS**) and the **NSC,** which was to serve as a direct link of communications between the White House and the newly formed CIA. He also initiated the **Korean War** without waiting for a congressional declaration of such, ordering U.S. troops to carry out the **UN's** recommendation of defending South Korea.

The Unification Church

This quasi-cult, the Holy Spirit Association for the Unification of World Christianity, was founded in 1954 by North Korea–born **Reverend Sun Myung Moon** with the help of **Fascist** Japanese **Yakuza** member and fellow rabid anti-Communist **Ryoichi Sasakawa** (and the American **CIA** and Korean CIA). In the 1960s and 1970s, the "Moonies" may have received massive indirect funding via bribes from **Lockheed** to its Japanese contacts (and without Lockheed's knowledge). The church and Sasakawa later co-founded (with others) the **World Anti-Communist League** and also helped out **New Right** Fundamentalist and **Gang of Four** member Richard Viguerie. Lately, some believe that the church may have financed Japan's anti-Semitic cult leader Shoko Asahara and his **Terrorist Aum Shinrikyo** sect. The Moonies, incidentally, have a near-monopoly on the processing and marketing of ginseng (and they no doubt used some of those ginseng profits to fund French Fascist Jean Le Pen and his National Front Party).

✝ ↬ ⚰

United Fruit Company

Formed in 1899, this Central American banana-republic company was actually a **Rockefeller** subsidiary and Guatemala's largest landholder for decades. Among its major shareowners was **John Foster Dulles,** who also served as its attorney. Dulles's brother, **CIA** director **Allen,** sat on the board of the **J. Henry Schröder Banking Corporation,** a lender to United Fruit. In 1950, Guatemala's democratically elected president Jacobo Arbenz Guzmán began expropriating uncultivated land held by **Multinational** corporations (like United Fruit) and redistributing them to his country's landless poor. Arbenz Guzmán further angered the United States by allowing the **Communist** Guatemalan Party of Labor to grow. In response, in 1954 the CIA (after running an extensive smear campaign with the help of United Fruit's PR man **Ed Bernays**) helped overthrow Arbenz Guzmán and installed a U.S.-friendly military dictatorship in Guatemala.

✝

U.S. Army

Being all that they can be, in the 1950s this infantry branch of the **Pentagon** allowed the **CIA** to experiment with **LSD**-25 on 1,500 "volunteer" GIs. In the 1960s, the U.S. Department of Defense wanted to create a decentralized computer network so that it wouldn't have a single "point of failure" network hub that could be targeted and disabled in a nuclear attack. This experiment, administered by the Defense Department's Advanced Research Projects Agency, became known as the ARPAnet, which gradually evolved into what is now the **Internet.** The army also uses cow plasma for emergency blood transfusions, which brings up eerie thoughts about all those **Cattle Mutilations** (and **Aliens**).

👣 △ ☼ ☉

Vietnam War

The U.S. "police" action of 1965 to 1975, in which the United States committed itself militarily to the tiny Southeast Asia country, fearing that if Vietnam turned to **Communism,** all the others around it would be sure to follow soon after. (This was the misguided **Cold War** theory, the Domino Effect.) By the time the United States pulled out completely, more than 55,000 Americans had been killed and more than 300,000 wounded in a nonofficial war that cost the United States more than $110 billion and eroded public confidence in its government.

✍ △ ▱

Official Memorandum

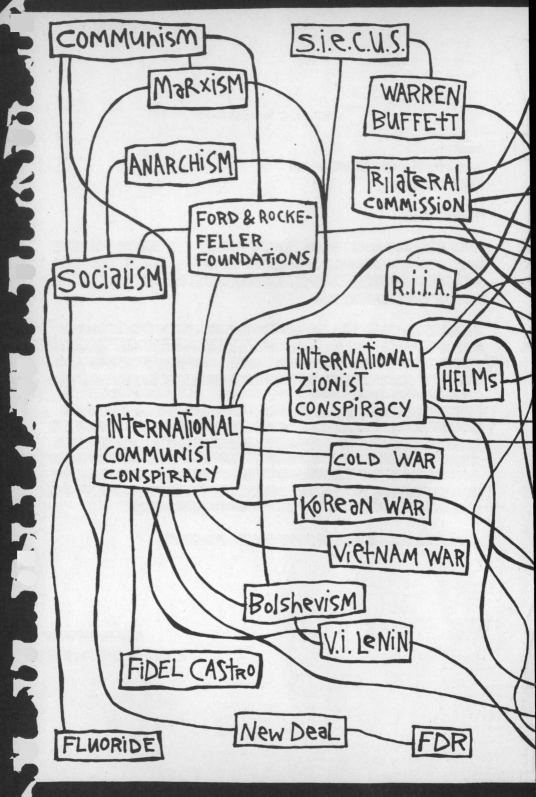

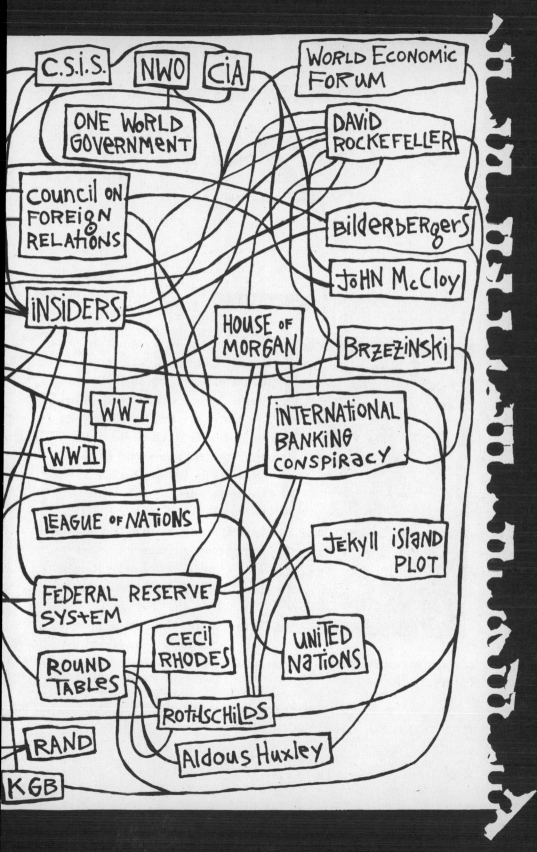

Conspiracy

To the unitiated, it sounds preposterous: Communists and the Establishment in cahoots? Working toward the same New World Order? But the Socialist Register gives life to their lie, showing how Insiders like David Rockefeller and his fellow Masters of the Universe have bankrolled one Commie-enacted societal upheaval after another (be it the overthrow of Russia's csars or Mao's brutal Cultural Revolution), all part of their plan to bamboozle the average Joe into thinking he's the next domino to fall and so the government better crack down on everybody—himself included—so as to avoid a state of nature.

Anarchism

Bilderbergers

Zbigniew Brzezinski

Suspected of being a **KGB** mole by some conspiranoiacs, at the very least Z.B. has played the role of yes-man stooge very well—to the **Round Table,** to the **Rothschilds** and the Warburgs, and to mentor **David Rockefeller.** In 1973, at Rockefeller's request, Z-Big man (fresh from **Nixon**'s cabinet as national security advisor) laid the groundwork for what became the **Trilateral Commission,** a kind of handmaiden to the **NWO** desires of the **Insiders** and the Establishment. He also served as **Carter**'s national security advisor and **Bush**'s campaign advisor.
〰 ☺ 🌐

It will soon be possible to assert almost continuous control over every citizen and to maintain up-to-date files, containing even the most personal details about health and personal behavior of every citizen in addition to the more customary data. . . . Power will gravitate into the hands of those who control information.

—Zbigniew Brzezinski, *The Technotronic Age* (1968)

Warren Buffett

A billionaire investor, Buffett's Omaha-based Berkshire Hathaway Inc. holdings and investment firm own a significant number of shares in *The Washington Post* (owner of *Newsweek*), **Coca-Cola, Disney/Cap Cities,** McDonald's, and General Dynamics (the **Military-Industrial Complex** defense-industry giant and manufacturer of the Trident and Seawolf nuclear submarines, the Titan IV space-launch rocket, and the F-III fighter jets, which were used in the 1986 bombings of Libya). Buffett's wife, Susie, was a strong booster for fellow Omahan Lawrence King, Jr., the Republican party activist behind the shutdown of Omaha's Franklin Community Federal Credit Union. Aka the Oracle of Omaha, Buffett, some conspiranoiacs claim, has been a longtime supporter (and funder) of Planned Parenthood, **SIECUS,** and the Zero Population Growth movement. Buffett's pals include **NBC** anchorman Tom Brokaw and zillionaire **Bill Gates.**
▩

Fidel Castro

Cuba's unabashed **Communist** leader since 1959, when he overthrew the U.S.-backed Fulgencio Batista dictatorship and nationalized all businesses (thereby curtailing a huge **Mafia-Multinational-CIA** cash cow of hotels, brothels, and casinos). Castro has been the target of at least eight CIA murder attempts. The CIA has tried to a) season his favorite stogies with a deadly toxin; b) powder his shoes with a powerful depilatory, on the theory that if his hair fell out, his machismo would decline and he'd have to step down from office; and c) infect the breathing apparatus of his scuba suit with tuberculosis bacteria, which might lead to a rare and fatal skin disease. Some say that Castro returned the favor by dispatching four hit teams to murder **John F. Kennedy.** The 1961 **Bay of Pigs** operation was a failed attempt to assassinate Castro that involved the CIA and the Mafia.

△

Center for Strategic and International Studies (CSIS)

A very conservative think tank affiliated with the **Jesuit**-founded Georgetown University (where **Bill Clinton** did some postgraduate work and where he learned all about how the world *really* works from **Insider** professor Carroll Quigley). The CSIS is closely allied with the **CIA,** the **Trilateral Commission,** and the **Bilderbergers**.

There does exist, and has existed for a generation, an international Anglophile network which operates, to some extent, the way the Radical Right believes the Communists act. In fact, this network, which we may identify as the Round Table Groups, has no aversion to cooperating with the Communists, or any other groups, and frequently does so.

—Carroll Quigley, *Tragedy and Hope*, 1966

CIA

♍ ★ ✝ 🏛 🐗 ⋙ △ ✐ ↬ ⚑ ☺ 🔀 ⊕ ☉

Cold War

🏛

The paranoid mentality is far more coherent than the real world, since it leaves no room for mistakes, failures, or ambiguities.

—Richard Hofstadter, "The Paranoid Style in American Politics" (1971)

Communism

✳ ✡

Council on Foreign Relations

♍ ↬ ☺ ⊕

Federal Reserve System

♍ ✡ ⊕

Fluoride

Deemed by 1950s Christian groups as "the devil's poison," fluoride became a public-health measure intended to prevent tooth decay by adding the compound to water supplies. Experimental programs involving artificial fluoridation at selected sites were conducted in the 1930s to test its benefits, but before completion of the programs the U.S. Public Health Service officially endorsed fluoridation in 1950. Since then, water supplies for

117

about 50 percent of the U.S. population use fluoride, with similar or even higher percentages in Canada, Ireland, Australia, and New Zealand. In 1960, the **American Dental Association** recognized **Procter & Gamble**'s fluoride-filled Crest toothpaste as effective against tooth decay. The **John Birch Society** and other superpatriotic groups, along with certain anti-federalist citizens in Utah and other fluoride-free states, say fluoridation is a **Communist** plot to sap Americans of their "precious bodily fluids" (a notion spoofed in Stanley Kubrick's 1964 film *Dr. Strangelove or: How I Learned to Stop Worrying and Love the Bomb*). Go ahead and laugh, but recent studies show fluoride may impair the functioning of the immune system and play a role in infant mortality and Down's syndrome births. While working on **WWII**'s Manhattan Project, scientists in upstate New York produced massive amounts of fluoride (as did a **Du Pont** chemical factory in New Jersey, where there was a huge wartime accident involving the release of fluoride into nearby drinking water). Fluoride, it turns out, was essential for the manufacture of nuclear-weapons-grade uranium and plutonium. After WWII, chemists from **I.G. Farben** told U.S. scientist Charles Perkins that the Third Reich had worked out a scheme involving the mass medication of drinking water as a means of controlling population—using sodium fluoride. Vindication of sorts for those who say Fluoride is yet another government plan for mass **Mind Control**.
☞ ☼

Ford and Rockefeller Foundations

Part of the Eastern Establishment's ruling elite, these tax-exempt organizations are used to protect **Insiders'** wealth and affect economic and political policies in their favor. In the past, these foundations fomented **Communism** and **Socialism** through the funding of groups like Students for a Democratic Society, the Yippies, and the Black Panthers. **John Foster Dulles** was a member of the **Rockefeller Foundation.** Both foundations also contribute to the **Tavistock Institute**.
〰 ▩ ⊕

Richard Helms

This scion of **Insiders** (his grandfather was a president of the **Federal Reserve** and the first director of the **Bank for International**

Settlements) became a major figure within the **CIA** and engineered many of its "dirty tricks" during the 1960s. Helms became a UPI reporter in 1935 (he interviewed **Hitler** in 1937), then served in the **OSS** during **WWII** and remained in intelligence work when it became the CIA in 1947. Before Helms took over as CIA director (1966–1973), he organized project **MK-ULTRA** and was generally obsessed with **Mind Control**.

🐀 ⊕

House of Morgan

✡ 🏠

Aldous Huxley

British novelist, occultist, and former intelligence agent, Huxley died on the exact same date—November 22, 1963—that **JFK** was assassinated. Huxley had his wife shoot him up with one final blast of **LSD**-25. Huxley envisioned a *Brave New World* and popularized the **Tavistock Institute**'s LSD program (as enacted by the **CIA**'s **MK-ULTRA** project). His grandfather, Thomas, was one of the founders of **Cecil Rhodes's Round Table** groups. Al also palled around with H. G. Wells and occult godfather **Aleister Crowley** and was a member of the homo-psychedelic Children of the Sun cult (whose other members included D. H. Lawrence and George Orwell). He was also the first director of the **NWO**-ish UNESCO (**United Nations** Educational, Scientific, and Cultural Organization) and served as a mentor to **Timothy Leary** (whom he met at Stanford). While in California, he helped set up the cultish **Esalen Institute**.

🐀 〰 ∽

> The twenty-first century . . . will be the era of World Controllers. . . . The older dictators fell because they could never supply their subjects with enough bread, enough circuses, enough miracles and mysteries. Under a scientific dictatorship, education will really work—with the result that most men and women will grow up to love their servitude and will never dream of revolution. There seems to be no good reason why a thoroughly scientific dictatorship should ever be overthrown.
>
> —Aldous Huxley, *Brave New World Revisited*

Insiders

△ ∽ ⊕

International Banking Conspiracy

♍ ✖ ✿ ★ ♒ ▱ ↬ ∽ ⚕ ⊕

International Communist Conspiracy

♍ ✳ ✡ △ ∽ ☺ ☿

International Zionist Conspiracy

♍ ✖ ✳ ✡ ∽ ▩ ⊕

The Jekyll Island Plot

✡

KGB/MGB

Founded by **Vladimir Lenin** (and known in its early days as the Cheka) to function as the Bolsheviks' "devastating weapon against countless conspiracies and countless attempts against Soviet power by people who are infinitely stronger than us," wrote Lenin. After **WWII,** the agency instigated a kind of Project **Paperclip** of its own: rounding up some 6,000 German scientists of the Third Reich and sending them to Moscow, where they were teamed up with Soviet scientists in order to help the Rooskies win the space race. The ex-**Nazi** experts also developed the Soviet fighter jet, the MiG, and during the **Korean War,** the former Nazis' expertise in psychological **Mind Control** was used on various prisoners of war in the hopes of developing a team of brainwashed Soviet agents who would return to the West and spread chaos. Given free rein to terrorize the Soviet populace, the KGB was also the longtime **Cold War** nemesis of the CIA and interrogated **Lee Harvey Oswald** on his trip inside the USSR.

🐾 △ ᴄ⊛ ✿

> Government is an association of men who do violence to the rest of us.
>
> —Leo Tolstoy

Korean War

★ 🐾

League of Nations

✡

Vladimir Lenin

✡

Marxism

✡ ☺

John McCloy

Warren Commission member, **Knight of Malta,** the architect of the postwar Nuremberg trials, and the former head of the **Council on Foreign Relations.** A kind of "godfather of the American Establishment" for his work as **World Bank** president and for his work in the late seventies, when **Henry Kissinger** and **David Rockefeller** enlisted his legal services to try to prevent the shah of Iran's American investments (in Rockefeller's **Chase** bank) from being nationalized by the Ayatollah Khomeini. McCloy also oversaw construction of the **Pentagon** and during **WWII** worked with future Supreme Court justice Earl Warren on setting up the Japanese-American internment camps in the United States.

🌐

New Deal

◎

Franklin D. Roosevelt's 1930s program for relief, recovery, and reform intended to solve the economic and social problems created by the **Great Depression**. The programs of the New Deal (1933–1939), considered by many critics and supporters alike to be **Socialistic** in nature, sought to restructure American banking, stimulate industrial recovery, assist victims of poverty, guarantee minimum living standards, and prevent future economic crises. The Federal Deposit Insurance Corporation, Social Security, and the contemporary American welfare system all stem from the New Deal.

New World Order

♍ ※ ∽ ☺ ⊕

We shall have world government whether or not you like it—by conquest or consent.

—James Warburg,
testifying before the U.S. Senate Foreign Relations Committee (1950)

One World Government

♍ ✡ ∽ ⊕

RAND Corporation

One of the first and most famous of all think tanks (those research and analysis institutions that serve as way stations for out-of-work politicians, academics who can't teach, and other talking heads and self-important pundits), this Santa Monica–based nonprofit corporation grew out of a postwar research-and-development project (hence, its name R&D, RAND) of the U.S. Air Force (in conjunction with the **Tavistock Institute** and the **Royal Institute on International Affairs**) and was a key player in the development of the **Internet**. In the 1960s, **John F. Kennedy**'s secretary of state, Robert McNamara, relied on RAND and its pioneering approach to problem-solving to figure out the country's policy on Vietnam: For example, McNamara would ask RAND's defense intellectuals to determine the exact number of ICBMs (intercontinental ballistic missiles) the nation needed. In the midst of the **Cold War,** alleges one conspiranoiac, RAND hired itself out to the Soviet Union to determine the terms of a possible U.S. surrender to the **Communist** superpower. Today, about 80 percent of RAND's income comes from the government.

△ ∿ ✿ ☉

Cecil Rhodes

✡

David Rockefeller

Son of oil baron John D. Rockefeller (America's first billionaire) and therefore a key part of the immense Rockefeller empire. David is the king of the **Insiders**: the head of the **Bilderbergers,** founder of the **Trilateral Commission,** a bastion of the Eastern Establishment, and the former chairman of **Chase Manhattan Bank** (formerly Chase National). In 1972, he instructed his crony **Zbigniew Brzezinski** to draw up the official plans for the creation of the **Trilateral Commission.**

∿ ⊕

Franklin Delano Roosevelt

❋ ✝

Rothschilds

♍ ✡ ★ ∿

Royal Institute of International Affairs (RIIA)

Founded in 1919 just after the Paris Peace Conference (following the end of **WWI**), this outgrowth of **Cecil Rhodes's Round Tables** was a precursor to the United States's **Council on Foreign Relations.** Also sometimes referred to as Chatham House.

∿

Full control of the drug trade must be completed in order that the governments of all countries who are under our jurisdiction will have a monopoly which we will control through supply. . . . Drug bars will take care of the unruly and the discontent, would be revolutionaries will be turned into harmless addicts with no will of their own.

—Royal Institute of International Affairs' alleged secret paper (1960s)

Sex Information and Education Council of the United States (SIECUS)

☯

A government organization founded in 1964 by Mary Steichen Calderone, then medical director of Planned Parenthood–World Population. SEICUS's symbol was the Taoist yin/yang representation of male and female sexuality, which, according to the **John Birch Society,** is an occult reference and evidence that SIECUS is part of a one world **Communist** plot to undermine American Christianity via organizations like NARAL (the National Abortion Rights Actions League), Planned Parenthood, UNESCO (**United Nations** Educational, Scientific, and Cultural Organization), and the YMCA and YWCA (Young Men's and Young Women's Christian Associations). **Warren Buffett** has given away part of his millions to SIECUS.

Socialism

✳ ✡ ∽

Trilateral Commission

♍ ∽ ☺ ⊕

United Nations

♍ ✡ ∽ ⊕

Vietnam War

★ △ ▱

World Economic Forum

Aka the Davos Conference and a kind of alternative **Trilateral Commission,** this annual six-day gathering (first held in 1971 as the European Management Symposium) was conceived in 1965 by Klaus Schwab, a fifty-eight-year-old Swiss business professor. Forum attendees consist of world politicians and business leaders, who pay Schwab a fee (on average, $20,000) to discuss better ways to promote and implement the idea that the elite set the global economic agenda and that free-market capitalism will win out over any and all governmental attempts to stop it.

✝ ⊕

WWI

✡

WWII

✡ 🦅

Davos Attendees

Warren Beatty, former Israel prime minister Benjamin Netanyahu, president of Egypt Hosni Mubarak, Palestinian leader Yasir Arafat, Microsoft CEO **Bill Gates,** Dell chairman and CEO Michael Dell, failed U.S. presidential candidate Steve Forbes, former Enron CEO Rebecca Mark, Nokia president and CEO Jorma Ollila, **General Electric** CEO and chairman Jack Welch, Britain's former chancellor of the exchequer Kenneth Clarke, chairman and CEO and president of ITT Travis Engen, Newt Gingrich, Boris Yeltsin's deputy national security chief Boris Berezovsky, UN secretary-general Kofi Annan, former National Urban League president Vernon Jordan, Unisys chairman and CEO James Unruh, Daewoo chairman Kim Woo-Choong, and Kellogg CEO and chairman Arnold Langbo.

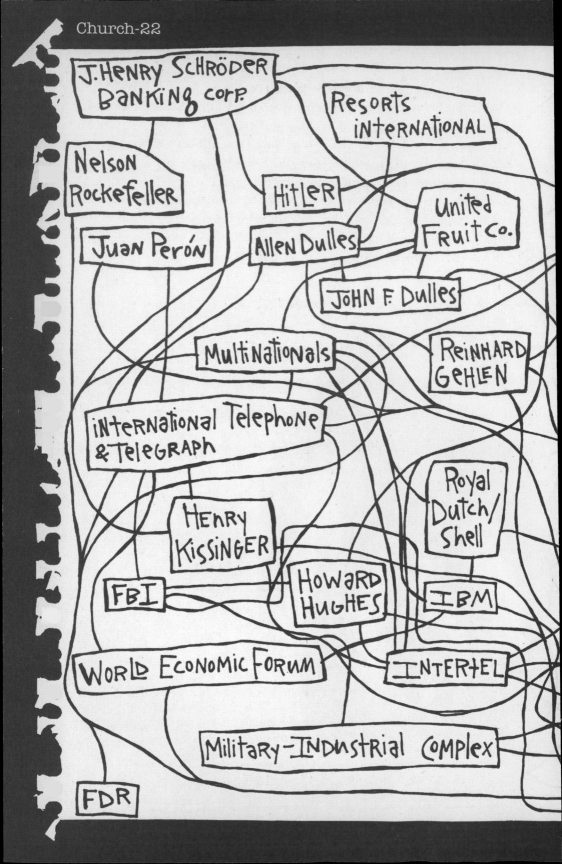

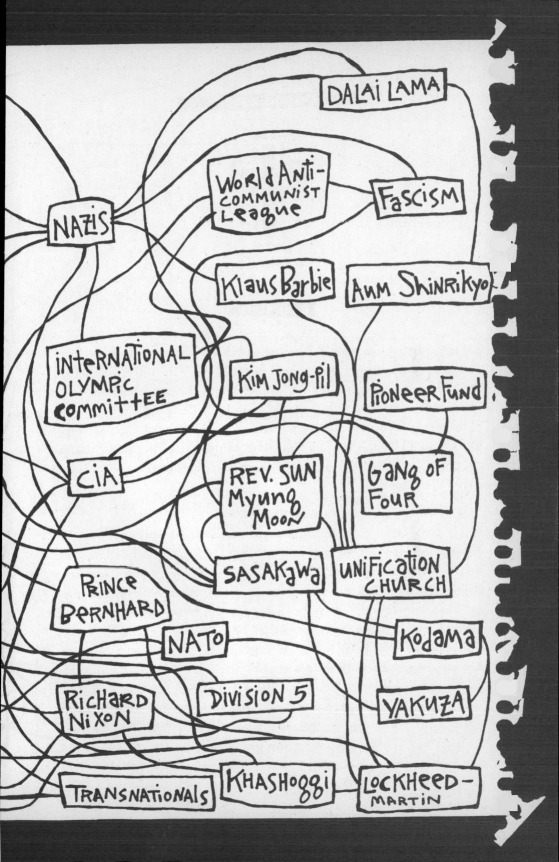

Conspiracy

So named because of the Fascistic reach of Reverend Sun Myung Moon's Unification Church and because ITT founder Sosthenes Behn served as inspiration for the wheeler-dealer conscience-free Milo Minderbinder character in Joseph Heller's *Catch-22*. Moon proved that a church does not really have to be about God or religion, and ITT—the world's first true Multinational—proved that a corporate-controlled state is far more profitable than a nation-controlled state.

Aum Shinrikyo

A 40,000-large quasi-Buddhist anti-Semitic paramilitary sect of Japan, founded in 1986 by Shoko Asahara. Allegedly funded in part by the **Unification Church,** the **Yakuza** (Japan's mafia), and the **World Anti-Communist League,** Aum Shinrikyo, which translates as "Supreme Truth," was responsible for the May 1995 sarin gas attack on the Tokyo subway lines that killed twelve (having targeted Tokyo because, in their minds, it was Japan's "Jewish" capital). Aum has also been tied to other gas attacks throughout Japan during the past several years, plus other murders and attempted murders, and is suspected of kidnappings and mail bombings. Close to one hundred Aum followers worked in Japan's self-defense forces (the country's military). Following the gas attack, police raided Aum's headquarters and uncovered a cache of AK-47s and a veritable **Biochemical Warfare** factory, where the cult's chemists synthesized the sarin used in the subway attack and where they were on the verge of manufacturing botulism, a substance even more deadly than sarin. The group may have gotten both toxins through the **KGB,** from scientists at Russia's **Bioprcparat**—its old Biochemical Warfare labs. Aum was also suspected of having developed an **Electromagnetic Radiation** weapons system, one perhaps inspired by Nikola Tesla's earthquake-inducing weapons-technology theories and that Aum may have tested on January 17, 1995, in Kobe (where an Asahara-predicted earthquake killed 5,000 people).

Klaus Barbie

CIA

Dalai Lama

Division 5

This legendary ultrasecret **FBI** assassination unit is said to have been in cahoots with **CIA** man **Clay Shaw** and his sinister Swedish front company, **Permindex.** Funded by the late Texas oilman Clint Murchison (no friend of JFK's, he), D-5 also, according to the pseudonymously written *NASA, Nazis and JFK,* worked with **NASA** and its ex-**Nazi** rocket scientist **Wernher von Braun,** to bring down the president.

Allen Dulles

John Foster Dulles

Fascism

FBI

Gang of Four

Not the band but the leaders of the Fundamentalist anti-Communist **New Right** political movement as led by: Richard Viguerie, whose direct-mail empire became the grassroots backbone of the New Right campaign and who seized on the abortion issue as the New Right's battering ram against liberalism and whose financial fortunes may have been helped by the work he did for the **WACL** and the **Unification Church**; Terry Dolan, the founder of the National Conservative Political Action Committee (NCPAC) who developed the art of negative campaigning and who later died of AIDS (NCPAC's messages were "designed to generate hatred and fear, repeated over and over again until they stick," said Dolan); Howard Phillips, who in 1975 founded the Conservative Caucus, a grassroots action group; and **Paul Weyrich,** who in 1973 first founded, with the financial backing of Joseph **Coors,** the **Heritage Foundation,** an ultraconservative think tank, then split off from the foundation a year later to help set up the Committee for the Survival of a Free Congress, a training program and market-research company for New Right candidates. As Weyrich told a New Right gathering in 1980, "We're talking about Christianizing America."

Reinhard Gehlen

Adolf Hitler

Howard Hughes

A dashing playboy aviator turned lascivious obsessive-compulsive, this tycoon inherited his dad's Hughes Tool Company and turned it into part of a billion-dollar empire. Hughes also owned Trans World Airlines, and as head of RKO Film Studios, he lured many of Hollywood's leading ladies (and aspiring starlets) into the sack, including Jean Harlow, Ava Gardner, Ginger Rogers, Katharine Hepburn, and Jane Russell. In 1948, the eccentric Texas billionaire (via his RKO studios) floated Walt **Disney** a cool $1 million interest-free loan. In 1966, he retreated to the penthouse suite of the Desert Inn hotel and casino in Las Vegas, where—tended by an entourage

of **Mormon** male nurses—he used his ties to the **Mafia,** the **CIA,** and **Richard Nixon** to buy up most of Sin City. Hughes—always a behind-the-scenes figure with a long political reach—is rumored to have known beforehand that **Bobby Kennedy** would be assassinated. It's also said that he may have indirectly caused the **Watergate** break-in: His former D.C. lobbyist, Lawrence O'Brien, had taken over as chairman of the Democratic National Committee, and Nixon, paranoid that O'Brien might find out about the $100,000 Hughes-to-Nixon contribution that his Mob buddy Bebe Rebozo had negotiated, sent his plumbers to raid the DNC headquarters. Hughes relied on *Mission: Impossible* spook and onetime G-man **Robert Maheu,** his "alter ego," to pimp him many a wanna-be Hollywood starlet and crush

A Gem of an Idea

Based on an unpublished text written in the 1970s by an obscure American chemist, the late Bruce Roberts, and which has since been recycled, reconfigured, and updated countless times and almost always anonymously, the Gemstone File aspires toward the ultimate: the Grand Unified Theory. It incorporates practically every major villain, cabal, and scandal of the twentieth century, but Roberts's true bête noire was Aristotle Onassis, whom Roberts blames for most of the West's postwar trials. And, according to Roberts, it was Onassis who ordered the killings of **JFK** and **Martin Luther King, Jr.,** was in cahoots with the **Mafia,** and who later took over **Howard Hughes**'s empire (even while Hughes made **Richard Nixon** his lapdog). The latest Gemstones include all of New Zealand and Australia's postwar turmoils within its all-encompassing theories.

any potential blackmailers. (This is the Hughes that has so fascinated conspiranoiac crime writer James Ellroy.) Toward the end of his hermetic life, he shot up codeine, ate Valiums like M&M's, wouldn't pick up anything without a Kleenex, and relied on the dubious care of his five Mormon male nurses. The Old Man died in 1976—dehydrated, malnourished, and with several broken-off hypodermic needles still under the skin of his wasted arms.

△

International Business Machines (IBM)

Aka Big Blue, IBM is the world's top provider of computer hardware and services (especially mainframe and midrange computers) and was essentially nurtured into success by the NSA (with whom IBM gladly exchanges information). IBM introduced the FORTRAN programming language in 1957 and floppy disks in 1971, and in 1995 IBM gobbled up software pioneer Lotus, developer of the 1-2-3 spreadsheet. A major donor to the Institute of Contemporary Studies, in 1980 Big Blue gave struggling twenty-two-year-old geek Bill Gates his big break when they chose his small start-up company to write an operating system for its new personal computer, what eventually became MS-DOS. Recently, Argentinians have accused Big Blue of bribing its government officials (from 1994 to 1995, to the tune of $20 to 40 million) in order to win a $250 million contract with the state-owned Banco de la Nación—a scandal that some Argentinians claim may have led to the deaths of at least six people, one of whom was president Carlos Saul Ménem's son.

✿ ⊕

International Intelligence Incorporated (Intertel)

An Indianapolis-based private intelligence, security, and investigative agency dubbed the Five Eyes and identified by its doodle-gram logo—a pentagram with a dot at each point. Allegedly birthed by the triumvirate of Meyer Lansky's Bahama-based Resorts International, the FBI's Division 5, and Britain's MI6, Intertel's staff has included former members of Scotland Yard and the Royal Canadian Mounted Police, plus agents from the CIA and the FBI (who also work with Intertel). **Nixon** used the company to do much of his undercover information-gathering. Other clients included **ITT, Howard Hughes,** and the Shah of Iran.

△

A good conspiracy is an unprovable conspiracy.

—Jonathan Vankin,
Conspiracies, Cover-Ups and Crimes (1991)

International Olympic Committee

★ 🏛

International Telephone & Telegraph (ITT)

Founded by Sosthenes Behn (the inspiration for the Milo Minderbinder character in Joseph Heller's *Catch-22*) and commonly known as ITT, this U.S.-based company was one of the first **Multinational** corporations. Before and during **WWII,** ITT supported **Hitler,** designing and building **Nazi** phone and radio systems and supplying crucial parts for German bombs, and after WWII, the company provided jobs for many an ex-Nazi. In the early 1970s, it engaged the **CIA**'s help in staging the coup that led to the 1973 overthrow and "assisted suicide" of Chile's president Salvador Allende (CIA cofounder **Allen Dulles** was a stockholder in ITT and a good friend of Behn's). This effectively gave ITT sole control over the Chilean economy, in which it had many investments. ITT is still a **Military-Industrial Complex** giant via its defense and electronics arm, which produces electronic-warfare systems, night-vision apparatus, radar-jamming devices, and tactical communications networks. CEO and president Travis Engen attends the **World Economic Forum**.

J. Henry Schröder Banking Corporation

🏹 ★

Kim Jong-Pil

Jong-Pil founded the Korean **CIA** and advised the **Reverend Sun Myung Moon** on the formation of the **Unification**

Church. His right-hand man in South Korea was former KCIA operative Kim Un Yong, the key aide to the head of the **International Olympic Committee,** former **Fascist** Juan Antonio Samaranch.

Adnan Khashoggi

A Saudi arms dealer and entrepreneur with very close connections to elements of the Saudi royal family and the leaders of Israel. A gambling addict, playboy, and former friend of **Richard Nixon**'s, as well as uncle to the late Dodi Fayed, Princess Diana's boyfriend, Khashoggi also served as **Lockheed**'s Mideast "consultant" and often did scut work for the **CIA.** In 1986, for example, Khashoggi helped raise the financing for the sale of Hawk missile parts to Iran (which was illegal at the time). This sale was one of the main components of **Oliver North**'s **Iran-Contra** plan. (Khashoggi helped Albert Hakim with the buying and selling of weapons for North.) The funding for the sale came from the **Bank of Credit and Commerce International** (BCCI), where Khashoggi maintained accounts and also shared the bank's attorney, the late Clark Clifford, onetime advisor to many U.S. presidents.
☺

Henry Kissinger

This German-American (and Jewish) advocate of atomic weapons, aka Henry the K, the Super Kraut, and the Iron Stomach, first sprang to national prominence as **Nixon**'s national security advisor during the **Vietnam War,** when he put forth the idea of a "winnable" nuclear war and set in gear the 1969–1973 carpet-bombing of Cambodia, killing 750,000 or so Cambodians and leading to the rise of the genocidal Pol Pot and his Khmer Rouge regime. In 1973, Kissinger won the Nobel Peace Prize. (Go figure.) During **World War II,** he worked in the **U.S. Army**'s Counterintelligence Corps (the one involved with Project **Paperclip**), the same unit

Catcher in the Rye writer **J. D. Salinger** apparently served in. He later spent 1952 at the **Tavistock Institute.** A protégé and cohort of **Nelson Rockefeller**'s, and a crony of **David Rockefeller**'s (Kissinger chaired the International Advisory Committee on Rock's **Chase Manhattan Bank**), Henry the K later headed up his own company, Kissinger Associates (handling clients like **General Motors** and **Hewlett-Packard**), while also serving as a member of **Banco Nazionale del Lavoro**'s international advisory board from 1985 to 1991, at a time when the BNL expedited loans to **Saddam Hussein** so that the Iraqi dictator could purchase goods from GM and Hewlett-Packard, goods that strengthened his war machine. Despite all his **Insider** connections, onetime **CIA** counterintelligence chief and conspiranoiac supreme James Jesus Angleton long suspected Kissinger of being a **KGB** agent. A **Bilderberger,** a member of the **Council on Foreign Relations,** and a consultant for Goldman Sachs and **NBC,** at various times in his career Kissinger has also worked for or been on the boards of **Coca-Cola, ABC, CBS,** and **ITT,** and another business associate of his was Japanese **Fascist Ryoichi Sasakawa.** In 1997, his son David, a former **Disney** executive who's now at **Bronfman**'s Universal Television (and who was also pals with JFK Jr.) landed his dad a quick gig with Mauschwitz CEO Michael Eisner to help placate China's **Communist** leaders over the release of the Martin Scorsese film *Kundun,* a pro-Tibet film about the **Dalai Lama.**
🐾 😐 🌐

Yoshio Kodama

Despite his post-**WWII** status as a class A war criminal—a designation given only to cabinet officers, ultranationalists, and high-ranking military men—the **CIA** had Kodama released from prison (and certain execution) because he possessed valuable inside information about Communist insurgents in China and Japan. Working as a CIA operative, Kodama helped rebuild the Japanese mafia (the **Yakuza**) along with close friend and fellow ultrarightist **Ryoichi Sasakawa.** Kodama became an influential *kura maku* (Japanese for those who wield power behind the scenes) and helped finance the Liberal-Democratic Party, which has guided Japan politically since its inception in 1955. Throughout the 1960s and 1970s, Kodama worked his connections—legal and otherwise—to open

135

Japanese markets to the U.S.-based **Lockheed** Aircraft Corporation. In the early 1980s, though, Kodama's luck soured and he was indicted for bribery, perjury, and violation of the exchange laws. He died of a stroke in 1984.

☙

Lockheed-Martin

Prior to their 1990s merger, Lockheed was a major supplier of goods to **Pandora** and to the **NSA.** Formerly known as the Skunk Works and now Lockheed, this aerospace and **Military-Industrial Complex** ogre is the nation's largest defense contractor. Lockheed produced the U-2 spy plane, the Hubble Space Telescope, and the F-117A Stealth jet. In 1972, desperate to unload some questionable product on the Japanese, Lockheed called in **Yoshio Kodama,** a **CIA** operative and a member of the Black Curtain, part of the **Yakuza** (Japan's Mob), to strongarm the sale of a fleet of TriStar jumbo jets to All-Nippon airlines. President **Nixon,** too, intervened on Lockheed's behalf, and—bingo!—Kodama walked off with millions and Nixon had Lockheed forever indebted to him (in return, Lockheed made sizable contributions to Nixon's campaign funds). More Lockheed planes were sold to Japan's air force after Kodama engineered the appointment of General Genda (the former Japanese **WWII** military commander who had orchestrated and overseen the attack on Pearl Harbor) as chief of the air force. Around this time, too, it has been alleged, Lockheed paid the Netherlands's **Prince Bernhard** (cofounder of the **Bilderbergers**) over a million to convince the Dutch to buy Lockheed's Starfighter warplanes and other aircraft. Arms-merchant smoothie **Adnan Khashoggi** also served as Lockheed's "Mideast consultant" during the seventies and eighties. Not surprisingly, Lockheed and other military-industrial complex corporations have been accused of having undue influence on **NATO**'s weapons contracts. Lately, Lockheed has been lobbying states like Texas and Arizona to implement its Information Management Systems (IMS) division, which would allow the defense industry giant to take over those states' respective welfare programs (monitoring and distributing food stamps, overseeing job-placement offices, et cetera).

△ ☼

Military-Industrial Complex

♏ ★ △ ⚰ ☺ ✿ 🎆

Reverend Sun Myung Moon

A North Korean–born self-proclaimed prophet, Moon founded the **Unification Church** in Seoul, Korea, in 1954 (with help from **CIA** operative **Ryoichi Sasakawa**). The Unification Church (aka the Moonies) has had many dealings with the CIA and, some believe, may have provided financial aid to Shoko Asahara and his **Aum Shinrikyo** cult. Moon brought his church to the United States in 1959 and was convicted of income tax evasion in an American court in 1982 and sentenced to eighteen months in prison. Japanese taxes were used to finance the Moonies and, after being laundered by the **Yakuza,** the **World Anti-Communist League,** which Moon, a devout anti-Communist **Fascist,** also helped get off the ground.

🏨 ↷ ⚰ 🎆

Multinationals Conspiracy

♏ △ 🌐

Nazis

♏ ★ 🏨 🐦 ⚰ ✿

Richard Nixon

U.S. president (1969–1974) and paranoiac supreme, in the theater of early sixties politics Nixon played the embittered Salieri to **JFK**'s charismatic Mozart. Early on in his career as a Republican congressman, Nixon made his name investigating allegations of **Communism** against government officials for HUAC. (His

most famous target was Alger Hiss.) As **Eisenhower**'s vice president, he and the **CIA** dreamed up the **Bay of Pigs** invasion—under the assumption that Nixon would succeed Eisenhower as the next president. Instead, Nixon was trounced (popularly, if not in actual numbers—JFK's victory margin was suspiciously slim) in the 1960 election by the young JFK. Nixon initiated the War on Cancer campaign of the late 1960s, and in 1971, as part of this campaign, he transferred part of the U.S. **Army's Biochemical Warfare** unit (at **Fort Detrick**) to the **National Cancer Institute,** a branch of the **NIH.** Nixon had a symbiotic relationship with **Lockheed** and frequently used his influence to help the company's sales to foreign nations. Lockheed returned these favors by making sizable contributions to Nixon's campaigns. In 1972, Nixon tried unsuccessfully to help **Prince Bernhard** of the Netherlands conceal the fact that he had allegedly been paid over a million dollars by Lockheed to persuade the Dutch government to buy its aircraft. Under threats of impeachment following the **Watergate** conspiracy, Nixon resigned in 1974. Nixon was friendly with the anti-Kennedy Texas oilman H. L. Hunt. Coincidentally, he also happened to visit Dallas (for a meeting with **Pepsi** "strategists") the day before Kennedy was shot. He remained particularly loyal, fiercely so, to CIA spook **E. Howard Hunt,** who served as recruiter for the Bay of Pigs and, later, as a Watergate plumber. He also stayed on very tight terms with **Henry Kissinger,** his national security advisor and secretary of state during the **Vietnam War.**

⚏ △ ⬪ ♰ ☺ ☼

North Atlantic Treaty Organization (NATO)

A post-**WWII** military and economic alliance of twelve Western nations—Belgium, Canada, Denmark, France, Iceland, Italy, Luxembourg, the Netherlands, Norway, Portugal, the United Kingdom, and the United States—all pledged to the "collective defense" and security against the **Communists.** Formed in 1948, NATO was awash with operatives from **Reinhard Gehlen**'s Org and was later joined by many other countries, including, in 1997, Russia and former Soviet satellite countries the Czech Republic, Poland, and Hungary (another small step toward a **One World Government** and the **NWO**). Militarily and otherwise, NATO is led by the United States, and critics have claimed that America's **Military-Industrial Complex** corporations, such as **Lockheed,** have frequently had undue influence on NATO's weapons contracts.

> Who is the enemy? The enemy is no faceless "they." The enemy is clearly identifiable as the Committee of 300, the Club of Rome, NATO and all of its affiliated organizations, the think tanks and research institutions controlled by Tavistock. There is no need to use "they" or "the enemy" except as shorthand. **WE KNOW WHO "THEY," THE ENEMY, IS.** The Committee of 300 with its Eastern Liberal Establishment "aristocracy," its banks, insurance companies, giant corporations, foundations, communications networks, presided over by a HIERARCHY OF CONSPIRATORS—THIS IS THE ENEMY.
>
> —**Dr. John Coleman,**
> *Conspirators' Hierarchy: The Story of the Committee of 300* (1992)

Juan Perón

Associate of **ITT** founder Sosthenes Behn and president of Argentina from 1946 to 1955 and from 1973 to 1974. Perón got plenty of financial and political support from **Fascist Licio Gelli, Mafia** kingpin and cofounder of Italy's **Masonic P2** lodge.

Pioneer Fund

ᛋ ᛏ

Prince Bernhard

✗

139

Resorts International

In 1968, the onetime Mary Carter Paint Company, purchased in 1958 by Lowell Thomas and Thomas Dewey (with a bit of financial help from **CIA** director **Allen Dulles**), quickly changed its name to Resorts International and transferred its business operations from paints to hotels and casinos (in Atlantic City and the Bahamas). Resorts, long linked to the CIA by conspiranoiacs of all stripes, later bought **Intertel,** the corporate private-security and intelligence firm (whose clients included **ITT,** the Shah of Iran, and **Howard Hughes,** and whose first president was Robert Peloquin, an ex–**Justice Department** investigator who served on the "Get **Hoffa**" squad). Resorts is also thought to have had ties to the **Mafia**'s Meyer Lansky. In 1954, Resorts's first owners, Dewey and Thomas, founded, along with future CIA director **William Casey,** Capital Cities Communications, the eventual owner of the **ABC** television network and now part owner of **Disney.**

〰〰 △

Nelson Rockefeller

★ ⛪

Franklin Delano Roosevelt

✳ ✍

Royal Dutch/Shell

The world's number two oil-and-gas company, a partnership of the Royal Dutch Petroleum Company of the Netherlands (home of **Bilderbergers**' cofounder **Prince Bernhard**, who worked for RD/S) and the Houston-based Shell Oil (the **Rockefeller** family

Going Too Far?

British anti-Semite C. H. Douglas claims **Hitler** was the illegitimate descendant of the **Rothschilds.**

Comedian-activist-weight-reduction-hawker Dick Gregory says the 1979–1981 murders of twenty-eight young black men and boys were carried out by federal scientists who were nipping off the heads of the victims' penises to be used for an anticancer serum.

subsidiary based in **George Bush**'s hometown). RD/S's board of director membership intersects with **Unilever, Daimler-Benz,** and **IBM,** and the company has a joint-venture deal with **Fiat.**

Ryoichi Sasakawa

A drug-dealing member of the *kura maku* and the **Yakuza,** who, according to declassified **U.S. Army** Intelligence documents, worked for the **CIA** in post-**WWII** Japan and helped build the **Unification Church.** In 1939 he flew to Rome in one of his own aircraft to meet personally with **Fascist** dictator Benito Mussolini and help arrange the Axis alliance between Italy, Germany, and Japan and was arrested in 1945 as a class A war criminal. No matter. He was released after agreeing to work for the CIA and was aided back to extreme wealth with the help of **John Foster Dulles** and General Douglas MacArthur, who sought to get the Japanese economy back on its feet and at the same time use Japanese war criminals like Sasakawa to fight Communists. Before his release, Sasakawa's cellmate was future Japan prime minister Nobosuke Kishi, who founded what would eventually evolve into the **World Anti-Communist League.** Sasakawa describes himself as "the world's richest Fascist." In the early 1950s Sasakawa helped his good buddy and fellow anti-Communist **Reverend Sun Myung Moon** form the Unification Church (a joint project of the Korean CIA and the American CIA), and later the two men, with Nobosuke's aid, helped lay the groundwork for what would evolve into the WACL. Toward the end of his life (Sasakawa died in 1995) he associated with **Henry Kissinger** and enlisted business partner **Robert Maxwell** in his quest for the Nobel Peace Prize(!).

🏠

Transnationals

♏ ✿ ⊕

The Open Conspiracy will appear first, I believe, as a conscious organization of intelligent, and in some cases, wealthy men. . . . In all sorts of ways, they will be influencing and controlling the ostensible government.

—**H. G. Wells,** *The Open Conspiracy—Plans for a Revolution*

Unification Church

★ ↩ ✝

United Fruit Company

★

World Anti-Communist League

Founded in 1966 by Japanese **Fascist Ryoichi Sasakawa,** the **Reverend Sun Myung Moon,** and the Korean CIA (and American **CIA**), with help too from Taiwan president Chiang Kai-shek and South Korea dictator Syngman Rhee, and once led by ex–**Secret Team** member General **John Singlaub,** the WACL functioned as a kind of fascistic anti-UN magnet and attracted ultramilitant right-wing fanatics from around the globe. Its members ranged from wigged-out U.S. congressmen, ex-CIA spooks, and former **Nazis** to Italian **Terrorists** (like the shadowy **P2**), Latin American death-squad types (like El Salvador's Robert D'Aubuisson), and racist Afrikaners. Dedicated to fighting **Communism** and promoting rightism, the league spread to nearly one hundred nations on six continents and had been associated with North American racist groups and neo-Facists and anti-Semites worldwide. Its U.S. headquarters were in the offices of Reverend Moon's Freedom Center. In 1996, the WACL changed its name to the World League for Freedom and Democracy and claimed to have changed its ways.

🏛 ↩ ✝

World Economic Forum

✍ 🌐

Yakuza

Basically Japan's **Mafia,** the Yakuza (which means "worthless") have been a part of Japanese society since the seventeenth century, have been very influential in Japan's politics, and have long controlled its country's pornography and prostitution.

🏛 ↩

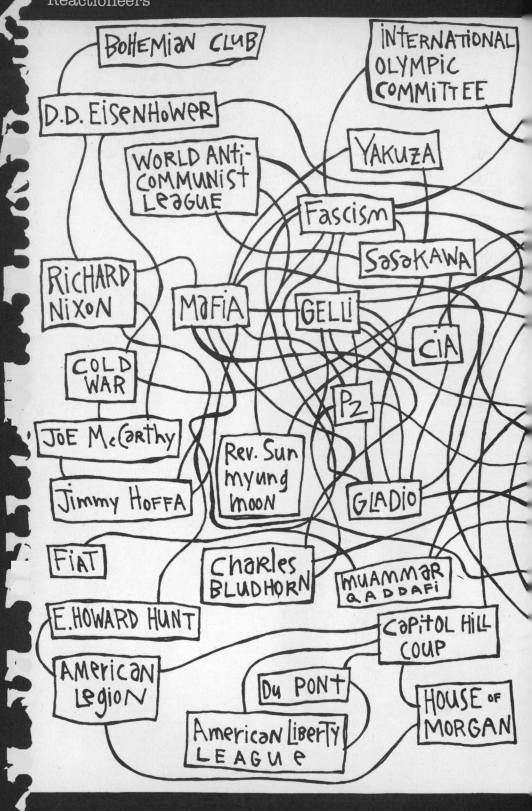

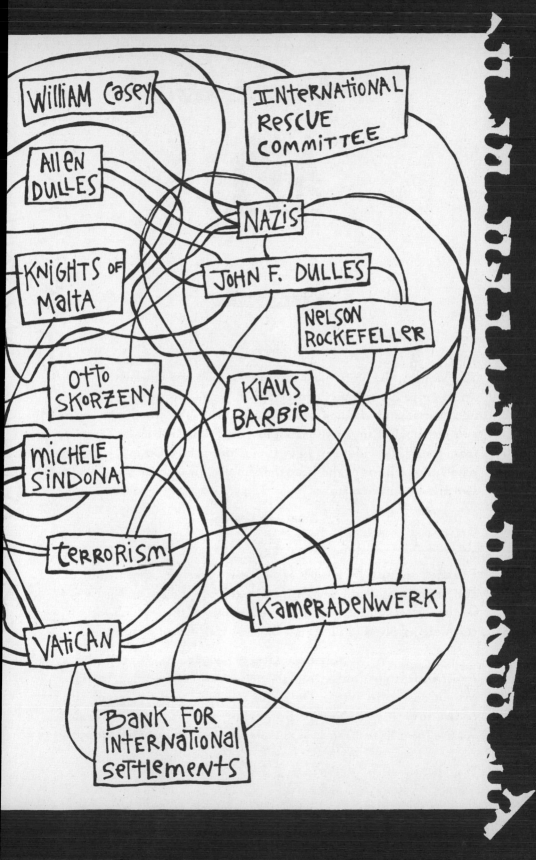

Conspiracy

The Vatican, the Mafia, and Fascists—is there any triumvirate in the world more dangerously conservative? Perhaps only the Nazis (and neo-Nazis) and staunch anti-Communists like Joseph McCarthy and the cabal of snobs who tried to oust Franklin Delano Roosevelt from the White House in 1933 (the Capitol Hill Coup). Unfortunately, the actions of the Reactioneers usually lead only to **Terrorism** and totalitarianism.

American Legion

Founded in 1919 by **House of Morgan** director Grayson Murphy and other aristocratic vets of the Great War, the legion's early goal was to "offset radicalism." Murphy and two of the legion's top officers were involved in the failed **Capitol Hill Coup** of 1933.

American Liberty League

A patriotic 1930s anti-Commie organization, founded by right-wing industrialist Irénée **Du Pont.** Du Pont and the league's two codirectors (former New York governor Al Smith and Du Pont executive John Raskob) were key players in the **Capitol Hill Coup.**

> Rumor is not always wrong.
>
> —Tacitus

Bank for International Settlements

❢ ★ ∞ ⊕

Charles Bludhorn

The late billionaire CEO of Gulf & Western (which he founded), Bludhorn served as a director on the board of an Italian company called Immobiliare, alongside Sicilian financier and Gambino **Mafia** crime-family consigliare, **Michele Sindona.** Bludhorn was also tight with Paul "the Gorilla" Marcinkus and **P2** boss **Licio Gelli,** and at one time he owned **MCA** (home of **Lew Wasserman** and **Ronald Reagan**).

▓

Bohemian Club

✖ 〰〰 ☺

Capitol Hill Coup

A little-known 1933 **Fascist** plot to overthrow president **Franklin Delano Roosevelt,** concocted by ivory-tower **Insiders** from the **Du Pont** empire and the **House of Morgan** and by the founders of the **American Liberty League,** along with founders and vets of the **American Legion** (who had the support of several **Knights of Malta**). Everyone involved was a hard-line right-winger who loathed FDR and his labor-friendly **New Deal** program. The coup was thwarted before it ever really get off the ground by **WWI** war hero, Major General Smedley Darlington Butler.

> Conspiracy refers to an act, conspiracy theory to a perception.
>
> —Daniel Pipes, author of Conspiracy (1998) and member of the Council on Foreign Relations

William Casey

★ ✏ ☺ ▨

CIA

♍ ★ ⛵ ✝ 🐘 〰〰〰 △ ✏ ➴ ▮ ☺ ▨ ⊕ ☉

Cold War

✍

Allen Dulles

★ ✝ 🐘 △

John Foster Dulles

★ ✝

Du Pont

Officially known as E. I. Du Pont de Nemours, Du Pont likes to be known as "the Armorers of the Republic," and it lives up to that moniker as the United States's number one manufacturer of chemicals. Originated in 1802 as an explosives maker, Du Pont entered into the petrochemical-and-oil big time with its acquisition of Conoco (manufacturer of paraquat, the highly toxic herbicide used to poison marijuana crops). Du Pont invented Teflon, markets Kevlar and Lycra, and owns the patent to 1984's transgenic "oncomouse." Its board of director membership intersects with **IBM,** and it has (or has had) joint ventures with **Merck** and **Dow.** The Du Pont family effectively owns the state of Delaware, controlling its state and local governments, its papers, and its radio and TV stations as well as its universities. All combined, the Du Pont conglomerate employs nearly 75 percent of Delaware, and Du Ponts have served in the military, as U.S. attorney general, as secretary of defense, as director of the **CIA,**

Organs of Conspiranoia

Spotlight, Crash Collusion, Conspiracy Update, The Eye, IllumiNet Press, Feral House, *Executive Intelligence Review,* A-albionic Research, Loompanics Unlimited, *Flashlight, Fate, The Unopened Files, Bizarre,* iF Magazine, *Strange.*

and as a Supreme Court justice. The firm's namesake company leader, Irénée Du Pont, founded the **American Liberty League** and, with company man John J. Raskob (**Knight of Malta** and **GM**'s board chairman), tried to forcibly oust **Franklin Delano Roosevelt** from office in 1933. Back in the 1930s, Du Pont joined forces with newspaper tycoon **William Randolph Hearst** to stamp out hemp (and marijuana). Du Pont also manufactured tons of **Fluoride,** which was used for the building of the **Manhattan Project**'s atomic bomb.
♒ ☼

Dwight D. Eisenhower

A heroic **WWII** general, Ike served as U.S. president during the blissful ignorance of the 1950s (1953–1961). (It's rumored that the powers-that-be at the **Bohemian Club** handpicked Ike as the country's 1952 Republican presidential candidate.) His secretary of agriculture from 1952 to 1960 was **Mormon** elder Ezra Taft Benson and his veep was **Richard Nixon**.
☉

Fascism

♍ ☀ ⚕ ✝ ➹ ⚱ ☺

Fiat

Fabbrica Italiana di Automobili Torino, the Italian car, aerospace, telecommunications, and bioengineering firm, is still owned by the Agnelli family (who founded the company back in 1899). No longer just manufacturing Alfa Romeos and Ferraris, Fiat has moved into robotics and publishing. During **WWII,** Fiat supplied Italy's **Fascist** dictator Benito Mussolini with cars, trucks, and planes. In the 1970s, in need of more funds, Fiat agreed to a deal with Libya's **Muammar Qaddafi.** In 1976, Fiat gave Qaddafi a 10 percent share in the company, which boosted the company's stock. In 1986, flush from its turnaround success, Fiat bought out Qaddafi (who had turned a $415 million investment into a $2.9 billion profit), and a year later Fiat was designated one of the United States's main defense contractors for **Reagan**'s SDI "star wars" program. Chairman (and **Bilderberger**) Giovanni Agnelli

149

was recently named godfather of supermodel Elle MacPherson's daughter.

Licio Gelli

Terrorist Italian **Mafia** kingpin, raging anti-Communist, **Knight of Malta,** and arms-dealing **Fascist** who founded Italy's Masonic **P2** lodge, with **CIA** assistance, in 1966. Gelli helped set up the CIA's **Gladio** project and later infiltrated the **Banco Nazionale del Lavoro,** which expedited loans to **Saddam Hussein.** He also put a great deal of money behind his close friend, Argentina president Juan Perón (1946–1955 and 1973–1974), and was a guest of honor at president **Ronald Reagan**'s 1980 inauguration. Known as "God's banker" because of his ties to fellow P2 member Paul "the Gorilla" Marcinkus, Gelli also set up deals with the **KGB**—and it may have been his playing the Rooskie spies against the Company spooks that led to the mid-1980s downfall of Banco Ambrosiano. Suspected of having ordered the death of Pope John Paul I, who seemed open to the idea of purging the **Vatican** of its links to the Mafia, the P2, and the **Freemasons.**
☺ ▩

Gladio

Before **WWII** had even ended, **OSS** officer and future **CIA** titan James Jesus Angleton began courting Italian **Fascists** with the idea of rigging Italy's future elections to prevent the Italian Communist party from winning control of the parliament. Code-named Gladio, this decades-long plot involved the **Mafia,** the **Vatican,** "ex"-Fascists of Italy, paid-off politicians and journalists, and **P2** founder **Licio Gelli,** all of whom conspired, under Angleton's direction, to create such an ongoing rash of left-wing **Terrorism** (which hit its peak with the kidnapping and murder of Commie-tolerant Italian prime minister Aldo Moro) that Italy's unsuspecting populace would—and did—demand a stronger, avowedly anti-Communist government.

Jimmy Hoffa

This Detroit thug became president of the Teamsters union in 1957—despite his connections to the **Mafia.** U.S. attorney general **Robert Kennedy** relentlessly hounded Hoffa about his Mafia ties.

In return, **Sam Giancana** ordered Hoffa to bug all of Bobby's hangouts—including Peter Lawford's cottage, where Kennedy and **Marilyn Monroe** were to have met on the night she died. In 1967, Hoffa was sent to prison for jury tampering (in other words, bribery) and mishandling the Teamsters' pension fund. He was freed in 1971 by President **Nixon** (Nixon's involvement and frequent cooperation with Hoffa and the Teamsters may be traced back to their shared animosity toward the Kennedys and the mediating role that Hoffa played between Nixon and the Mafia). Hoffa disappeared on July 30, 1975, leading to rumors that the Mob either ground him up and passed him through a fat-rendering machine or buried him in the south end zone of New Jersey's Meadowlands Stadium (now Continental Arena).

△

House of Morgan

✡ ✍

E. Howard Hunt

A veteran of **Watergate** and the **Bay of Pigs,** a Company man, and alleged to be one of the three mysterious tramps who were seen lurking on the grassy knoll in Dallas on the day of **JFK**'s murder, the ubiquitous Hunt was also reported seen lurking around Mexico City's Cuban embassy on the day that a man claiming he was **Lee Harvey Oswald** appeared there in September 1963 demanding a visa to go to Cuba immediately. A favorite of **Nixon**'s, during the 1950s Hunt—then with the **CIA**—trained Cuban exiles in the art of espionage. Later he served in Southeast Asia alongside the **Triads** (who were setting up shop in the **Golden Triangle**) and under **Air America** boss Paul Helliwell. One of his old agency partners was none other than William Peter Blatty, author of *The Exorcist*. Hunt's father was a 32nd-degree **Freemason** and founder of the New York chapter of the **American Legion** (the coconspirator group in the 1933 **Capitol Hill Coup** to oust FDR).

△ ◻

International Olympic Committee

★ ✝

International Rescue Committee

★

Kameradenwerk

★

Knights of Malta

✖ ⚑ ☺

Mafia

♏ ✳ 〰 △ ✑ ☺ ▦

Joseph McCarthy

Senator from Wisconsin (1947–1957), McCarthy spearheaded the anti-Communist "witch hunt"—style investigations of the House Un-American Activities Committee during the early 1950s. Probably the most notoriously rabid opponent of the **International Communist Conspiracy** in this century, McCarthy's crusade was aided by national paranoia about Communist expansion and conspiracies stemming from the **Korean War** and the growing **Cold War,** and he was at one time represented by Teamster **Jimmy Hoffa**'s lawyer, Ed Williams. An ideological descendant of the Know-Nothing dopes (an anti-immigrant, anti-Catholic party of the mid-1800s), McCarthy was provided with morphine by former drug commissioner **Harry Anslinger** before eventually wasting away in an insane asylum. One of his former HUAC investigators was **Richard Nixon.**

Reverend Sun Myung Moon

✝ ⤳ ⚑ ▦

Nazis

♏ ★ ✝ 🐾 ⚑ ✿

Richard Nixon

✝ △ ✑ ⚑ ☺ ✿

P2

✳ ☺ RIGHT

Muammar Qaddafi

The heavy-handed leader of Libya, Qaddafi rose to power in a bloodless coup in 1969 after having graduated form the Libyan Se-

cret Service (which was set up by ex-**Nazi Otto Skorzeny**). Committed to unifying the Arab world, opposed to Israel and the United States, and a longtime supporter of various **Terrorist** groups (another trainer of Libyan terrorists was **Secret Team** teammate and renegade **CIA** agent Edwin Wilson, who also sold arms to Qaddafi and was then jailed for it), in 1976 Qaddafi rescued the **Fascist**-tolerant Italian automobile maker **Fiat** out of certain bankruptcy when he invested $415 million into the troubled company. In 1977, Qaddafi offered sanctuary to cult leader David "Moses" Berg and his **Children of God,** who were being investigated in California and New York for child molestation. Iraqi arms dealer **Ihsan Barbouti** designed a chemical weapons plant for Qaddafi.
☞ ☺

Nelson Rockefeller

★ †

Ryoichi Sasakawa

†

Michele "the Shark" Sindona

Sindona started out as a **Mafia** lawyer before joining Italy's **Masonic P2** lodge. He and Paul "the Gorilla" Marcinkus, president of the **Vatican Bank,** invested in **Procter & Gamble** and laundered drug money for the Mob and the Latin American **Cali-Medellín Cocaine Cartels.** Sindona was a guest at **Nixon**'s 1972 presidential inauguration and also sat on the board of Immobiliare, alongside **Charles Bludhorn,** late CEO of Gulf & Western.

Otto Skorzeny

⚐ ★

Terrorism

✳ ★ ☺

There have been many conspiracies, but history has shown that few have succeeded.

—Niccolò Machiavelli, *The Prince*

Vatican

♍ ✖ ✳ ⚲ ⚱ ☺ ☉

World Anti-Communist League

✝ ⚭ ⚱

Yakuza

✝ ⚭

Official Memorandum

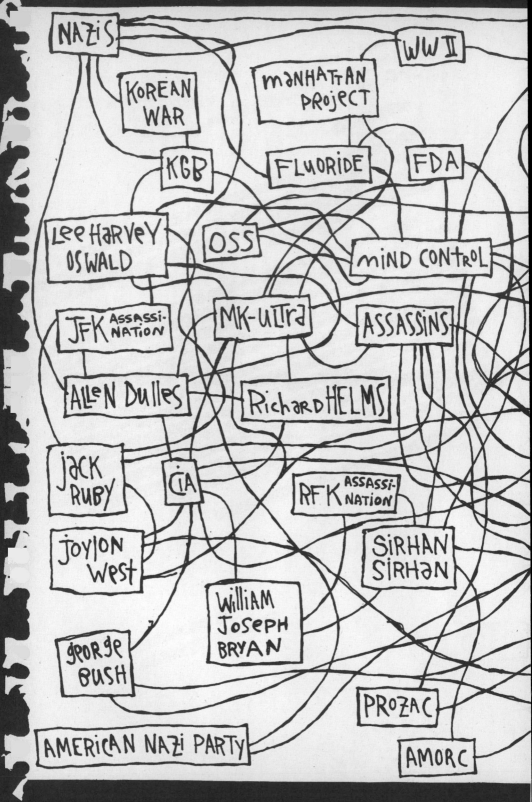

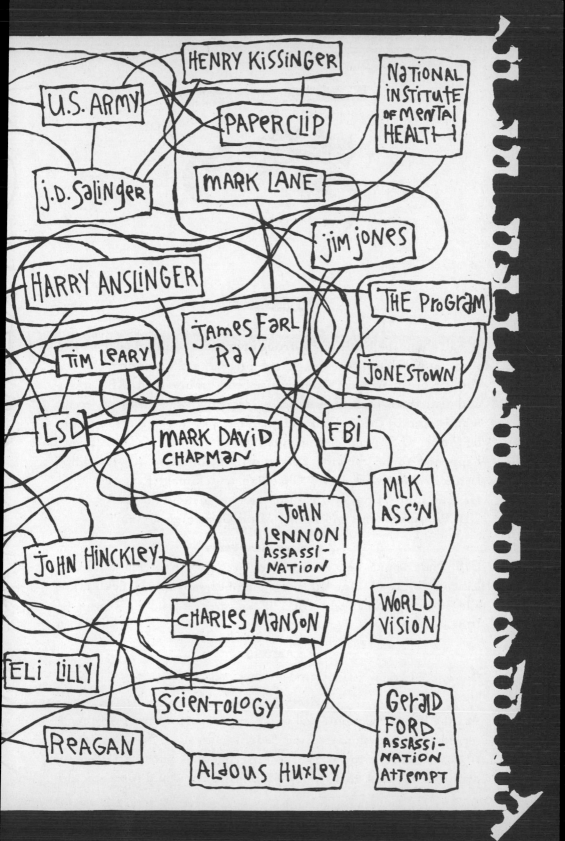

Conspiracy

It's all about the battle to control our minds. Inspired by the 1962 film *The Manchurian Candidate*, based on Richard Condon's thriller about Korean War–era Communists who brainwashed U.S. troops and sent them back to America as assassins (who'd kill on command), and by the odd coincidence that *Catcher in the Rye*, the classic by former U.S. Army counterintelligence operative J. D. Salinger, happened to be the one possession in common between John Lennon killer Mark David Chapman and Ronald Reagan's failed assassin John Hinckley, Jr., this chapter details the CIA's MK-ULTRA experiments and similar Mind Control programs.

American Nazi Party

U.S. **Nazi** wanna-bes, founded in 1959 by craven racist George Lincoln Rockwell. One latter-day member was **John Hinckley,** the alleged lone gunman who tried to assassinate President **Reagan** in 1981.

AMORC

✖

Harry Anslinger

Aka the King of Codeine and the Marquis of Morphine, Anslinger served as commissioner of the Federal Bureau of Narcotics from 1931 to 1961. During **WWII,** he experimented with the **Office of Strategic Services** on a version of hashish that would force spies to reveal all they knew. Later, when the **CIA** asked for help with its **MK-ULTRA** program, Anslinger happily lent the Company one of his narcotics agents, George Hunter White. In 1955, in San Francisco, White set up Operation Midnight Climax, in which he hired junkie prostitutes to lure johns back to their hotel for a little bit of sex and a whole lot of **LSD** (unbeknownst to the johns, whom White watched from behind a two-way mirror). Anslinger also provided **Joe McCarthy** with morphine and was married to the niece of **Andrew Mellon** (owner of Mellon National Bank, the bank of choice since 1928 for anti-cannabis company **Du Pont**).

Assassins

✖

William Joseph Bryan

A Los Angeles psychiatrist who treated **Sirhan Sirhan** with hypnosis before Sirhan assassinated **Robert Kennedy**. Bryan, who ran a therapeutic clinic called the American Institute of Hypnosis, claimed that he'd also hypnotized Albert DeSalvo, the Boston Strangler. A possible **CIA** operative, Bryan served as technical consultant on *The Manchurian Candidate*.

Mark David Chapman

The "lone gunman" who killed ex-Beatle **John Lennon** on December 8, 1980. Immediately after shooting Lennon in the back, Chapman calmly sat down and started reading **J. D. Salinger**'s *Catcher in the Rye*. Chapman's psychiatrist, Dr. Bernard Diamond, also treated **Robert Kennedy**'s alleged **Assassin, Sirhan Sirhan**. Chapman had also worked as a YMCA camp counselor (in **Terrorist**-rich Beirut, of all places) and flirted with neo-**Nazis**.

Church of Scientology

Cheery if litigious pseudo-religious crew created by **L. Ron Hubbard** in 1954. Supersensitive to and vengeful of its doubters, the "church" effectively uses blackmail, harassment, and the threat of litigation to silence its numerous critics. In 1993, the IRS granted Scientologists tax-exempt status—under very questionable circumstances: In the late 1970s, Hubbard's wife, Mary Sue, and ten other Scientologists, went to jail, convicted for electronic eavesdropping and breaking into IRS offices. In 1996, one of its members quietly purchased the Cult Awareness Network, creating a huge conflict of interest (to put it mildly). CAN then hired the self-appointed cult "expert" J. Gordon Melton, a Scientolapologist and Santa Barbara librarian, as its executive director—in 1997, for example, Melton came out in defense of Japan's **Aum Shinrikyo** cult. And in a case of a **Mind Control** kettle calling the brainwashing pot black, the "church," which loathes psychiatrists, has waged a long-running smear campaign against **Prozac** and its manufacturer, **Eli Lilly & Co.**, contending that the popular antidepressant pill induces suicide and aberrant behavior. In 1995, Clearwater, Florida, Scientologist Lisa McPherson died while under the care (or lack of care) of Scientologists in a case that's still being investigated.

〰 ∽ ☉

CIA

♏ ★ 👌 ✝ 🏛 〰 △ ▱ ∽ ✝ 😐 🔲 🌐 ☉

Allen Dulles

★ ✝ 🏛 △

Eli Lilly & Co.

Global pharmaceutical corporation headquartered in Indianapolis, Lilly introduced insulin in 1923, created the sedative Seconal in the

How's Your E-Meter?

Members of **Scientology** include Kirstie Alley, Tom Cruise and his wife, Nicole Kidman, John Travolta and his wife, Kelly Preston, Isaac Hayes, Juliette Lewis, Danny Elfman, Jenna Elfman, Chick Corea, Anne Archer, and the late Sonny Bono.

Those who say they only took classes or later left the Church include Mikhail Baryshnikov, William Burroughs, Van Morrison, Al Jarreau, Leonard Cohen, Emilio Estevez, the late Rock Hudson, Demi Moore, Christopher Reeve, Patrick Swayze, Marcia Clarke, Brad Pitt, and Jerry Seinfeld (plus several ex-members who later joined up with **Heaven's Gate**).

1930s, and produced almost three-quarters of the Salk polio vaccine in the 1950s. In 1954, Lilly successfully manufactured its first batch of **LSD** for the **CIA**'s **MK-ULTRA** experiments. Lilly also makes Darvon, a cannabislike drug. Former president and CIA director **George Bush** was the company's director from 1976 to 1977. In 1982, Lilly became the first company to market a biotechnology product, Genentech's Humulin, a human insulin copycat. Lilly has been criticized for sometimes using homeless alcoholic men to test out its latest experimental drugs.

〰 ☺ ✺

FBI

♏ ❋ ✝ 〰 △ ✺ ⊕ ☉

Fluoride

✍ ✺

Food and Drug Administration (FDA)

Public health agency delegated to determine, among other things, which drugs are healthful enough for Americans. The FDA regulates food, cosmetics, medicines, and medical devices, as well as various radiation-emitting products, like microwave ovens. In the 1950s, the FDA cooperated with the **FBI** in the harassment and persecution of agitsexprop radical Wilhelm Reich and bent over backward for the **CIA** during its **Mind Control** programs of the 1940s to 1970s. There's a huge ethically muddy crossover of FDA scientists and administrators to pharmaceutical companies, creating the perception, if not the reality, that the FDA is merely, in the words of former senator Howard Metzenbaum, the "handmaiden" of the pharmaceutical industry.

✺

Gerald Ford Assassination Attempt

On September 5, 1975, **Manson** Family member Lynette "Squeaky" Fromme attempted to assassinate President Gerald Ford in Sacramento, California. If Fromme's assassination attempt had succeeded, Ford's successor would have been **Insider** extraordinaire, Vice President **Nelson Rockefeller.** The attempt took place in front of the City of Francis's St. Francis Hotel, located across Mason Street—indicating a possible connection to London's notorious **Hell Fire Club,** a **Masonic** group publicly known as "the Friars of St. Francis of Wycombe."

Richard Helms

✍ ⊕

John Hinckley, Jr.

In 1981, Hinckley, allegedly a member of the **American Nazi Party,** tried to assassinate **Ronald Reagan** while doped up on Valium, supposedly to impress *Taxi Driver* star Jodie Foster, whom he had been stalking. Hinckley's father, John Hinckley, Sr., was a **World Vision** official and a friend of Vice President **George Bush.** What's more, Bush's son Neil had a lunch date scheduled with Hinckley's brother Scott on the day John Jr. shot Reagan. Some suspect that Hinckley may have been yet another "zombie assassin" carrying out orders under the influence of hypnotism, pharmacology, or other **Mind Control** programs—orders perhaps triggered by **J. D. Salinger**'s *Catcher in the Rye,* one of Hinckley's few possessions (and the same book **Mark David Chapman** sat down to reread right after he gunned down **John Lennon**).

☺

Aldous Huxley

✍ ♒ ∽

John F. Kennedy Assassination

On November 22, 1963, President **John F. Kennedy** was assassinated in Dallas, Texas—an act of **Terrorism** that shocked and demoralized the American public. Before leaving on that fateful trip, Kennedy had been warned by several congressmen not to go to Dallas, and even JFK himself was worried about the trip. Dallas had the reputation as a city controlled by powerful extremist right-wingers like the **John Birch Society.** On the morning of November 22, for example, JFK read a full-page advertisement in the *Dallas Morning News* that heavily condemned his "soft" policy toward Cuba. This advertisement was placed by the American Fact Finding Committee, whose leading sponsors included members of the John Birch Society and the son of influential Texas tycoon H. L. Hunt (who loathed Kennedy). Kennedy was killed near the end of a motorcade through downtown Dallas, as his car moved through a park between Dealey

Plaza and the Texas School Book Depository. Several shots were fired at intervals, hitting Kennedy as well as Texas governor John Connally. Kennedy's head basically exploded, and Connally was seriously wounded but survived. Hours after they were shot, an unstable ex-marine and **Communist** sympathizer, **Lee Harvey Oswald**, was caught, arrested, and charged with the murder. The very next day Oswald was gunned down—under heavy police custody, and in front of a live national TV audience—by another seemingly crazed and vengeful lone gunman, **Jack Ruby.** Given the maddening mass of confusing and contradictory evidence, it's hardly surprising that JFK's assassination immediately spawned one conspiracy theory after another. Physical evidence from the scene of the murder was carelessly handled and may have been tampered with; the rifle supposedly belonging to Oswald may have been switched with another gun; an incriminating palmprint was found long after the intitial dusting; bullets and bullet fragments were lost and replaced; and Kennedy's body was removed from Dallas at gunpoint by the Secret Service. Some even suspect that JFK's body was switched with another corpse or that surgery was done to alter his wounds. (Not to be left out of the JFK assassination mill, self-exiled anti-**Castro** Cubans say JFK was murdered by Chinese Communists who plotted the hit while in Cuba.) The autopsy was performed in Maryland by inexperienced doctors, who were badgered throughout by military "observers." To this day, much of the evidence from the autopsy is missing, including Kennedy's brain; and in 1979, a **CIA** agent was found tampering with the remaining evidence, mostly photographs of the president's head. No matter. The **Warren Commission,** mostly JFK haters and assorted **Freemasons** who were appointed (by **LBJ**) to investigate the

163

murder, ignored most of this evidence and instead focused on the "facts" that pointed to Oswald as the sole killer. Despite the efforts of New Orleans attorney Jim Garrison and others, the lone gunman theory remained the official one until 1979, when the congressional Assassinations Committee concluded that a conspiracy had been involved. One theory is that the assassination was actually a Freemason ritual enacted as part of a plan to bring about the **New World Order** (the triple underpass of Dealey Plaza was the site of the first Masonic temple in Dallas). Many of Nixon's future **Watergate** team—Frank Sturgis and **E. Howard Hunt,** to name just two— were roaming around Dallas the day after the murder. Nixon was also friends with other Kennedy haters like the late Texas oilman **Clint Murchison** and billionaire H. L. Hunt (who later paid for publication of a book called *Krushchev Killed Kennedy*).

△

John Lennon Assassination

The ex-**Beatle** singer and songwriter was gunned down on December 8, 1980, by **Mark David Chapman** in front of the Dakota, his elegant New York City apartment building.

I Killed JFK! No, *I* Killed JFK!

In 1980, when Texas police arrested Charles Harrelson, an associate of **Jack Ruby** and **Mobster Santos Trafficante,** and the father of *Natural Born Killers* star Woody Harrelson, the cops said Harrelson admitted to taking part in the murder of **John F. Kennedy.** Later, Harrelson, now in prison for the murder of a federal judge, told a Dallas TV station: "At the same time I said I'd killed the judge, I said I'd killed Kennedy, which might give you an idea as to the state of my mind at the time. It was an effort to elongate my life."

In 1993, Illinois cop killer James Files, who also claimed to have served in Laos as a **U.S. Army** paratrooper and to have trained Cuban exiles for the **Bay of Pigs,** fessed up, saying *he* blasted away from the grassy knoll while Chicago mobster Charles Nicoletti fired away from the Dal-Tex building.

Jim Jones

Known as the "messiah from Ukiah," Jones was the founder of the now-infamous People's Temple, a cult he first set up in Ukiah, California, in 1965. A dark and charismatic self-proclaimed prophet, Jones spoke of a **Socialist** utopia and soon attracted Christian missionaries from **World Vision.** Jones also settled in with the local director of the **John Birch Society** (no surprise, given that Jones's father had been a member of the **Ku Klux Klan** in Indiana) and let the society use Temple members to get out the vote for **Nixon.** Paranoid even then in small-town Ukiah, Jones often used doubles of himself and had his followers rehearse fake mass suicides. In 1977, Jones moved his People's Temple to a remote compound in Guyana, where, on November 18, 1978, Jones supposedly convinced more than 900 of his followers to commit suicide en masse.

∽

Jonestown Massacre

On November 18, 1978, 913 people, mostly followers of religious cult leader **Jim Jones,** were found dead in the cult's Guyanese compound. Of the 913 Kool-Aid "suicides," 910 showed signs of gunshot wounds, strangulation, or needle marks (on their shoulder blades!). The bodies of the cult members were later cremated or left in the jungle to rot—no autopsies were ever performed. The Reverend Jones himself was alleged to have blown his brains out. However, his gun was found a full 200 feet from his body, and photos of his apparent corpse did not bear Jones's characteristic tattoos. Green Berets (who'd been trained by **Bo Gritz**) and **CIA** Vietnam operatives worked the cleanup shift at the Jonestown massacre site. It's speculated by some that the Berets—and/or **CIA** man Richard

Jonestown Redux

Jonestown has lately been repopulated with thousands of Hmong refugees from Laos (the Hmong grew most of the opium for the **CIA**'s **Golden Triangle** drug operations), and **World Vision** "missionaries" have stepped in to help out.

Dwyer and/or the Temple's posse of white armed guards, who ate well, disciplined everybody else, and came and went freely—may have actually carried out the mass extermination (although Dwyer has always denied any involvement). It has been suggested that the massacre/suicide order may have been sparked by the investigations of U.S. congressman Leo Ryan, who went to Guyana to investigate allegations of brutality, only to be murdered along with four others prior to the slaughter. Some theorize that the real purpose of Jonestown was an **MK-ULTRA**-style **Mind Control** and brainwashing experiment for training robot assassins (one footlocker contained more than 11,000 doses of Thorazine). Alternatively, the "utopian community" was a racially motivated experiment designed to demonstrate a new way to handle uppity black nationalists.
∽

KGB

✍ △ ∽ ☼

Henry Kissinger

† ☺ ⊕

Korean War

★ ✍

Mark Lane

An attorney for civil rights leader **Martin Luther King, Jr.**'s **Assassin, James Earl Ray,** Lane was a confidant of and legal counsel for cult leader **Jim Jones**: the two allegedly discussed the idea of smuggling Grace Walden, a witness with a potential alibi for Ray, into the **Jonestown** compound. (Lane, however, denies there was ever any such talk and claims the **U.S. Army** instigated this rumor to smear him.) Lane also represented the **Liberty Lobby,** Willis Carto's militia-friendly neo-**Nazi**-ish group, as well as Jane Fonda, **Lee Harvey Oswald**'s mother, **John Hinckley, Jr.,** and *American History X* director Tony Kaye. Lane was in Guyana at the time of the **Jonestown** mass suicide, leading some conspiranoiacs to wonder just how it is he managed to escape the massacre.
△

Timothy Leary

The Pope of Dope and unofficial guru of psychedelia in the 1960s and 1970s, Leary, a psychologist, first tried **LSD** in the early sixties while teaching at Harvard. He also invented "the Leary," a personality test later used by the **CIA** to quiz possible Langley employees. At Harvard, he and fellow psychedelic enthusiasts **Aldous Huxley** and Allen Ginsberg turned on Beatnik pals William Burroughs and Jack Kerouac. Leary later brainstormed with Marshall McLuhan to come up with the drug movement's most famous slogan: "Tune in, turn on, drop out." Leary then turned on American painter and former lover Mary Pinchot Meyer, sister-in-law of *Washington Post* editor Ben Bradlee. Meyer, whose husband was a CIA man, slept with **JFK**. (Meyer was shot twice in the head and killed in 1964, and her murder remains unsolved.) In 1974, after several months in jail, Leary agreed to rat out his fellow acid enthusiasts, for which the **FBI** cruelly assigned him the code name "Charlie Thrush."

〰〰
〰〰

LSD

❀

This synthetic hallucinogen, developed in Switzerland by Sandoz Pharmaceuticals researcher Albert Hofmann, was introduced in America via the **CIA**'s **MK-ULTRA** project, which tested the drug on all sorts of subjects, with and without their knowledge: college students at Cornell University via the Society for the Investigation of Human Ecology; marines at the Atsugi Naval Base (where **Lee Harvey Oswald** was stationed); black patients at the Lexington Narcotics Hospital; and whoring businessmen lured into the Midnight Climax operation in San Francisco.

167

(The **U.S. Army** Chemical Corps also tested LSD on 1,500 "volunteer" GIs.)
⋙

Manhattan Project

This **WWII** research project, rumored to have been thought up by partyers at the **Bohemian Club,** led to the development of the atomic bomb. Most of the work was done at **Los Alamos National Lab.** Certain members working on the bomb were also simultaneously involved in the development of a **Mind Control** "truth drug" at St. Elizabeth's Hospital in Washington, D.C., as part of the **CIA**'s **MK-ULTRA** project. The project started off in New York City, where scientists in upstate New York produced massive amounts of **Fluoride** for the project (as did a **Du Pont** chemical factory in New Jersey, where huge amounts of fluoride accidentally were released into nearby drinking water), since fluoride was essential for the manufacture of nuclear-weapons-grade uranium and plutonium.
✿ ☉

I'm so skeptical that I find it beyond me to deny the possibility of anything.

—Budd Hopkins, *Intruders,* 1987

Charles Manson

A swastika-tattooed late-sixties cult leader and racist, some say Charlie, aka the Wizard, got his **LSD** (indirectly) from **Timothy Leary.** A onetime aspiring musician and partying buddy of Beach Boy Brian Wilson, Manson was at least morally responsible for the gruesome 1969 Tate-LaBianca murders in which five members of his "family" descended on the rented Beverly Hills home of Sharon Tate (the eight-months-pregnant wife of film director Roman Polanski) and the home of Leno and Rosemary LaBianca. His possible petty motive for the Tate murder: that the Manson crew was really after Vojtek Frykowski, a notorious acid dealer who was banging San Francisco Folger's coffee heiress Abigail Folger (who might've also been sleeping with Charlie). The possible warped motive for the LaBianca

killings: according to Manson, they deserved it because they dealt in kiddie porn. A self-styled **Jesus** figure, some say that Manson preached his mishmash interpretation of **Beatles** lyrics, the Book of Revelations, **Hitler,** and **Scientology** (and commissioned the Tate-LaBianca killings) hoping that it would incite a racial black-and-white battle of Armageddon (hence the writings-in-blood at the victims' homes, "Death to Pigs" and "Healter-[sic] Skelter"). After the ashes cleared from this racial war, a white master race would emerge (the blacks being clueless on what to do or where to go) and Charlie would be their king. While on parole in San Francisco in 1967, Manson may have crossed paths with **CIA Mind Control** psychiatrist **Dr. Louis Joylon West.** While in prison before the infamous murders, he hooked up with the **AMORC Rosicrucians** (the same branch that so obsessed **Robert Kennedy's Assassin Sirhan Sirhan).** Days before the Tate-LaBianca murders Manson visited Big Sur's **Esalen Institute.** A rumored member of the Process, ex-Scientologist Robert DeGrimston's black magic sect, and a definite **Nazism** enthusiast, Manson had his last name appropriated by the goth-rock group **Marilyn Manson.**
∞ ∾

Martin Luther King, Jr., Assassination

☀ △

Mind Control

Primarily the use of drugs, hypnosis, radiation (often of the **Electromagnetic Radiation** kind), ELF (Extreme Low Frequency), **Microwave,** or radio waves to alter or control a person's mental faculties—all of which have been employed, wittingly and unwittingly, by the **CIA,** the **NIH, NIMH,** the **Stanford Research Institute,** and many other organizations.

〰 ⤳ 😒 ✧ ☉

MK-ULTRA

The **CIA**'s psychopharmacology project (1953–1964) run by **Allen Dulles** and **Richard Helms** (who dreamed it up). MK-ULTRA was an effort to concoct a drug that could so alter human behavior as to create an agent with no free will (the ultra Mind Kontrol Manchurian Kandidate—get it?). Helms hoped that the CIA would one day have a small army of these unlikely, normal-seeming, on-call **Assassins** capable

Ante-ULTRA

Project Chatter: Forerunner to **MK-ULTRA,** this "offensive" *Mind Control* program (1947–1953) of the U.S. Navy was designed to solicit information from people without the use of physical force—and experimented with mescaline.

Dr. Hubertus Strughold: Top **Nazi** scientist smuggled out of Germany via Project **Paperclip,** Strughold oversaw Dachau's notorious aviation medicine experiments (injecting inmates with gasoline, malaria, or typhus; dunking prisoners into icewater-filled tubs, et cetera—all to see how long it took for people to die under such conditions). Strughold later resettled in Texas and was lauded by **NASA** as the "father of space medicine."

Bluebird/Artichoke: The **CIA**'s first **Mind Control** program involving drugs (Bluebird was renamed Artichoke in 1951—but was essentially the same project), with the goal of forging an "exploitable alteration of personality" in a person, which eventually gave rise to **MK-ULTRA.**

Dr. Ewen Cameron: President of the World Psychiatric Association until he died in 1967, Cameron ran the infamously cruel early-1960s "psychic driving" experiments, conducted at the **CIA**'s request and expense at Montreal's Allain Memorial Institute at McGill University. Cameron's mind-deconditioning-and-reconditioning technique (ab)used unsuspecting involuntary patients (depressed housewives, manic college students). First they were given huge doses of **LSD,** maybe some electroshock, some were lobotomized, and most were later subjected to tape-recorded messages played—up to 250,000 times—under their pillows at night.

of murder on command. The program involved not just psychedelic drugs but brainwashing, sensory deprivation, hypnosis, ESP, lobotomy, and electroshock. It continued from 1965 until 1973 under the name MK-SEARCH, and the idea for such a candidate was inspired, in part, by the work of ex-**Nazi** scientists who were absorbed by the USSR's **KGB** and the work they seemed to be up to in Asia during the **Korean War.**

National Institute of Mental Health (NIMH)

Offshoot of the **NIH,** the NIMH has long been under the chairmanship of various **Freemasons** (most notably, Robert Hanna Felix, a 33rd-degree Mason and an **MK-ULTRA** mastermind, the director of NIMH from 1949–1963), and it was an early and eager **CIA**-bankrolled participant in MK-ULTRA and other experimental **Mind Control** programs (involving **LSD** and other hallucinogens) during the 1950s and 1960s. LSD proponent-guru **Timothy Leary** received the better part of his 1950s psychedelic research money from the NIMH. Once a NIMH (and **RAND**) consultant, and the screenwriter of the 1983 parapsychological horror film *The Entity,* former **UCLA** parapsychologist Barry Taff coauthored a *UFO* magazine article that claimed **Aliens** are responsible for various nefarious forms of Mind Control—a thesis some conspirologists have

Conspiranoia! Culture

Located near the infamous Texas School Book Depository in Dallas resides the Conspiracy Museum, a monument to conspiranoid thinking dreamed up by eighty-five-year-old Harvard alumnus and architect R. B. Cutler, a self-proclaimed "assassinologist" and practitioner of Zen. Cutler scoffs at the simplicity of the "lone gunman" theory and claims that **Oswald** wasn't even Oswald: He was a **CIA**-trained double agent by the name of Alek Hidell. Besides, Cutler adds, three men shot and poisoned **Kennedy** (one firing with a gas-powered umbrella pistol). Cutler's museum features video kiosks, a conspiracy-themed bookstore, and—the pièce de résistance—a 108-foot-long mural that traces the history of American conspiracies from the failed assassination attempt on Andrew Jackson to the downing of Korean Airlines Flight 007.

cleverly turned on its head, saying that Taff is really part of an elaborate **DOD-**CIA-NIMH-RAND cover-up and that his embrace of **Alien Abductions, Crop Circles, Cattle Mutilations,** and other *E.T.*-like visitations are nothing but a cleverly bizarre white-wash of *real* government-funded Mind Control projects.
✡ ☉

Nazis

♍ ★ ✝ ⛪ ⚰ ✡

Office of Strategic Services

★

Lee Harvey Oswald

The alleged lone gunman accused of assassinating President **John F. Kennedy** on November 22, 1963—and who was murdered by **Jack Ruby** a day later. Oswald served as a U.S. marine at Atsugi Naval Base in Japan (home of the U-2 spy plane and some of the **CIA's MK-ULTRA LSD** experiments). Oswald also served under CIA flightman **David Ferrie** in a Civil Air Patrol Unit. In the late fifties, he developed **Communist** sympathies and defected to the USSR, where he was interrogated by the **KGB.** Interestingly, Oswald was on the **Red Cross**'s payroll during his stay in Russia. He returned to the United States in 1962 (courtesy of the CIA) but continued to agitate on behalf of Communist causes. He spent the summer before JFK's assassination in New Orleans, working for the Fair Play for Cuba Committee and hobnobbing with creepy members of the Company and the **Mob** (his uncle was a bookie in **Carlos Marcello**'s organization). Oddly, the leader of anti-**Castro** exile group **Alpha 66,** Antonio Veciana, has claimed that Oswald sometimes sat in on their meetings, although Oswald was supposedly pro-Castro. New Orleans businessman and CIA agent **Clay Shaw** hired an attorney for Oswald, but that turned out to be unnecessary. As a child, Oswald's favorite TV show was *I Led Three Lives,* about an **FBI** counterspy.
△

We may not ever know with certainty the Name or the Names. But we do have a much darker, more complex, less innocent vision of America, produced by the murk that has been churned up by the dissidents.

—Ron Rosenbaum on JFK assassination theories, *Time*, 1992

Paperclip

★ ☼

The Program

Also known as the Plan and the Black Genocide Program, some speculate that the rise of both **AIDS** and crack may be related to this alleged three-part **FBI/CIA** scheme. According to this theory, inner-city African-Americans (and Hispanics) are being systematically murdered: first through the distribution of drugs (heroin in the 1970s, crack in the 1980s) and then through the calculated spread of the deadly sexually transmitted disease AIDS. A number of black leaders, including California representative Maxine Waters and comedian-activist Dick Gregory, suspect, as do their constituents, that crack cocaine (and coke) may be part of the Program.

Shock Troop

Six years after an assassin killed her son, on June 30, 1978, Alberta Christine King and church deacon Edward Boykin were shot dead in an Atlanta church by Ohio State University dropout Marcus Wayne Chenault. A Chenault associate later told **The New York Times** that he and the Dayton, Ohio, native were part of the Troop, a radical religious sect who felt that black civil rights ministers were falsely leading black people and should therefore be killed. Authorities later claimed there was no link between the Atlanta killings and the mysterious deaths of two Dayton ministers around the same time, and said Chenault was a crazy lone gunman. Oddly enough, the Troop's leader, Hananiah Israel, later relocated to Guyana, only miles from where **Jim Jones** had founded **Jonestown.** There Hill and his followers set up their own little utopia and called it Hilltown.

Others suspect that the ebola virus, the deadly superinfectious agent, and AIDS may have been spawned in Africa as a result of a CIA-**Pentagon Biochemical Warfare** experiment.

James Earl Ray

The **Assassin** convicted of shooting civil rights leader **Martin Luther King, Jr.,** on April 4, 1968. Ray, who died in 1998, always claimed that he had not acted alone, an account confirmed by confessed murderer **Jules Kimble.** (In 1997, two detectives said they traced Ray's mysterious Raoul, the man Ray claimed set him up, to an associate of **Jack Ruby.**) Ray's lawyer, at his first trial, was the **Mob**-connected Percy Foreman. Later, Ray was represented by **Mark Lane,** who also represented cult leader **Jim Jones.**

△

Anyone who has ever delved into assassination theory . . . must finally conclude that nothing is certain: nothing can be believed.

—Betsy Langman and Alexander Cockburn, *Harper's*, January 1975

Ronald Reagan

A **Freemason** and a **Knight of Malta,** this onetime B-movie actor and former client of MCA president **Lew Wasserman** went on to two terms as U.S. president (1981–1989). In the 1930s, his roommate and traveling companion was bisexual **Nazi** agent and statutory rapist Errol Flynn. As president, Reagan waged the "Just Say No" **War on Drugs** campaign while at the same time those in his administration seemed indirectly responsible, at best, for the flood of **Iran-Contra-**connected crack cocaine that was flooding the nation's streets. A friend of Fundamentalists and a staunch anti-Communist, Reagan loved to cite Scripture, whether invoking it in support of his advocacy of nuclear power and weaponry or just as a rallying tool to stamp out Commies. The **New Right** flourished under his watch.

∽ ⚸ ☺ ▩

Robert Kennedy Assassination

In the midst of his 1968 presidential campaign, in which he was a virtual lock to defeat **Nixon,** Kennedy was killed by **Sirhan Sirhan,** a crazed "lone gunman." Also there that fateful night, however, was **Lockheed** employee Thane Eugene Cesar, an alleged right-wing Kennedy hater and **Nazi** enthusiast who was moonlighting that evening as a security guard and who was seen standing immediately to Kennedy's right—with his gun drawn. The night before he was killed, Kennedy had dinner with Roman Polanski, his wife Sharon Tate, and John Frankenheimer, director of *The Manchurian Candidate.*

△

If one does not account for occasional mistakes and incompetence, then nearly every . . . political murder could appear to be a conspiracy, particularly if a civilian investigator—with limited access and resources—is looking for one.

—Dan E. Moldea,
The Killing of Robert F. Kennedy: An Investigation of Motive, Means and Opportunity (1995)

Jack Ruby

The lone gunman who killed **Assassin Lee Harvey Oswald**—President **Kennedy**'s lone gunman killer—in front of a live national TV audience on November 23, 1963, the day after JFK's assassination, despite Oswald's being under "heavy" police custody. A former gun smuggler (his client was Cuba), Ruby ran the gambling and narcotics operations in Dallas for Chicago **Mafia** boss **Sam Giancana,** once ran errands for Al Capone, and in 1959 worked as an **FBI** informant. His fellow gunrunner was **David Ferrie,** who'd brought Ruby into the **Bay of Pigs** fiasco. Ruby later hired Ferrie at his Carousel Club strip joint. Ruby died in jail of cancer, which he claimed had been injected into him.

△

J. D. Salinger

The pathologically private, germophobic, and homeopathic author of the 1951 classic novel *Catcher in the Rye* (the one book found in the possession of lone gunmen **John Hinckley, Jr.**, and **Mark David Chapman**), now living as a recluse in a small New England town and exposed by Joyce Maynard as a bit of an old lech. In **WWII**, Salinger served in the **U.S. Army**'s Counterintelligence Corps—rumored to have been the same unit as **Henry Kissinger**'s.

Human culture has always been manipulated by mind control, i.e., the monopolization, concealment, and destruction of information and the control of man's primary tool of information processing: the mind. In the twentieth century, however, the technological tools for attaining total control have been delivered into the hands of a small coterie, the scientists and the men who hold their leashes, and those tools have been turned upon the mostly unsuspecting populace, who have been manipulated, prodded, worked on, deluded, and destroyed, usually in the name of achieving a peaceful, i.e., a controlled society.

—Jim Keith, *Mind Control, World Control* (1997)

Finders Keepers

When Florida cops picked up six undernourished kids in a public park in Tallahassee in 1987, they unwittingly shed light on a sick Washington, D.C.–based group of allegedly pedophilic kiddie-porn preverts called the Finders. Possibly satanic, possibly murderous, and straight out of one of Andrew Vachss's Burke novels, the Finders have been linked by some conspiranoiacs to the Monarch Project, a joint **CIA–U.S. Air Force Mind Control** program designed to transform dissociative children into mini–Manchurian Candidates.

Sirhan Sirhan

Yet another lone gunman, this Jerusalem-born Palestinian was convicted of the 1968 assassination of democratic presidential candidate **Robert Kennedy** (according to authorities, Sirhan shot Kennedy as a protest against his pro-Israel stance). His postassassination psychiatrist was **William Joseph Bryan,** who claimed to have hypnotized Albert DeSalvo (the Boston Strangler) and who served as a consultant on *The Manchurian Candidate*. Among Sirhan's noodlings were references to the **Rosicrucian** order **AMORC.** Sirhan is also alleged to have been involved with the Process, a group founded by ex-**Scientologist** Robert De Grimston, and he may have even attended parties thrown by alleged fellow Process enthusiasts Sharon Tate and Roman Polanski (the night before he was killed, Bobby Kennedy had dinner at Polanski's mansion).
△

U.S. Army

★ △ ✿ ☉

Dr. Louis Joylon West

Aka Dr. Jolly West, a psychiatrist, was the man brought in to determine the mental state of **Lee Harvey Oswald**'s killer, **Jack Ruby.** A friend of **Aldous Huxley,** West conducted **LSD** research for the **CIA**'s **MK-ULTRA** program, and in the early 1970s, as director of **UCLA**'s Neuropsychiatric Institute, his treatment plans for the aborted Center for the Study and Reduction of Violence (originally proposed by governor **Ronald Reagan** and Earl Brian) included chemical castration and psychosurgery (and on children, no less). He also served as defense psychiatrist for Patty **Hearst.** In the 1980s, West took part in the **Stanford Research Institute**'s "remote viewing" **Project Grill Flame** experiments.
〰〰

World Vision

The Christian world's largest evangelical relief and development order, founded in 1950 by stadium preacher Billy Graham's fellow Youth for Christ organizer, Bob Pierce. World Vision is located in Southern California, but the group's foot soldiers show up in all of the world's worst places—in third

world refugee camps and near **CIA** covert operations in Southeast Asia, Lebanon, and the Honduras–Nicaragua border. World Vision missionaries are suspected of gathering information for the CIA while they proselytize about **Christ.** They were frequent visitors to cult leader **Jim Jones,** first in California and then in Guyana. John **Hinckley,** Sr., father of John Jr., the lone gunman who tried to kill **Reagan** in 1981, was a World Vision official.
☞

WWII

✡ ✍

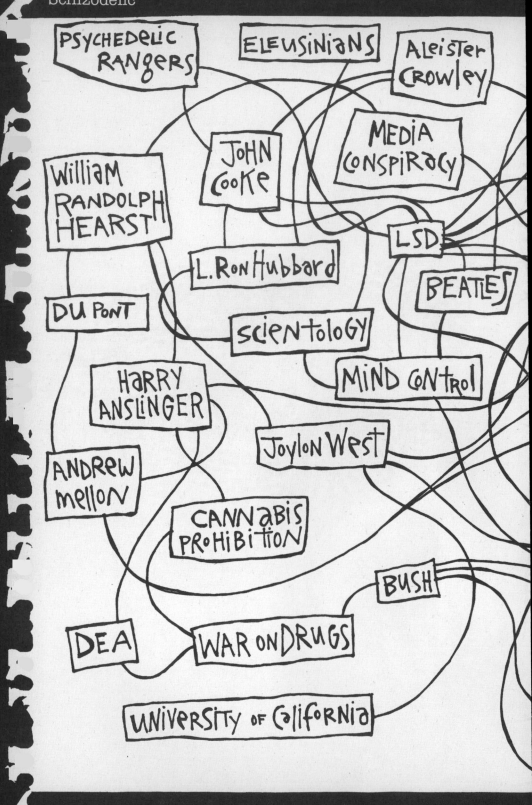

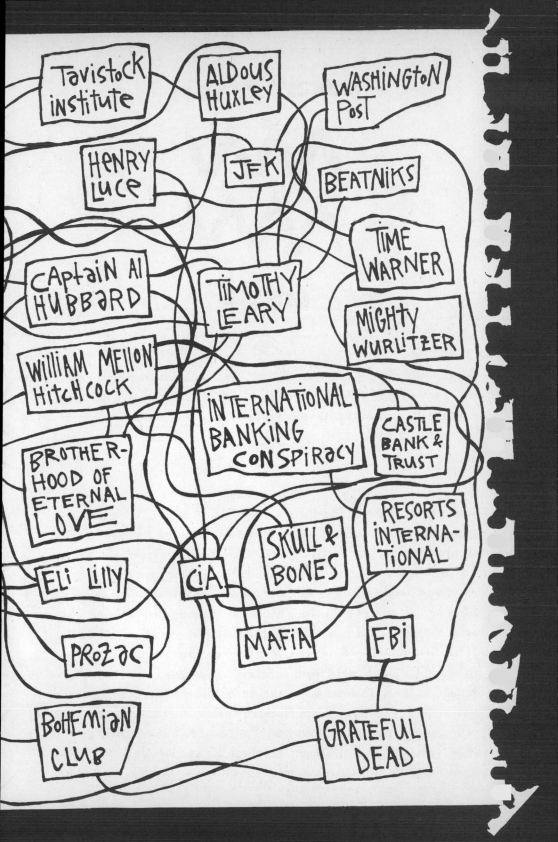

Alas, how different might it all have been had LSD not first ended up in the damnably spotted hands of the CIA? Probably a tad more psychedelic and a little less schizophrenic.

Harry Anslinger

The Beatles

John, Paul, George, and Ringo—and Theo Adorno. To some con-spiranoiacs, the Fab Four were but malevolent agents of psychedelia shipped stateside by Britain's nefarious **Tavistock Institute,** whose "British invasion" mission was to seduce America's youth with their numbing **Satanic** atonal beat and, worse, to encourage the use of **LSD** and all things hallucinogenic. Their groundbreaking *Sgt. Pepper's Lonely Hearts Club Band* (1967), for example, was slammed by the **John Birch Society** as being part of a **Communist** plot and awash in **Mind Control** tricks. And contrary to popular belief, conspira-noiac Dr. John Coleman avows that it was Theo Adorno, an obscure philosopher-composer from Germany's Frankfurt School who long railed against capitalism but whom Coleman says was actually an ex-Nazi, special friend of Queen Elizabeth II, and stooge of the Tavi-stock Institute, who actually penned all of the Beatles' music and lyrics (and led the world down that rotten path to heavy metal, punk, and New Wave, too).

☙

Rock 'n' roll music encourages kids to take drugs . . . it's part of our plot. . . . Drugs are the most efficient way to revolution.

—Timothy Leary, 1969

Beatniks

Counterculture movement of the 1950s and 1960s spearheaded by (mostly white) junkies, gays, poets, and other assorted bums, such as Jack Kerouac, William Burroughs, and Allen Ginsberg. The beatniks became a spawning ground for the civil rights movement and the pro-drug activism of the 1960s.

Bohemian Club

✖ ⛪ ☺

Brotherhood of Eternal Love

A radical idealistic California acid cult, this late 1960s to early 1970s hippie mafia, founded and led at first by ex—motorcycle gang members, manufactured and distributed **LSD** worldwide and took in nearly $200 million. In their quest for that ever-elusive high of highs, their brilliant alchemical chemist Nick Sand (perhaps at the behest of the **CIA**) invented STP (Serenity, Tranquility, Peace), a superpowerful LSD-like drug that was anything *but* serenity, tranquility, or peace, instead cranking up a user's paranoia and hallucinations to the point of insanity. Before the mysterious Ronald Stark took over the brotherhood's operations (Stark bragged about his connections to the CIA and the **Yakuza**), the group first turned to **Timothy Leary,** who in turn introduced them to **Mellon** family heir **William Mellon Hitchcock,** who became the group's patron. By 1972, the brotherhood had run its course: Hitchcock had left, Stark had moved on, and most of its key members were either in jail or on the run.

183

William Joseph Bryan

George Bush

A scion of Texas oil and East Coast privilege, Bush paid his dues as **Nixon**'s appointed head of the National Republican Committee (1972), as **CIA** director (1975–1977), as head of **Eli Lilly & Co.**, and as vice president under **Ronald Reagan** (1980–1988) before taking control as commander in chief and U.S. president (1988–1992). He was a **Freemason**, a member of the **Council on Foreign Relations** and the **Trilateral Commission**, and a proud member of the **Skull & Bones** society (allegedly, as part of his initiation, Bush's Skull hazers made him lie naked in a coffin with a ribbon tied around the family jewels and shout out every last morsel of every one of his sexual experiences). In 1942, his father was charged by the U.S. government of operating front groups for the **Nazis**; and in **WWII**, his grandfather advised the British on covert "psychological" operations. In 1961, Bush was CEO of Zapata Off Shore Oil, married to Barbara Bush, and living in Houston. A year later the **Bay of Pigs** invasion of Cuba turns into a fiasco, but, more interestingly, two of the CIA's ships bore the names the *Houston* and the *Barbara J* and the Cuban resupply mission's code name was Operation Zapata. Fellow Bonesman and CFR member **William Casey,** who was also Bush's business partner, convinced Reagan to pick Bush as his running mate. The Bush family had ties to the family of would-be Reagan assassin **John Hinckley**: George Bush was a friend of John Hinckley, Sr., and his son Neil had a lunch date scheduled with John Hinckley, Jr.'s brother on the day that John Jr. shot Reagan. As vice president, Bush was involved in the U.S. effort to build up **Saddam Hussein**'s war machine. He was also heavily mixed up in the **Iran-**

Contra affair. As president, Bush continued Reagan's futile **War on Drugs** and appointed former steroid freak Arnold Schwarzenegger (a dedicated Republican fund-raiser) chairman of the Presidential Council on Fitness and Sports. In 1991, he launched the **Gulf War,** ostensibly in retaliation for Saddam Hussein's 1990 invasion of Kuwait. But right after the end of the Gulf War, the Bush administration quietly and illegally repatriated more than 5,000 Iraqi soldiers to Oklahoma City for "humanitarian" purposes—many of the Iraqis were officers, and more than a few were experts in demolition. In 1990, Bush appointed former University of Nebraska chancellor Ronald Roskens to head the **U.S. Agency for International Development** (a CIA front) one year after Cornhusker regents had canned Roskens for what some conspiranoiacs allege was because of his rumored ties to a supposed CIA-run homosexual call-boy/child-abuse ring that may have been set up by Roskens's associate, Omaha banker Lawrence King. One of Bush's favorite phrases during his election and term in office was **"New World Order."** Bush called Nixon his "mentor." Charter Trilateral Commission member (and **David Rockefeller** crony) **Zbigniew Brzezinski** was Bush's campaign advisor. Bush has also been linked to Italy's Fascistic **Propaganda Due Lodge** and to David Berg's bizarre cult known alternately as the **Children of God** and the Family of Love, if only because they once sang for him after he toured the aftermath of 1992's Hurricane Andrew.

△ ✐ ↝ ⚲ ☺ ✿ ⊕

Cannabis Prohibition

The country's first **War on Drugs**, this early 1920s to 1930s campaign to stamp out reefer madness was led by **Harry Anslinger**, director of the Federal Narcotics Bureau (a precursor to the DEA), and propagandistically supported whole hog by newspaper magnate **William Randolph Hearst.** Hearst, it turned out, had invested too, too much money in **Du Pont**'s expensive wood-pulping process that allowed hemp to be made into paper.

Castle Bank & Trust

Set up in the mid-1960s by **CIA** vet, **Air America** founder, and **Bay of Pigs** paymaster Paul Helliwell (who was also

E. **Howard Hunt**'s boss in the **Golden Triangle** and who later helped set up **Disney**World), this Nassau, Grand Bahamas, front institution served as a cash Laundromat for the Agency's Golden Triangle heroin profits, money then used to fund various and sundry paramilitary high jinks. Castle also washed clean the deposits of **Mafia** dons and drug dealers (like the **Brotherhood of Eternal Love**). Other Castle clients included **Richard Nixon, Howard Hughes,** Hugh Hefner, Creedence Clearwater Revival, and Tony Curtis.

◇

CIA

♏ ★ ⌂ ✝ ⛪ 🐾 △ ◇ ↩ ⚔ 😊 🔳 🌐 ☉

John Starr Cooke

A polio-stricken scion of wealth and an in-law and pal to **CIA** player Sherman Kent, Cooke first dabbled in the cultish arts (Cooke became **Scientology**'s first "clear" in the United States before leaving the group and its founder, **L. Ron Hubbard,** in the 1950s) and then sank himself into the occult—as a psychic, and a channeler, and the owner of a tarot deck that supposedly once belonged to **Aleister Crowley.** Then Cooke found his true calling: After dropping **LSD**-25, he made it his mission to get the whole world high. His **Psychedelic Rangers** became his undercover agents for such change, and from his base in Cuernavaca, Mexico, he led acid-tinged séances and welcomed into his compound visitors like singer-songwriter Leonard Cohen and Andrija Puharich, future publicist for Israeli spoon-bending psychic Uri Geller.

↩

Aleister Crowley

Immortalized for heavy metalheads by Ozzy Osbourne, this British occult figure of the mid-twentieth century sometimes preferred to be called "the Beast 666." A good-natured bisexual **Satanist,** Crowley served in the British Secret Service and was a heroin addict and obsessive practitioner of Tantric sex magick. He believed that he was the antimessiah of the apocalypse. He flirted with the **Thule Society,** designed the **Babylon Working,** and claimed that he could summon the Loch Ness Monster at will from his Boleskin House, which bordered Nessie's lake (the same house in which Led Zeppelin drummer and occult enthusiast, John Bonham, drank himself to death). He was friends with **Aldous Huxley** and a former member of the **Hermetic Order of the Golden Dawn** but was kicked out by the group in 1910 because of his obsession with sexual rites. He later ascended to Outer Head of the Ordo Templi Orientis. During **WWI,** while living in New York City, Crowley wrote pro-German propaganda for the Germans—scribblings he later said were part of his assignment for **MI6.**

☞ ∿

Drug Enforcement Agency (DEA)

An agency of the Department of Justice that heads the enforcement of laws governing narcotics and controlled substances, the DEA (an offshoot of the Federal Narcotics Bureau, which was lorded over by **Harry Anslinger** in the 1930s) was created in 1973 in an effort to consolidate several other federal agencies and enforce the Controlled Substances Act of 1970. The DEA runs point in the **War on Drugs** but is often thwarted, some argue, by the illicitly complicit drug-underworld activities of the **CIA** and its "agents."

🌐

Du Pont

🏛 ☼

Eleusinians

✖ ※ ∿

Eli Lilly & Co.

👄 🙂 ☼

FBI

♏ ※ ✝ 👄 △ ☼ 🌐 ☉

The Grateful Dead

According to a 1968 file from the **FBI** (and be warned, quotes like this one are often taken out of context—but who cares!), Deadhead founder Jerry Garcia was hired by the feds "to channel youth dissent and rebellion into more benign and nonthreatening directions" via their atonal rock music and **LSD** and cocaine use. Oddly enough, in 1995, the Dead's guitarist Bob Weir was offered membership to the superexclusive ultra-Republican boys' camp, the **Bohemian Club.**

William Randolph Hearst

The king of yellow journalism and the central subject of Orson Welles's *Citizen Kane.* In 1924, Hearst (1863–1951) allegedly murdered film director Thomas Ince. In the 1930s, Hearst teamed up with Federal Narcotics Bureau chief **Harry Anslinger** to stamp out marijuana, less for moralistic reasons and more because hemp production threatened to displace the pulp-sulfide processing of wood into paper, a process developed by **Du Pont** and intended for Hearst's newspapers and into which Hearst and Du Pont had sunk millions. Bedazzled by the *Elmer Gantry*—style tent revivals of the young Billy Graham, Hearst gave the fledgling preacher a huge boost in 1949 when he dispatched the infamous "Puff Graham" telegram to his editors, demanding that they jam Graham down their readers' throats. Grandfather of future kidnapping (and possible **Mind Control**) victim Patty Hearst.

William Mellon Hitchcock

The grandson of Gulf Oil founder, William Larimer Hitchcock, and nephew of industrialist **Andrew Mellon,** Hitchcock served as patron of **LSD** guru **Timothy Leary** and allowed his New York estate, Millbrook, to become LSD central during the sixties (a kind of upstate version of Andy Warhol's Factory). After moving from Millbrook out to California, he helped finance the **Brotherhood of Eternal Love** and invested some of his and the brotherhood's millions into the infamous **Resorts International** and its rumored **CIA-Mafia**-connected casinos. Mr. Billy, as acid freaks liked to call him, also may have squirreled away a chunk of drug money in the Bahamas' **Castle Bank & Trust,** the financial institution of choice for other drug dealers.

Captain Alfred Hubbard

Known as the "Johnny Appleseed of **LSD**," this former **OSS** man worked for **Harry Anslinger**'s Federal Narcotics Bureau, the **Food and Drug Administration,** Hoover's **FBI,** and the **CIA.** After he first dropped acid in 1951, Hubbard made it his lifelong goal to turn on as many people as he could to LSD's potentially beneficent effects (as treatment for alcoholism and schizophrenia). Seemingly good-natured, Hubbard hobnobbed with other acid gurus (like **Timothy Leary**), but he also distrusted hippies and Communists—and all that work for the various fed agencies makes one wonder what his *real* goals were.

L. Ron Hubbard

A former navy officer and onetime **LAPD** investigator turned sci-fi writer, Hubbard went on to write *Dianetics* and found the **Church of Scientology**. He was also a devotee of **Aleister Crowley**'s occult philosophy and work and, together with **John Whiteside Parsons,** reenacted Crowley's **Babylon Working.** For several months, Hubbard was an active member of Parsons's **Ordo Templi Orientis** (an occult group that also included Crowley), and even met his second wife there. Dubbed the "fat boy" by his onetime star disciple, **John Starr Cooke,** Hubbard often told his sci-fi-writer chums that the surest way to wealth was to start your own religion. Though he reportedly died in 1986, trashy sci-fi novels with Hubbard's name on them still manage to be churned out.
‏👓 ☉

Aldous Huxley

✍ 👣 〰

International Banking Conspiracy

♍ ✖ ✡ ★ ✍ 📏 👓 〰 ⚕ 🌐

World Psychedelic Institute

After a stint at Millbrook, Leary cohort and **Aldous Huxley** pal Michael Hollingshead returned to London and in 1965 founded this short-lived but hugely influential den for dope smokers and acid heads—Roman Polanski, the Rolling Stones, the Yardbirds, and **Beatle** Paul McCartney all scored their acid here.

John F. Kennedy

The U.S. president from 1961 to 1963 and the so-called King of Camelot. In 1960, JFK defeated **Richard Nixon.** In 1961, Kennedy launched the disastrous **Bay of Pigs** operation. Staunchly Catholic, JFK nonetheless bonked numerous women besides his wife, Jacqueline Bouvier Kennedy, including **Marilyn Monroe,** Angie Dickinson, and **Mafia** moll Judith Exner. (JFK may also have inadvertently bedded down with an agent from East Germany's secret police, Ellen Rometsch, a suave hooker who may have been working for the Stasi.) Joseph Kennedy, JFK's father, made his millions as the East Coast distributor of illicit liquor during Prohibition, with sugar supplied to him by **Sam Giancana** and his Chicago Black Hand Mafia Outfit and by New York's Syndicate rep, Frank Costello. During the 1960 presidential election, Giancana guaranteed his old pal Joe that his son John F. would win Chicago—and he did, ensuring JFK's victory, by the smallest margin ever. JFK maintained a questionably close relationship with *The Washington Post*'s Ben Bradlee, who rarely challenged the president in the D.C. paper. Kennedy also had ties to Hollywood and the Mafia: He was a friend of Rat Pack singer **Frank Sinatra,** who introduced him to one of his mistresses, Judith Exner. Kennedy shared Exner and Monroe with Mob boss Giancana, and it's speculated that these affairs may have led to stronger ties between Kennedy and the mobster. Kennedy may have made more enemies by supporting the civil rights movement, planning to end the **Vietnam War,** and threatening to dismantle the **CIA.** In 1961, JFK founded the **Peace Corps.** △

Timothy Leary

LSD

Henry Luce

Cocaine-snorting founder of *Time* and *Life* (the future **Time-Warner** media megaconglomerate and, in Luce's day, home to many **CIA** agents posing as journalists—part of the Agency's **Mighty Wurlitzer** propaganda machine). Luce used his power to blatantly foist Billy

Graham and his conservative brand of Christianity upon Eisenhower-era America. (In 1954, *Time* ran a slathering puff piece on Graham, putting the revivalist evangelist on its cover.) Luce was also a **Freemason,** a member of Yale's **Skull & Bones** society, and a good friend of fellow Bonesman and CIA chief **Allen Dulles.** At first, Luce cooperated with the **Kennedys,** running puff pieces on **JFK** and **Robert.** But after JFK's assassination Luce sided with his old Bones pal, Dulles, and the other members of the **Warren Commission**—who needed popular support for their lone gunman position. So *Life,* under publisher and former CIA consultant C. D. Jackson (who ran psychological warfare operations in **WWII** and later became known as "chief of the **Cold War**"), snapped up the rights to the Zapruder home-movie footage of the JFK assassination, then published picture frames of it out of sequence—showing JFK's head flying forward. A properly sequenced Zapruder film shows the president's head falling backward after he was shot. *Life*'s series just happened to back up the Company line that Kennedy was killed by a lone gunman firing from behind. (The Zapruder family lawyer, as of 1999, was Bob Bennett, who also served as legal adviser to President **Bill Clinton.**) Luce and his wife, Clare Boothe (who later served on President **Reagan**'s Foreign Intelligence Advisory Board, was a **Knight of Malta,** and sat on the board of **Reverend Sun Myung Moon**'s *Washington Times* newspaper), dropped **LSD** liberally, at least half a dozen times.

△ ▨

Mafia

♏ ❋ ▥ △ ✎ ☺ ▨

Media Conspiracy

♏ ✿ △ ➳ ✧

Andrew Mellon

Cofounder, with his father and brother, of Mellon National Bank in Pittsburgh. This billionaire financier (1855–1937) and his bank funded **Du Pont** in the 1930s (during its antihemp days). In 1921, he resigned as president of Mellon National Bank to become the secretary of the treasury for presidents Harding, Coolidge, and Hoover. His niece married Federal Bureau of Narcotics commissioner **Harry Anslinger,** the man who led

191

the assault on marijuana (and hemp). Mellon's distant descendants include **Richard Scaife** and **William Mellon Hitchcock.**

The Mighty Wurlitzer

The **CIA**'s decades-long **Cold War**—era propaganda campaign whose long-running raison d'être was to smear the USSR at every media opportunity, which the Agency did by producing books, films, and articles by the thousands—most of which were rife with misinformation, disinformation, or out-and-out lies. Orchestrated by **OSS** vet Frank Wisner (who exfiltrated and repatriated many a **WWII Fascist** to the United States—hard-line anti-Communist murderers from the Latvian Thunder Cross, the Hungarian Arrow Cross, et cetera—whom he employed at Radio Liberty and Voice of America), the Wurlitzer, so-called because Wisner liked to say that, like the famous jukebox, he could call up any Media outlet in the world and have them play the CIA tune, also planted its agents at various CIA-cooperative magazines, TV networks, and newspapers (most notably at William Paley's **CBS,** Arthur Sulzberger's *New York Times,* and at **Henry Luce's Time-Life**). Fodor's travel guides started out as a Wurlitzer front, and journalists who once participated in the Wurlitzer or worked knowingly with CIA spooks include conservative columnist **William F. Buckley,** *Ms.* magazine founder Gloria Steinem, and **PBS** newsman Bill Moyers.
△ ▓

On the one hand, the conspiracy theory searches for the truth. On the other, many truths are repeatedly shown to be the products of fictions, plots, and lies.

—S. Paige Baty, *American Monroe: The Making of a Body Politic* (1995)

Mind Control

🐦 ∞ 😌 ✿ ☉

Prozac

Introduced in 1988, one of the first and most effective of the new anti-depressant drugs on the market for the nearly 20 million bummed-out Americans. Some consider Prozac the **Mind Control** drug of the

1990s. Prozac is manufactured by **Eli Lilly & Co.**, which sold about $3 billion worth of the pill in 1998 alone. Both Prozac and Eli Lilly have been the target of an ongoing **Scientology** smear campaign, which says the pill induces suicide and aberrant behavior.

Psychedelic Rangers

The brainchild of the cultish **John Starr Cooke**, this cadre of acid assassins sought to revolutionize world society (and humankind's inner spiritual nature) via the transcendental powers of **LSD**. To do that, they zeroed in on certain individuals (like comedian-activist Dick Gregory and Yippie leader Jerry Rubin). The rangers, under Cooke's directions, initiated potentially influential first-timers with ungodly doses of LSD (2,000 to 3,000 microgram hits of the stuff—when 100 to 250 usually did enough damage), hoping their mind-blowing experience would sway them to the rangers' cause, and in turn they'd then sway the public, too. Ranger Michael Bowen helped organize the January 14, 1967, Be-in, the Gathering of the Tribes—a thousands-strong San Francisco drugfest and prelude to Woodstock.

∽

Resorts International

✝ △

Scientology

🐀 ∽ ☉

Skull & Bones

🕯 ☺

Tavistock Institute

∽ 〰 ▦ ⊕

Time Warner

The world's largest entertainment and information company (now headed up by Jew Gerald Levin) after Time Warner merged with Ted Turner's media company (TBS, TNT, CNN). The company includes Warner Brothers Pictures, a Hollywood studio incorporated in 1923 by the Warner brothers (Sam, Jack, Harry, and Albert—all Jews), and Time-Life, its New York publishing company arm, known for its influential flagship publications *Time* and *Life* and its Establishment bias, was founded by cocaine enthusiast **Henry Luce** in the 1920s. In 1957, *Life* devoted seventeen pages to the divine wonders of the magic mushroom (the psilocybin psychedelic), a story written by J. P. **Morgan** & Co. vice president R. Gordon Wasson. Time-Life harbored **CIA** writers from the Agency's **Mighty Wurlitzer** anti-Communist propaganda machine.

△ 🏿

University of California

This gargantuan educational corporation maintains eight primary campuses: UC-Berkeley, UCLA, UC-San Diego, UC-Santa Cruz, UC-Santa Barbara, UC-Irvine, UC-Davis, and UC-Riverside. UC has the nation's second-largest library (behind the Library of Con-

Synergy, Baby!

Take *Batman and Robin*. This is how it often works. First, there's the Batman comic book series (published by DC Comics, of which **Time Warner** owns half). Then there's the Warner Bros.–produced movie (the fourth in the highly lucrative series). Then the Warner Bros. *Batman* soundtrack, the endless barrage of plugs for the film on the WB network (or on TNT or TBS) or on the cover or in the pages of the Time Inc. magazines *Entertainment Weekly, Time, In Style, People*, or *Life*. Then there's the Batman and Robin marketing blitz on the World Wide Web (via Time Warner's massive website, Pathfinder). There might be a novelization of the movie that will then be sold through Time Warner's Book-of-the-Month Club. There will most certainly be the many Batman and Robin toy action figures from Hasbro (of which Time Warner owns 14 percent), and there might even be a related lawsuit against the film or its makers that will be aired on Court TV someday (Time Warner owns 33 percent of the cable network). And there's sure to be a Batman and Robin ride at any one of Time Warner's Six Flags Theme Parks. But if you manage to miss all that, or avoid it, don't worry, Time Warner is sure to broadcast *Batman and Robin* repeatedly on its HBO (Home Box Office) cable outlet.

gress) and the largest public university publishing company. From 1953 to 1968 UC-Berkeley and the **National Cancer Institute** conducted **Biochemical Warfare** research with the **U.S. Army.** The Internet was also developed there (in part), and in conjunction witht the **U.S. Army** (now it's the Department of Energy). The University of California runs the **Los Alamos National Laboratory.**
〰〰 ☼

War on Drugs

First taken up by **Harry Anslinger** and his Federal Narcotics Bureau in the **Cannabis Prohibition** days of the 1930s, then opened up fifty years later in 1970 (right about the time of the Controlled Substances Act of 1970, which oddly coincided with the **CIA**'s gradual shutdown of its **MK-ULTRA Mind Control** experiments using **LSD**—a Frankenstein the Agency created and then saw spiral out of its control; hence, make the drug illegal). The modern battle peaked in enthusiasm and hype during the **Reagan** and **Bush** "Just Say No" 1980s.
✐ ☺

The Washington Post

Washington, D.C.'s preeminent daily newspaper, owned by Katharine Graham (a Jew), and whose chief shareholder is **Warren Buffett.** The *Post* also owns *Newsweek.* Graham's late husband worked for the **CIA** at one time, as did the *Post*'s editor, Ben Bradlee, an intimate pal of President **John F. Kennedy.** Later, during **Nixon**'s presidency, the paper burnished its image by breaking the **Watergate** affair—and Bradlee became one of the president's chief enemies.
△ ▦

Dr. Louis Joylon West

🦅

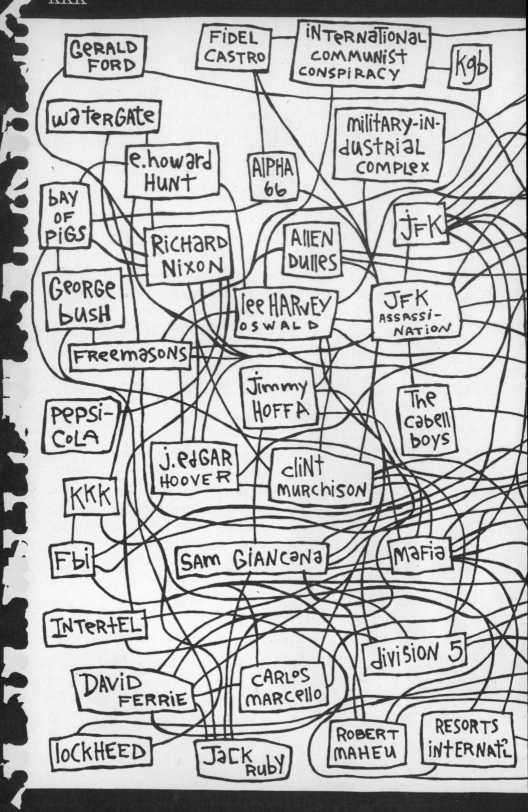

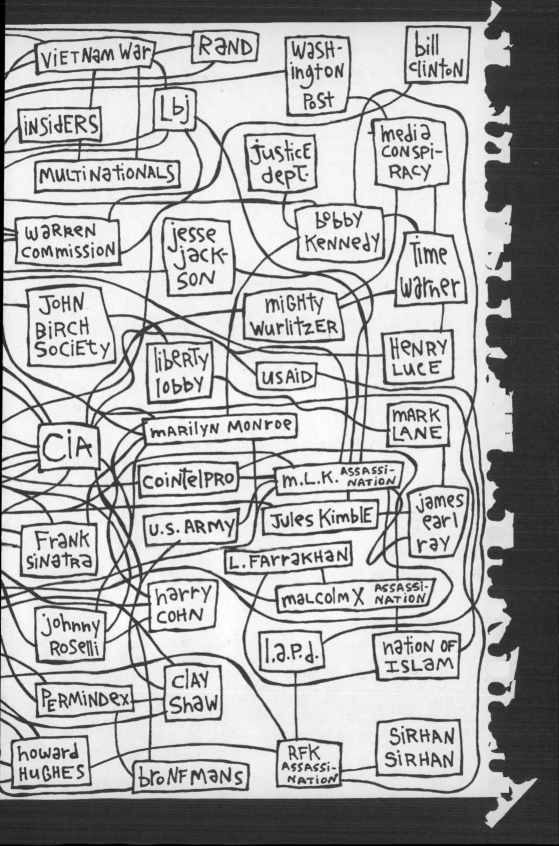

△

Conspiracy

Not the Ku Klux Klan but Killing Kings and Kennedys. The latter being John F. and Robert Kennedy and the former being Martin Luther King, Jr., Malcolm X, and—again—JFK, the King of Camelot (and later the death of Elvis Presley, the King of rock 'n' roll). (Not to mention the political assassination of Edward Kennedy's presidential aspirations after the 1969 car "accident" in Chappaquiddick, Massachusetts, in which Kennedy survived but his date, Mary Jo Kopechne, did not.) The JFK assassination in itself is a kind of be-all and end-all—and catch-all—of conspiracy theories, a morass of potential coconspirators real and unreal, most of whom eventually link up with someone else who slept with someone else who worked with some other person who ties in somehow to the murder of Malcolm X or Bobby Kennedy or Martin Luther King, Jr. The birth of the lone gunman, perhaps the first successful Manchurian candidate.

The debate is no longer whether JFK was killed by Lee Oswald acting alone or as part of a conspiracy—it is instead, which conspiracy is correct?

—Gerald Posner,
Case Closed: Lee Harvey Oswald and the Assassination of JFK (1993)

Alpha 66

A motley crew of **CIA**-funded anti-**Castro** Cubans and Cuban exiles, employed for various assassination attempts on Fidel and the
Bay of Pigs. The group's leader, Antonio Veciana, claims **Oswald**
often sat in on Alpha meetings. Alpha's still active in Florida—if a
tad geriatric.

Bay of Pigs

Nixon-concocted and **JFK**-approved, this April 1961 botched attempt to invade Cuba and assassinate **Fidel Castro** involved the
CIA, the **Mafia,** anti-Castro Cuban exiles known as **Alpha 66,** and
many others. Cooked up behind President **Eisenhower**'s back, Vice
President Nixon plotted with the CIA (and the Mob) on how to off
Castro (who in 1959 had overthrown the U.S.-backed Batista dictatorship, then nationalized all businesses and closed the lucrative
Mob-controlled hotels, casinos, and brothels—all to the great dis-
may of the Mafia, the CIA, and the **Multinationals**). JFK subsequently inherited the Nixon-CIA plot (both Nixon and the Agency
had expected Nixon to win the 1960 election), but though JFK
wanted to eliminate Fidel, he didn't want U.S. forces to carry out
the invasion, only Cuban exiles, which, after the mission failed miserably, became a major sticking point with Nixon, the CIA, and the
anti-Castro exiles. In 1961, **George Bush** was CEO of Zapata Off
Shore Oil, married to Barbara Bush, and living in Houston. Two of
the CIA's Bay of Pigs ships bore the names the *Houston* and the *Barbara J* and the Cuban resupply mission's code name was Operation
Zapata.
☺

The Bronfmans

✡ 👁 ▦

George Bush

〰〰 ✏ 👁 ⚔ ☺ ✿ 🌐

The Cabell Boys

CIA deputy director Charles Cabell was fired in 1962 by JFK.
Charles, who loathed JFK and whose brother at the time of
JFK's **Assassination** was Dallas mayor Earl Cabell, later

joined **Robert Maheu**'s detective agency—and reportedly sat in on JFK assassination meetings with Maheu and **Mafia** bigwig **Sam Giancana**.

Fidel Castro

✍

CIA

𝕀𝕡 ★ ✍ ✝ ⚒ ☞ 〰 ▱ ➳ ⚕ ☺ ▨ ⊕ ☉

> The genuine, honest-to-golly vast conspiracy afoot these days is composed of the millions and millions of Americans who are conspiring to blame their troubles on some vast conspiracy.
>
> —Arthur Hoppe, *San Francisco Chronicle*, June 1997

Bill Clinton

U.S. president who never met a donor (or a doughnut) he didn't like. A member of the **Council on Foreign Relations**, the **Trilateral Commission**, and the **Bilderbergers**, a **Rhodes** scholar, and the former governor of Arkansas. Not long after Louisiana congressman Hale Boggs publicly expressed his doubts about **FBI** procedure and the **Warren Commission**'s findings on the **JFK assassination**, his plane disappeared without a trace over Alaska—and the man who drove Boggs to the airport that fateful day was none other than future president Bill Clinton. In his 1992 democratic nomination acceptance speech, he thanked conspiracy realist and **Insider** Carroll Quigley (Bubba's favorite teacher at Georgetown U). While governor, Clinton seemed to have turned a blind eye to the **Iran-Contra** drugs-and-guns resupply planes that regularly flew in and out of **Mena,** Arkansas. In the 1993 raid on David Koresh's Branch Davidians compound in Waco, Texas, several of his former bodyguards just happened to be among the handful of federal agents who were killed there. A **GATT** booster and a fan of **NAFTA** (sentiments he shares with the leaders of the **Transnationals**), Clinton has more than a few detractors, like the indefatigably hateful **Richard Scaife,** who suspects that Clinton arranged the "suicide" of Vince Foster and the airplane-crash death of Ron Brown. Clinton survived the Whitewater and Paula Jones fiascos only to be impeached, though not ousted from office, by the findings of independent counsel **Kenneth Starr**—over a semen-stained dress, a wet cigar, and a few white lies.

✐ ☺ ⊕

Harry Cohn

President of Columbia Pictures from 1932 to 1958. Known as a heavy gambler and "the meanest man in Hollywood," Cohn relied on his connections to **Mafia** musclemen like mobster Lucky Luciano and Frank Nitti to break up Tinseltown's union strikes. One of his best friends was Mafioso **Johnny Roselli,** who, in 1928, introduced him to East Coast mobster Longie Zwillman (who'd discovered Jean Harlow). Zwillman lent Cohn the $500,000 he needed to buy out his brother Jack's stake in Columbia.

▦

COINTELPRO

The **FBI**'s COunter INTELligence PROgram set up in the 1960s to discredit and bring down dissident groups, especially the civil rights and women's movements and members of the New Left.

In 1971, G-men from **COINTELPRO** broke into the home of sci-fi writer Philip K. Dick (the movies *Blade Runner* and *Total Recall* were based on two of his books) and stole many of his files, heightening his already acute paranoia, and leading, perhaps, to *VALIS*, his book and theory about a Vast Active Living Intelligence System put on Earth by three-eyed **Aliens** from Sirius to aid and monitor our evolution.

Division 5

✝

Allen Dulles

★ ✝ ⛪ 🐾

Louis Farrakhan

Born Louis Walcott in Bronx, New York, Farrakhan started out as a calypso singer. Now the leader of the **Nation of Islam,** Farrakhan has been hounded by allegations throughout his career that he had a hand in **Malcolm X**'s death. Before Malcolm X's assassination, Farrakhan wrote a series of articles in the Nation of Islam's newspaper in which he branded Malcolm X a "dog" and said he deserved death; and in a clip from the 1995 documentary *Brother Minister,* Farrakhan at one point asked a 1993 NOI meeting in Chicago, "Was Malcolm your traitor or ours? And if we dealt with him like a nation deals with traitors, what the hell business is it of yours?" Even Betty Shabazz, Malcolm X's widow, accused Farrakhan of having played a role in her husband's killing (allegations that Farrakhan denies). In 1995, he told of having been abducted by **Aliens**—an experience that inspired his 1995 Million Man March on Washington, D.C.
☉

FBI

♍ ※ ✝ 🐾 ♒ ☼ ⊕ ☉

David Ferrie

A creepy quasi-transsexual **Mafia**-linked **CIA** flightman who commanded **Lee Harvey Oswald**'s Civil Air Patrol unit, Ferrie is suspected of having flown to safety the "hit team" responsible for the **JFK assassination.** He is the business and pleasure pal of **Clay Shaw,** as well as the sidekick of the mobster **Carlos Marcello** and **Jack Ruby** (who gave him a job at his Carousel Club strip joint).

Gerald Ford

Picked for the vice presidency by **Richard Nixon** (after Spiro Agnew resigned in disgrace), Ford stepped into the Oval Office's big seat in 1974 when Nixon also resigned in disgrace (due to the **Wa-**

tergate scandal). Ford served as president from 1974 to 1977. A **Freemason,** Ford also served on the **Warren Commission.** It's speculated that Nixon may have rewarded Ford with the vice presidency for keeping his knowledge of Nixon's involvement in the **JFK assassination** under wraps. In 1975, Ford pardoned Nixon for his Watergate crimes. **Henry Kissinger** was Ford's secretary of state. Ford's presidency (and 1976 presidential campaign) was doomed in part by the bad advice given to him by future **Federal Reserve** chairman **Alan Greenspan,** who at that time was chairman of the Coucil of Economic Advisers.

Freemasons

♍ ❋ ✡ ⚥ ☺

Sam Giancana

A **Mafia** gangster who helped run the Mob in Chicago and Las Vegas, Giancana started out as a hit man for Al Capone, then served as the liaison between the Mafia and the **CIA.** Giancana shared a pair of occasional mistresses with the promiscuous **JFK:** movie star **Marilyn Monroe** and Judith Exner. Giancana, aka Mooney, also used **Frank Sinatra** as a middleman between him and the president

**Gerald Ford,
Editor in Chief**

Before signing off on the **Warren Commission** report, Ford altered one key sentence in the 1964 paper that strangely confirmed the lone gunman theory. The staff wrote: "A bullet had entered his [**JFK**'s] back at a point slightly above the shoulder and to the right of the spine." Ford's version read: "A bullet had entered the back of his neck at a point slightly to the right of the spine." And the final edit stated: "A bullet had entered the base of the back of his neck and slightly to the right of the spine." Effectively, Ford's teeny-tiny changes, which did not come to light until 1997, solidified the only-**Oswald**-did-it theory that a single bullet had passed through Kennedy and wounded Texas governor John Connally. Ford said that his changes "had nothing to do with a conspiracy theory."

and Monroe and Angie Dickinson as innocent couriers between him and JFK. His other "business associates" included Texas oilmen and rabid JFK haters H. L. Hunt and the late **Clint Murchison,** as well as **Lyndon Johnson.** He claimed to have secured the number of votes needed in Chicago that assured JFK's narrow 1960 presidential victory over **Nixon**—as a favor to Kennedy's dad, Joseph, with whom Mooney bootlegged liquor during Prohibition. Giancana claimed that the CIA at one point asked him to knock off first **Castro,** then Kennedy, and that the **FBI** offered him $1 million to kill Martin Luther King, Jr.

Jimmy Hoffa

J. Edgar Hoover

Howard Hughes

E. Howard Hunt

Insiders

International Communist Conspiracy

Intertel

Reverend Jesse Jackson

John Birch Society

An anti-Communist group founded in 1958 by retired candymaker Robert Welch. Fittingly, their headquarters are located in the Wisconsin hometown of Communist witch-hunter **Joe McCarthy.** The Birchers are a major ideological influence on the Militia Movement and are notorious for their conspiranoid theories. Cult leader **Jim Jones** was a member, as was Ralph Davis, a member of the board of

directors for **Wackenhut Securities,** and Willis Carto, founder of the 1980s **Populist Party** and the **Liberty Lobby.** Former **KKK** Grand Dragon Tom Metzger started off as a John Bircher before founding the White Aryan Resistance (WAR) in San Diego in the 1980s. **Paul Weyrich,** cofounder of the **New Right** and the **Heritage Foundation** and a **Gang of Four** member, used to write a column for one of the society's weekly publications, *Review of the News.*
†

> I never believed that Oswald acted alone, although I can accept that he pulled the trigger.
>
> —**Lyndon Baines Johnson,** *The Atlantic* (July 1973)

John F. Kennedy Assassination

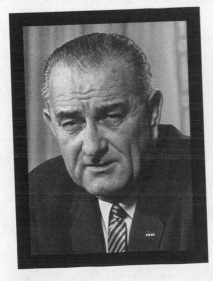

Lyndon Baines Johnson

A Texas oilman and the 36th president (1963–1969) of the United States, Johnson was at times a conservative, at times a liberal, but always a **Freemason.** Succeeding to the presidency after the murder of **John F. Kennedy,** Lyndon Johnson authorized the **Warren Commission** to look into the assassination. During his term, he stepped up U.S. involvement in the **Vietnam War** and launched the **Socialist**-tinged welfare program known as the Great Society. His advisors included entertainment-industry bigwigs like Arthur Krim (late president of United Artists) and **Jack Valenti,** whom LBJ appointed in 1967 as head of the **Corporation for Public Broadcasting.**

Based on the evidence that I've been shown, I would think that it would be very difficult for something of that magnitude to occur on his [Lyndon Johnson's] watch and he not be privy to it.

—Dexter Scott King on Martin Luther King, Jr.'s, assassination, ABC's *Turning Point*, 1997

Justice Department

Created in 1870. During his 1961 to 1964 stint at the department, attorney general **Robert Kennedy** used his position to indict (and anger) powerful crime figures like **Jimmy Hoffa** and **Carlos Marcello.** During the **Reagan** administration, U.S. attorney general Ed Meese and others at the Justice Department allegedly forced software company Inslaw's husband-and-wife owners out of business by not paying for the **PROMIS** software that Inslaw had designed for them, instead seizing PROMIS for themselves. **Clinton** Justice Department official Webster Hubbell was later assigned to investigate the Inslaw affair but resigned one month later—perhaps due to an arrangement between his boss,

Clinton, and **George Bush,** who supposedly agreed never to rat on each other's infidelities (Bush's involvement in the **Iran-Contra** mess and Clinton's involvement in the same).

☺

John F. Kennedy

〰〰

Robert Kennedy

John F. Kennedy's younger brother, the U.S. attorney general (1961–1964) who aggressively prosecuted Teamsters boss **Jimmy Hoffa** and the **Mafia.** No stranger to corruption himself, Bobby may have used his relationship with Time-Life's Henry Luce to try to place articles that looked kindly on himself and less kindly on his adversaries. Like his elder brother, he dallied with movie star **Marilyn Monroe.**

KGB

🔫 🐀 👓 ☼

Jules Kimble

An incarcerated murderer and racketeer, Kimble admitted to participating in the 1968 murder of civil rights leader **Martin Luther King, Jr.**, with the help of the **CIA.** Kimble claimed that he was part of a King assassination team that included himself, fall guy **James Earl Ray,** seven CIA men (three of them disguised as Memphis police), and a mysterious figure whom both Ray and Kimble call "Raoul." Kimble was an associate of mafioso **Carlos Marcello** and was also linked to the **Ku Klux Klan.**

Ku Klux Klan

✳ ✝

Mark Lane

🐀

Liberty Lobby

California businessman and ultra-right-wing wacko Willis Carto's contribution to society. Founded in 1957, the Liberty Lobby is a patriotic front for racists and anti-Semites that has popularized many an outlandish anti-Semitic and **Communist** conspiracy theory (which the lobby disseminates via its organ, *The Spotlight*). It was at one time represented legally by **Mark Lane,** who also advised **Jim Jones** and **James Earl Ray.** The Liberty Lobby is vaguely tied to accused Oklahoma City bomber Timothy McVeigh, in light of the fact that McVeigh had with him a phone card issued by *The Spotlight*. In 1981, **Reagan** unsuccessfully tried to appoint former Liberty Lobby lobbyist Warren Richardson to the post of assistant secretary of health and human services, despite (or because of) Richardson's anti-Semitic views.

✝

Lockheed-Martin

✝ ✡

Los Angeles Police Department (LAPD)

The LAPD's investigation squad on the **Robert Kennedy** case was headed by Manuel Pena, who allegedly served on an LAPD "international development" unit, the **U.S. Agency for International Development**—a **CIA** cover program that was often referred to as the "Department of Dirty Tricks." AID was renowned throughout the Agency for its nefarious rackets (tortures, assassinations, drug-running operations) in Latin America and Southeast Asia. It was here, too, at the LAPD, where the nation's first SWAT team was developed, in the mid-1960s, by future LAPD chief Daryl Gates.

Henry Luce

〰 ▦

Mafia

𝕿 ✳ ⛰ 〰 ✐ ☺ ▦

Robert Maheu

Maheu and his private-investigation firm, Maheu, Inc., served as the real-life models for the popular TV series *Mission: Impossible.* As the right-hand man of tycoon **Howard Hughes,** Maheu was in charge of pimping for his boss and chasing off blackmailers. A former **FBI** man, he was on the **CIA** payroll and often worked for Chicago **Mafia** boss **Sam Giancana,** who at one time assigned Maheu to tail **Bobby Kennedy** (in the hopes of blackmailing the anti-Mafia attorney general).

Malcolm X Assassination

On the verge of moderation and about to join hands with **Martin Luther King, Jr.,** this black Muslim civil rights leader was shot and killed by **Assassins** as he addressed four hundred supporters at New York's Audubon Ballroom on February 21, 1965—reputedly ordered by Malcolm's ex-mentor, the **Nation of Islam** leader Elijah Muhammad. Others think that maybe the three murderers were put up to their task by the **FBI.** Malcolm X was long under investigation by the feds as a leading spokesman for the Nation of Islam and an advocate, in his early days, of black separatism (Malcolm X coined the phrase "by any means necessary" to describe his quasi-militant philosophy). Following a 1964 pilgrimage to Mecca, Malcolm announced that he had become an orthodox Muslim and founded the Organization for Afro-American Unity to rival the Nation of Islam. The FBI continued to hound his family after his death. In 1995, the feds arrested Malcolm X's daughter, Qubilah Shabazz, and accused her of hiring Michael Kevin Fitzpatrick to kill **Louis Farrakhan,** the leader of the Nation of Islam, who has long battled mumblings that he played a role in Malcolm X's death (which he denies).

Carlos Marcello
New Orleans's Mob boss during the 1950s and 1960s. One of Marcello's most loyal footmen was **David Ferrie,** suspected of having flown **JFK**'s hit team to safety after the assassination. A frequent target of attorney general **Bobby Kennedy,** who successfully deported him to Guatemala, Marcello had made a serious threat against JFK's life prior to his assassination (only to be dismissed by the **FBI**).

Martin Luther King, Jr., Assassination

✳ 🦅

Media Conspiracy

♍ ✡ ♒ ∽ ☼

The Mighty Wurlitzer

♒ ▨

Military-Industrial Complex

♍ ★ ✝ 👤 😊 ✿ ▨

Marilyn Monroe
Born Norma Jean Mortenson (or Baker), Monroe gained remarkable popularity when she appeared nude on a calendar and soon the bottle-blond actress with the breathy voice was an international sex symbol and American icon. Sadly, her low self-esteem compromised her ability to say no—and men the world over used and abused and exploited her to no end. The

CIA may have used her to blackmail various world leaders (like Indonesia's President Sukarno), and everyone from **John F. Kennedy, Frank Sinatra, Sam Giancana, Robert Kennedy,** and **Harry Cohn** had or claimed to have had sex with her. In mid-1962, apparently fearful of all she knew about CIA-**Mafia** operations, the Agency asked Giancana to off her. On August 5, 1962, Monroe mysteriously "overdosed" on barbiturates in Los Angeles, shortly after being visited by several men. Some say that one of the last to have seen her was Robert Kennedy or maybe Peter Lawford (who served as a go-between between Marilyn and both Kennedys, and in whose cottage Monroe was found dead). But Giancana, in his biography, said that it was a pair of Mafiosi thugs who gave her a fatal anal shot of doctored Nembutal.

Multinationals

♏ ✝ ⊕

Clint Murchison

Murchison was a close friend of **J. Edgar Hoover** and fellow Texas oilman billionaire H. L. Hunt (all of whom shared Murchison's dislike for their president, **John F. Kennedy**). **Nixon** was an acquaintance, too, as was Mafioso Meyer Lansky. A major funder of the **FBI**'s clandestine and legendary **Division 5** hit squad, Murchison also poured some of his dough into **Clay Shaw**'s **Permindex**, the equally legendary front company for drug-running and **Assassins.** (His son, Clint Jr., once owned America's Team, the NFL's Dallas Cowboys). Among the myriad businesses he owned, the most peculiar was the mysterious Great Southwest—one of whose clients after JFK's assassination was Marina **Oswald,** Soviet wife of Lee Harvey.

Nation of Islam

❋ ☉

Richard Nixon

✝ ⛰ ✎ ⚱ ☺ ☼

Lee Harvey Oswald

🐃

Pepsi-Cola

Drink Pepsi, Get Stuff! During the late 1960s and early 1970s, when **Richard Nixon**'s law firm was representing Pepsi, **Coke**'s archrival set up a bottling plant in the capital of Laos, Vientiane. The **CIA,** according to **Bo Gritz** and others, allegedly used this Pepsi factory (with the soda company's knowledge and blessing, it seems) as the heroin-processing plant for their **Golden Triangle** drug operations. On November 21, 1963, the day before **JFK** was shot to death in Dallas, Nixon met with Pepsi strategists—about what remains uncertain.

✑

Permindex

A mysterious Swedish trade-exposition company allegedly founded by the **Bronfmans'** lawyer Louis Bloomfield in 1957, with its main U.S. branch located in downtown New Orleans's World Trade Mart, which was run by **CIA** man **Clay Shaw.** Permanent Industrial Exhibitions (Permindex) was merely a drug-funded front for an **Assassins**-for-hire operation. Among the shadowy company's backers were Texas oilmen **H. L. Hunt** and the late **Clint Murchison**—neither of whom much liked **JFK**.

RAND

✍ ∽ ✿ ⊙

James Earl Ray

🦅

Resorts International

✝ 〰

Robert Kennedy Assassination

🦅

Johnny Roselli

This Chicago mobster, a protégé of the powerful Mob boss Lucky Luciano, also worked as a bootlegger goon with Al Capone and West Coast **Mafia**—Hollywood ambassador Jack Dragna (the Mob boss of all the 1930s and 1940s Los Angeles bookies and gambling-house managers). A sometime film extra, Roselli served as the liaison between Columbia Pictures

211

president **Harry Cohn** and East Coast mobster Longie Zwillman, and was known as quite the fashion boy around Tinseltown. He was represented by the same lawyer as **Robert Kennedy**'s assassin **Sirhan Sirhan.** In his leisure time, he caroused with singer **Frank Sinatra**'s rowdy entourage, the Rat Pack. He also claimed he slept with Judith Exner, and to have shared her with **John F. Kennedy** and his boss, **Sam Giancana.** At one point, Roselli served as the Mafia-**CIA** liaison in the plan to assassinate Cuban dictator **Fidel Castro.** However, just before he was due to testify to the congressional Assassinations Committee in 1976, Roselli was found strangled and dismembered, floating in a metal drum off the Florida coast.

Jack Ruby

Clay Shaw

A New Orleans businessman (president of **Permindex**) and **CIA** agent, Louisiana's conspiranoiac district attorney Jim Garrison accused Shaw of participating in a conspiracy to kill President **John F. Kennedy.** A cross-dresser himself, Shaw was known to be a friend of transsexual pilot **David Ferrie.** Permindex was very tight with the **FBI**'s legendary renegade assassin cabal, **Division 5,** and it was Shaw to whom **Nazi** rocket scientist and future **NASA** man **Wernher von Braun** surrendered in 1945.

Frank Sinatra

Informally known as Il Padrone and the Chairman of the Board, and now an American icon, Sinatra had many friends, including President **Kennedy** and a number of Mafiosi (such as **Johnny Roselli**), who caroused with Sinatra's Rat Pack (aka the Knights of the Toupee: Dean Martin, Peter Lawford, Sammy Davis, Jr., et al.). Sinatra was also longtime buddies with **Charles "Lucky" Luciano** and Meyer Lansky, and his two Hoboken pals, the Frischetti brothers, were cousins of Al Capone. Sinatra was also one of **Marilyn Monroe**'s many lovers. In the 1940s, Old Blue Eyes was accused of being a red **Communist.** It's rumored that his Oscar-winning comeback role in *From Here to Eternity* was strong-armed away from **Harry Cohn** (who

hated Frankie) courtesy of his friends in the Mob. Sinatra later introduced Kennedy to one of his mistresses, Judith Exner. Mobster **Sam Giancana** tabbed Sinatra as his liaison between his Chicago Mafia Outfit and JFK.

Sirhan Sirhan

Time Warner

U.S. Agency for International Development (USAID)

A **CIA** front specializing in propaganda campaigns in developing nations, the USAID works very closely with **World Vision.** In 1977, its population program director announced the Agency's (aborted) intent to sterilize a quarter of the world's women (mostly those in developing and third world countries). In 1990, President **George Bush** appointed former University of Nebraska chancellor Ronald Roskens to head the USAID, one year after Cornhusker regents had canned Roskens. In 1991, USAID, along with the **International Monetary Fund,** the **World Bank,** and **International Banker** George Soros, handed over the restructuring of the Russian economy to the Harvard Institute for International Development, which effectively drove Russia into the ground financially, leading to its economic collapse in 1998.

U.S. Army

Vietnam War

Warren Commission

The 1964 body assigned to investigate President **Kennedy**'s assassination for the possibility of a conspiracy. The commission concluded that both **Lee Harvey Oswald** and **Jack Ruby** had been acting alone, found no evidence of a conspiracy, and cleared the **CIA** of any connection to Kennedy's murder. The commission was approved by Kennedy's former vice president, the newly minted president **Lyndon Johnson**—who was a **Freemason,** as were many other Warren Commission members (**Allen Dulles, Gerald Ford,** Supreme Court Chief Justice Earl Warren, et al.). Another commission member, Representative Hale Boggs of Louisiana, publicly expressed his doubts about the Warren Commission and **FBI** procedures. Not long afterward, the plane he was flying in disappeared without a trace over Alaska. On his very last trip to the airport Boggs was driven there by none other than future president **Bill Clinton.** The commission's "no conspiracy" conclusion reassured many Americans.

The Washington Post

〰〰 ▦

Watergate

On June 17, 1972, a small group of **Nixon**'s men—most of them familiar faces from the **Bay of Pigs** fiasco—broke into the Democratic National Committee HQ in Washington, D.C.'s Watergate hotel and office complex in order to plant a few bugs. Some say that it was Nixon's paranoia that led him to order the raid, that he'd hoped to find out whether the Democrats had info that could be used to blackmail him. Others theorize that Nixon and the **CIA** were trying to blackball each other. After all, it was former CIA security chief James McCord who led the blatantly bungled operation, then pinned the blame on Nixon. Another CIA veteran, Alexander Butterfield, was the man who tipped off the Senate investigating committee about the incriminating tape recordings that Nixon had made of himself, thus helping to seal Nixon's political coffin in

The Nazi Commission

According to conspiranoiac writer John Judge, the actual author of the Warren Commission's report was Otto Winnacker, formerly one of **Hitler**'s official historians of the Third Reich.

1973. The most famous "third-rate burglary attempt" in U.S. history, all five of the Watergate crooks were connected to CREEP (the Committee to Re-Elect the President). Precipitated perhaps by Nixon's reaction to the publication of the Pentagon Papers and his apparent desire to smear Papers whistleblower Daniel Ellsberg's public image (and the DNC's).

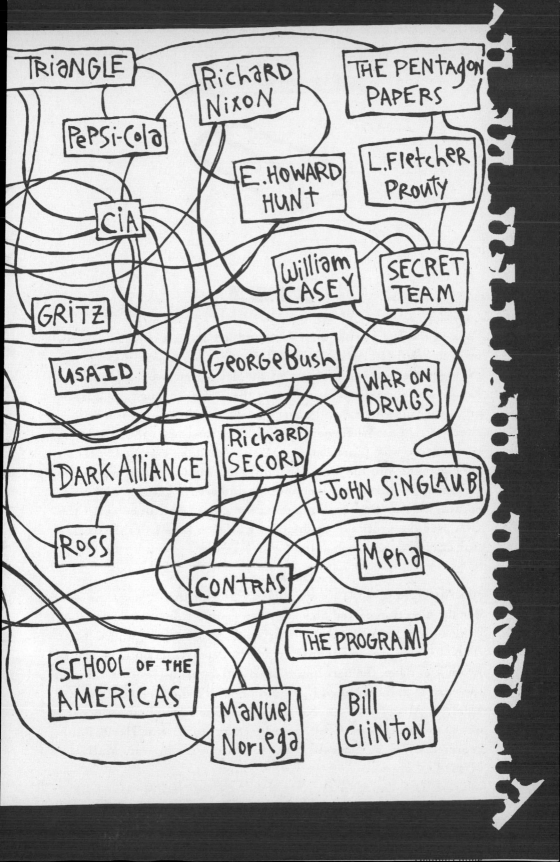

The Golden Alliance

Conspiracy

Back in the late 1940s, the CIA stumbled on to a covert cash-cow crop in Southeast Asia's Golden Triangle: opium. And soon began the Agency's worldwide export of the drug, first processing it into heroin and then distributing it, via the Mafia, throughout Europe and the United States, and using profits from its sales to fund other sneaky activities. When heroin got old in the early 1980s, the CIA entered into what journalist Gary Webb called the Dark Alliance: an arrangement with the Cali-Medellín Cocaine Cartels in which the Company facilitated the distribution and sale of cocaine and crack cocaine in America's vulnerable inner cities. And once again the CIA used the profits from their drug sales to keep its other operations in full swing (such as the Contras).

Air America

Aka Air Opium, this 1960s to 1970s **CIA** "airline," for a time under the direction of Ted Shackley, flew opium from various Laotian collection spots in the **Golden Triangle** to Vientiane, where it was then allegedly processed into heroin at a **Pepsi-Cola** bottling plant. From Vientiane, the heroin was distributed worldwide (often inside the corpses and coffins of U.S. soldiers who'd died in the **Vietnam War**), to Miami mobster Santos Trafficante's San Francisco network, to U.S. troops fighting in Vietnam, to **Nugan Hand Bank** representatives in Australia, and to Europe's Corsican **Mafia** in Marseilles, France.

Bank of Credit and Commerce International (BCCI)

Aka the Bank of Crooks and Criminals International and the Bank of Cover for Collecting Intelligence (in honor of Britain's **MI6** intelligence agency), the BCCI laundered money to and from drug dealers, **Terrorists,** spies, and blackmailers and was renowned for having set off the largest banking scandal in world history. Operating out of branches in Pakistan and Switzerland, the BCCI siphoned off its profits to help ship matériel (via MI6 and **Monzer Al-Kassar**) to **Saddam Hussein** and **Muammar Qaddafi** and Afghanistan's **Mujahedeen** "freedom fighters." Founded and directed by many of the same people (allegedly including former **CIA** director **Richard Helms**) who created Australia's **Nugan Hand Bank** and then ran it into the ground, and established for the same nefarious purpose (laundering drug money and then using the cash to fund covert operations elsewhere), BCCI went belly-up in the late 1980s (billions of dollars in debt, with $20 billion more that's never been located) and its treasurer was convicted on charges of laundering drug-trafficking money.
∽ ☺

George Bush

〰 △ ∽ ⚊ ☺ ✿ ⊕

Cali-Medellín Cocaine Cartels

The cabal of Colombian drug lords who specialize in the production and distribution of cocaine, and who, by the 1980s, achieved the kind of wealth, power, and control over their industry (and Colombia) that would make the mouth of any **Transnational** water with envy. The once-impregnable Medellín Cartel has had to deal with the arrests of several of its leaders and the deaths of others, but the Cali Cartel has more than ably picked up the speedball—and continues to manufacture and distribute blow via its own Colombian employees as well as street gangs; the **Mafia** in New York City, San Francisco, Los Angeles, Miami, and Houston; and on to the rest of the country. It's said that the planes used by the cartels to carry drugs to the North came back loaded with cash and arms, both for the **Contras** and the cartels. Some of the cartels' lieutenants were trained at the **School of the Americas.**
☺

219

William Casey

★ ⚰ ☺ ▩

Castle Bank & Trust

♒

CIA

℞ ★ ✍ ✝ ⚰ 🐾 ♒ △ ⚯ ⚲ ☺ ▩ 🌐 ☉

Citicorp

✧

This global U.S. financial-service company (founded in 1812) owns Citibank, and its board of director memberships intersect with **Unilever,** Philip Morris, Exxon, and **GE.** CEO John Reed revolutionized the use of ATMs in the mid-1980s and, at best, allowed his friendship with the former president of Mexico, Carlos Salinas, to be exploited by Carlos's brother Raul, who was arrested in 1995 on charges of murder and "inexplicable enrichment." Known as Mr. Ten Percent and "the leech" among the leaders of the Mexico and **Cali-Medellín Cocaine Cartels,** Raul had somehow parlayed a $190,000-a-year salary into bank accounts (in banks outside of Mexico's jurisdiction) totaling more than $200 million, accounts handled by—who else?—Citibank, the Citicorp subsidiary under investigation by the U.S. **Justice Department** for possibly laundering drug money.

Bill Clinton

△ ☺ 🌐

The white press is pointing fingers at the black community saying we're paranoid and quick to see conspiracy at every turn of the corner. Where have they been for the last thirty years? Can I just mention the Tuskegee syphilis study, COINTELPRO, Watergate, Iran-Contra. Hello, America?

—Don Washington, jazz musician, *The New York Times*, October 1996

Contras

These U.S.-backed counterrevolutionary insurgents, led by Eden Pastora and perversely sanctioned by President **Ronald Reagan** as "freedom fighters," battled Nicaragua's left-wing Sandinista government during the early 1980s. Agents for the **CIA** (both active and retired) ran overt and covert operations in Nicaragua in order to help the Contras (mining harbors, blowing up fuel tanks, running arms to them, and training them in sabotage, assassination, kidnapping, and blackmail). Weapons manufactured at the **Cabazon Indian Reservation** were exported to the Contras, reportedly with the help of **Wackenhut Securities** employees. The CIA, along with **Oliver North** and the **National Security Council,** also illegally sold U.S. arms to Iran and then diverted the profits from those sales to fund the Contras' ongoing campaign. The Contras also sold and distributed cocaine and crack cocaine (along with various CIA agents and members of the **Cali-Medellín Cocaine Cartels** and other U.S.-based street gangs). Panama's **Manuel Noriega** also assisted by smuggling coke and laundering drug money (skimming off some of both for himself before sending on the cash and coke—and weapons—to the Contras).
⚱ ☺

The Dark Alliance

Former *San Jose Mercury News* journalist Gary Webb's theory that the crack cocaine epidemic that hit the United States in the 1980s (and beyond) was the result of the **CIA**'s having sponsored and encouraged drug trafficking in the predominantly African-American sections of Los Angeles and other big cities: The Agency got its cocaine from the **Cali-Medellín Cocaine Cartels** and then, via members of the **Contras** (or via Contra-friendly Nicaraguan drug middlemen), dealt the drug to low-level African-American drug dealers like **Ricky "Freeway Rick" Ross.** Ross then hired street gangs like the notorious rivals the Crips and the Bloods, who first broke the coke down into rocks, i.e., crack cocaine, and then sold the drug on the streets, primarily to other African-Americans (and Hispanics). As the demand increased, the profits shot up and the CIA got richer and richer, and so, too, did the Contras. And like killing two birds with one rock, the CIA was ridding itself (and society at large—white society) of a class of people who, in the Agency's eyes, really didn't do much for the rest of the world anyway—a fringe benefit that fit in perfectly with the **Program,** the fear among some blacks that groups like the CIA are doing whatever they can to eliminate the black race altogether. 😐

Golden Triangle

The jungle area where Burma, Thailand, and Laos intersect, the Triangle derives its name from the wealth generated by its opium trade. It is where the **CIA** (along with the **U.S. Agency for International Development**) and local tribal lords (along with the Chinese **Triads**) set up a cooperative—and lucrative—drug-smuggling operation in the late 1940s, which lasted till the early 1970s. Opium grown in the Golden Triangle was flown via **Air America** to Vientiane, Laos's capital, where it was allegedly processed at a **Pepsi-Cola** bottling plant (another CIA front) and made into heroin. The smack was then flown to U.S. troops fighting in Vietnam, the United States (sometimes packed into the body bags of U.S. soldiers), and the **Mafia** in France. Ted Shackley and many of his buddies from the CIA-**Military-Industrial-Complex** cabal known as the **Secret Team** were also alleged to have been directly or indirectly involved: Ed Wilson, Al Hakim, **Richard Secord, William Casey,** and **John Singlaub.** Rumor has it that there are no (and never were

You Say Potato . . .

The **CIA**'s exoneration of itself (to which the major media followed its lead), first from a 1985 Associated Press story and then from former *San Jose Mercury News* reporter Gary Webb's Dark Alliance articles (and book) that outlined the Agency's involvement in the 1980s and 1990s crack cocaine epidemic, may hinge solely on . . . semantics. Their 1982 "Memorandum of Understanding" directive did indeed prohibit the Company's full-time career "officials" from engaging in criminal activities, but "agents, assets and non-staff employees" could do whatever they wanted—licit or illicit. Such spook doublespeak gave them a legitimate out when reacting to—and even investigating—their own role in the **War on Drugs.**

any) POWs or MIAs left in Southeast Asia, but the **Reagan** and **Bush** administrations continued to exploit the families and comrades of the so-called missing Americans in order to continue funding fake rescue missions that were really fronts for the Agency's Golden Triangle drug runs.

Bo Gritz

A macho-man survivalist, **Freemason,** and self-professed gun nut who refuses to pay taxes (since he's broken his "contract" with America), Gritz served as the model and inspiration for Sylvester Stallone's jingoistic *Rambo* character and franchise. In 1992, he ran for president on the **Populist Party** ticket. Gritz worked in the **Golden Triangle** during its **CIA–Air America** opium-and-heroin heyday and trained the Special Forces unit that was sent in to mop up the mess in **Jonestown** (he trained many of the Afghani **Mujahedeen** "freedom fighters," too).

✝

E. Howard Hunt

⛰ △

International Banking Conspiracy

♍ ✘ ✡ ★ ✍ 〰 ∾ ✞ ⊕

Mafia

♍ ✳ ⛰ 〰 △ ☺ ▨

Mena

In the early 1980s, during **Bill Clinton**'s governorship, the remote airstrip of this tiny Arkansas town was used to run drugs, weapons, and cash. The money and weapons went to the **Contras**; the drugs came from the **Cali-Medellín Cocaine Cartels** and were sold in the United States. According to some conspiranoiacs, certain Arkansas associates of Clinton's were paid off with secretive "green flights"—drug-tainted money that was then laundered through: 1) Vince Foster at the Rose Law Firm in Little Rock, and 2) at the **Arkansas Development Finance Authority** (ADFA). Both Foster and the ADFA were connected to Hillary Clinton, Bert Lance of the **BCCI**, James and Susan McDougal of Whitewater fame, and Webster Hubbell.

☺

MI6

✡ ∾ ▦

Mujahedeen

Afghani "freedom fighters" who battled the Soviet Union for control of their own land, the Mujahedeen were armed by the **CIA** and supplied with funds scammed through the **BCCI** and the CIA's **Cali-Medellín Cocaine Cartels** drug sales and **Contra** money-laundering operations.
☺

Richard Nixon

✝ ⛪ △ ♟ ☺ ☀

Manuel Noriega

The dictator of Panama from 1983 to 1989 and distinguished 1967 graduate of the **School of the Americas.** Noriega was arrested by U.S. troops in 1989 and is now serving a life sentence in a U.S. prison on drug-trafficking charges. Noriega acted as bagman-liaison between the United States and the **Cali-Medellín Cocaine Cartels** smuggling ring (which also included Amiram Nir of Israel's secret police, the **Mossad**). Through an arrangement with the United States (primarily **George Bush** and **Oliver North**), the cartels ran cocaine to the United States in return for U.S. arms and money, which were flown to the **Contras** in Nicaragua. In 1986, in return for this Contra cooperation, the generosity of **USAID** to Panama happened to jump from a previous high of $1.3 million to $74 million. Federal authorities charged that Noriega and his family concealed large portions of their drug profits in Capcom Financial Services, the trading company tied in with the **BCCI.** But by 1989 Bush had begun to weary of Noriega's hubris, and perhaps fearful that his relationship with the pockmarked colonel might come to light, Bush ordered up a U.S. military invasion and had the sap hauled up north and imprisoned.
☺

Nugan Hand Bank

An Australian **CIA** front founded in 1974 by Frank Nugan and former Indochina CIA operative Michael Hand, the bank laundered money from the Agency's **Golden Triangle** opium-and-heroin drug runs. Future CIA director William Colby was on Nugan Hand's board of directors. Nugan Hand was also used to destabilize Australia's 1970s government (which it did—in 1975, the CIA forced the ouster of Australia's prime minister, Edward Whitlam) and pay for CIA spying jags in Angola and the Middle East. The bank collapsed in 1980 after Hand was found shot dead in his Mercedes in Sydney (ruled a suicide—sure).

The Pentagon Papers

Coauthored by **CIA-Pentagon** liaison **L. Fletcher Prouty,** who claimed the Papers were generated by the Agency to shift responsibility for the **Vietnam War** away from the CIA and their illicit **Golden Triangle** drug operations and on to the Department of Defense. The Papers, leaked to *The New York Times* by former RAND analyst Daniel Ellsberg, exposed the fraud that Defense Secretary Robert McNamara, **Lyndon Johnson,** and other pro-war White House cronies had perpetrated on the United States, and demonstrated the lies to which they'd resorted to justify U.S. involvement in Southeast Asia.

～

Pepsi-Cola

△

The Program

🐗 ☼

L. Fletcher Prouty

Company spook and **CIA-Pentagon** middleman, Prouty coauthored the **Pentagon Papers**, and also wrote the *Secret Team,* an exposé of the renegade intelligence-community and defense-establishment cabal he had helped to create in the 1960s. Fletch was the model for **Oliver Stone**'s "Mr. X" in the film *JFK,* for which he also served as advisor and consultant.

Ricky Ross

Aka Freeway Rick, Ross acted as the **CIA-Contra** go-between for the buying and selling of crack cocaine in South Central Los Angeles, a racket begun in the early 1980s. A small-time African-American drug dealer, Ross scored his cut-rate coke

from Nicaraguan exile Danilo Blandón, whose supplier was fellow Contra-friendly Nicaraguan Norwin Meneses (who both got their blow from the **Cali-Medellín Cocaine Cartels**). By 1985, Blandón was unloading up to one hundred kilos of cocaine a week on Ross, whose network in turn cooked the powder into crack and then sold it to the Crips and the Bloods—L.A.'s two most notorious gangs, which led to both (primarily) black-on-black gang warfare and a drug epidemic (perhaps part of the **Program,** the government's plot to gradually wipe out African-Americans). All the while the CIA used the profits from Blandón and Meneses to fund the Contras' war in Nicaragua against the Sandinistas.
☺

Savings & Loan Debacle

Late 1980s financial mess set in motion when in 1989 **Charles Keating**'s Phoenix-based American Continental Corporation filed for bankruptcy. Keating and his wildcatting cronies ran their S&L into the ground with too many high-risk loans and investments and flagrant profiteering. Keating also made grotesque campaign contributions to numerous politicians. The government bailout of Keating's other financial institution, the Lincoln S&L in San Diego, cost U.S. taxpayers nearly $2 billion. Billions in taxpayers' money was (and still is being) spent to save failing S&Ls whose collapses were partly due to investment in junk bonds sold by people like Ivan Boesky, Keating, and Michael Milken.
‡

School of the Americas

A **U.S. Army** infantry school located in Fort Benning, Georgia, this institution has trained more than 58,000 Central and South American military officers and soldiers in the ways of torture, kidnapping, blackmail, murder, **Terrorism,** interrogation, and surveillance. Aka the School of the Assassins and the Latin American West Point, its graduates include Panamanian dictator **Manuel Noriega** (Class of '67); General Hugo Banzer Suarez (Class of '56), military dictator of Bolivia (1971–1978); and Roberto D'Aubuisson (class of '72), El Salvador's notorious death-squad leader, nicknamed "Blowtorch Bob" (after his favorite instrument of torture) and so brazen that he ordered the 1980 assassination of Archbishop Oscar Romero.

☺

Richard Secord

A veteran of the **CIA**'s **Air America** operations during the **Vietnam War** and later a mercenary for hire. When President **Reagan** and Vice President **Bush** decided to help Iraq's **Saddam Hussein** in his war against Iran, they had the CIA enlist Secord. In turn, Secord called on **Wackenhut** to provide services and protection for himself and his Iraqi colleague, arms dealer **Ihsan Barbouti,** while they moved matériel in and out of the United States during the eighties. Secord and another arms dealer, Al Hakim (at the behest of **Ollie North**), also smuggled Soviet-made weapons, bought from **Monzer Al-Kassar,** to the **Contras.** Secord oversaw the route of the Contra supply planes from the United States to Central America, and on the way back **Manuel Noriega** smuggled **Cali-Medellín Cocaine Cartels** coke and laundered money onboard Secord's flights.

☺

> The CIA and other intelligence organizations learned early in their existence that the best means of creating the illusion of legitimacy was to provide the reality of legitimacy—that is, to run a straightforward business in one portion of the office, and do the secret work either in the back room or elsewhere.
>
> —Joseph C. Goulden,
> *The Death Merchant: The Rise and Fall of Edwin P. Wilson,* 1984

The Secret Team

A cabal of thirty or so Company spooks, drug lords, **Multinational** moneygrubbers, soldiers of fortune, and ideologues. According to Col. **L. Fletcher Prouty,** the onetime **CIA-Pentagon** liaison officer and author of the exposé *The Secret Team,* these are the folks who *really* run the U.S. government. This idea was later seized upon with a vengeance by conspiranoiac lawyer Daniel Sheehan, who claimed that most members of the team (Prouty included) started out in the **Golden Triangle,** men like Ted

Shackley, Ed Wilson, Al Hakim, **Richard Secord, William Casey,** and **John Singlaub.** Secret Teammates or not, these men later used their expertise in the 1980s **Iran-Contra** operations.

General John Singlaub

Before taking over as leader of the **Fascistic World Anti-Communist League,** Singlaub commanded a renegade **CIA Golden Triangle**–area unit that allegedly included members of the **Secret Team.** A late 1960s outfit in Laos, this little "off-the-shelf" program brought back together some of the Company stars of Operation 40—a supplemental Cuba-to-U.S. drug-smuggling and Let's-kill-**Castro** club involving superspook Ted Shackley and mobsters **Johnny Roselli** and **Sam Giancana.** In Laos, Singlaub not only served with Shackley and CIA man Ed Wilson, he also, according to some conspiranoiacs, tutored future **Iran-Contra** schemer **Oliver North** and North's **Contra** arms-runner, **Richard Secord.** In the early 1980s, Singlaub pipelined Chinese **Communist** guns to the Contras.

Triads

Originally formed in 1674, this Chinese secret society is still a strong presence in Hong Kong. The Triads specialize in illegal operations involving drugs (especially opium), prostitution, and extortion. Sales of their drugs helped provide financial backing for Sun Yat-sen's Kuomintang Nationalist Party in pre-Communist China. Gang members also worked closely with **CIA** agent **E. Howard Hunt,** when they were running opium and heroin out of the **Golden Triangle** region.

US AID

△

Vatican Bank

Created in 1942 by Pope Pius XII, this Institute for Religious Works belongs not to the Vatican city-state but to the pope and is the vast tax-exempt and hugely profitable financial half of the Holy See. In the 1980s, the bank's president was Paul "the Gorilla" Marcinkus, an ape-shaped onetime bodyguard to two popes and Chicago-born archbishop who used his authority to launder drug money and counterfeit stocks for the **P2** and the **Mafia.** Marcinkus, with the help of "God's banker," **Licio Gelli,** and Gelli's fellow P2 stud, **Michele Sindona,** helped finance the **CIA**'s **Fascist** anti-Communist **Gladio** project (via Milan's Banco Ambrosiano). When Ambrosiano collapsed around 1982 (following the "suicide" of its president, Roberto Calvi), records turned up showing Marcinkus's links to the Bahamas' Cisalpine Bank, which appeared to have been a financial Laundromat for drug money coming in from the **Cali-Medellín Cocaine Cartels.** (Marcinkus briefly served as the mayor of Vatican City, after stepping down as president of the bank, before retiring to Cicero, Illinois.)

Vietnam War

★ ✍ △

War on Drugs

〰 ☺

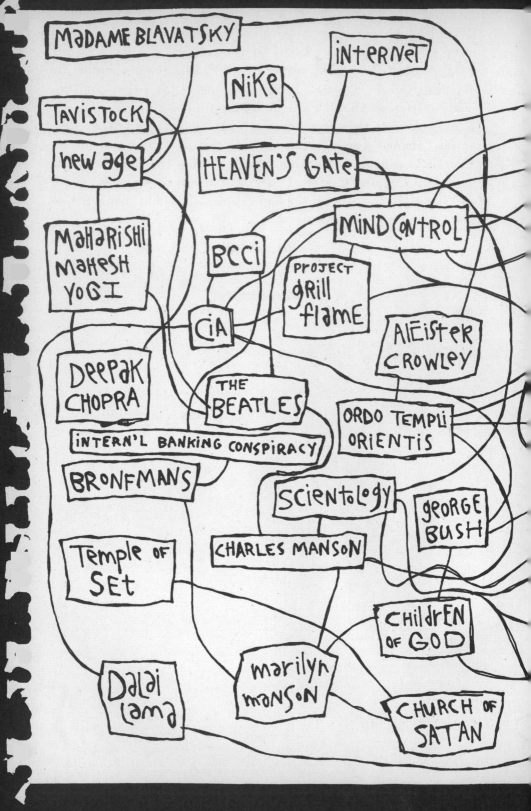

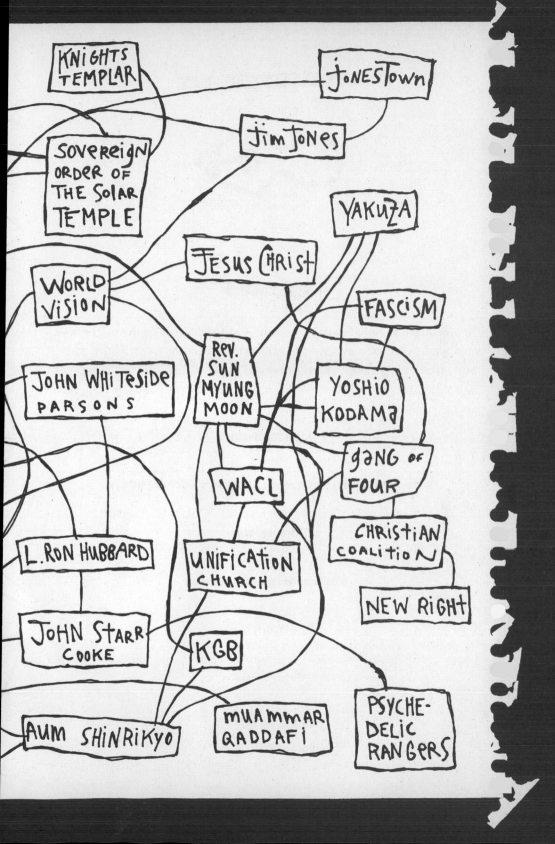

Conspiracy

Yet another form of mind control, Culture Club explores the occult groups of the past and the cults and cultish groups of the present, like Scientology, Jim Jones's People's Temple, and Japan's Aum Shinrikyo, and the ties of many of these groups to the New Age and the New Right.

Aum Shinrikyo

✝ ✿

Bank of Credit and Commerce International (BCCI)

▱ ☺

The Beatles

〜

Madame Helena Blavatsky

✡ ⚔ ∿

The Bronfmans

✡ △ ▨

George Bush

〜 △ ▱ ♦ ☺ ✿ ⊕

Children of God

This cult, a mix of witchcraft, astrology, and pseudo-Christianity, was founded in the 1970s by David "Moses" Berg, a virulent anti-

Semite who believed in an **International Zionist Conspiracy** and once proclaimed "God is a pimp." Berg and his Children posed as benign flower children when, in reality, they were extremely promiscuous: Not only did adults fornicate with adults but kids slept with kids and adults slept with kids, too. The Phoenix family—River, Joaquin, and Rain (and the other siblings and their parents)—were Children of God followers. Another member to have grown up in the cult was Rose McGowan, the exhibitionist girlfriend of rock star **Marilyn Manson**. In 1978, Berg changed the name of the group to the Family of Love, and under that appellation Berg and his crew were invited to the White House at Christmas in 1992 to sing for First Lady Barbara Bush. Later, when President **Bush** toured Florida after Hurricane Andrew, the family sang for him, too. Disbanded after a Halloween-night raid in 1993 in Argentina, the family resurfaced a year or so later in Libya, where Berg and his remaining followers received aid and comfort from, of all people, **Muammar Qaddafi**. Although Berg died in 1994, his followers carry on and were last seen fighting the courts in Scotland. ☺

Number of—

Post-**JFK Assassination** victims: 100+

Those who've died under suspicious circumstances who may have had incriminating evidence on **Clinton**'s alleged criminal activities: 30 and growing

Strategic Defense Initiative scientists who died of unnatural causes: 21

Those named in Danny Casolaro's Octopus conspiracy who've died or disappeared: close to 40 (and counting)

Clinton bodyguards who've died: 13 and growing (four at Waco—all with similar gunshot wounds to the left temple)

"Reality" is what we take to be true. What we take to be true is what we believe. What we believe is based upon our perceptions. What we perceive depends upon what we look for. What we look for depends upon what we think. What we think depends upon what we perceive. What we perceive determines what we believe. What we believe determines what we take to be true. What we take to be true is our reality.

—Gary Zukav,
The Dancing Wu Li Masters: An Overview of the New Physics, 1979

Deepak Chopra

A fiendishly charming India-born M.D. and celebrity guru (to Madonna, Demi Moore, the late Princess Diana, and *X-Files* star Gillian Anderson, among many others), a lecturer, motivator, and author (of *The Seven Spiritual Laws of Success* and the *Playboy* essay "Does God Have Orgasms?"), Chopra came to North America in the late 1970s as the ever-so-humble Lord of Immortality, when he led the charge westward as front man for the **Maharishi Mahesh Yogi**'s Transcendental Meditation movement. Now also known as the Bearer of True Enlightenment, Chopra preaches a mishmash of Eastern **New Age** metaphysics and Western-based medicine.

∽

Christian Coalition

A Fundamentalist right-wing religio-political organization, based in Chesapeake, Virginia, and founded by religious broadcaster **Pat Robertson** after his failed 1988 presidential campaign. The coalition, picking up from where the **New Right** left off, is a powerful lobby for U.S. political conservatism whose stated goal is "to give Christians a voice in government again."

✝

Church of Satan

A rather benign San Francisco—based sect of devil devotees founded by Anton LaVey in 1966 (LaVey's was the first **Satanic** church to be granted tax exemption). Since LaVey's death in 1998, however, the church has been bedeviled by internecine squabbles and a leadership vacuum. In 1994, goth-glam rocker **Marilyn Manson** was granted high priesthood in the church. Other satanic dilettantes and members included Jayne Mansfield, Laurence Harvey (star of *The Manchurian Candidate*), Sammy Davis, Jr., and L.A. rock-poster artist Chris "Coop" Cooper.

CIA

♍ ★ ⌂ ✝ 🕍 ☄ 〰️ △ ▱ 📍 ☺ ▦ 🌐 ☉

John Starr Cooke

〰️

Aleister Crowley

〰️ 〜

Dalai Lama

⚶ ✝ 〜 ☉

Fascism

♍ ✳️ ⚶ ✝ 🕍 📍 ☺

Gang of Four

✝ 📍

Heaven's Gate

Self-proclaimed deity Marshall Applewhite's Christian cult, he and thirty-eight of his small band of **Internet**-crazy, E.T.-believing followers (twenty-one women and eighteen men) committed suicide in late March of 1997, convinced that they were linking up with their **Alien** mother spaceship that was drafting behind the Hale-Bopp comet. Applewhite had at one time dabbled in **Scientology**. Appropriately, the group took **Nike**'s Just Do It slogan to heart, all of them ritualistically choosing a

fresh pair of Phil Knight's white-swoosh-on-purple-background sneakers as their final footwear of choice.
⊙

L. Ron Hubbard

〰 ⊙

International Banking Conspiracy

♍ ✖ ✡ ★ ✍ 〰 ✐ ∿ ⚲ ⊕

Internet

A computer network created in 1969, an almost accidental outgrowth of ARPAnet (the Advanced Research Project Agency net), this **Pentagon** experiment was designed to invent a noncentralized communications system that could survive a nuclear attack. The **RAND** Corporation and **UCLA** were instrumental in the early development of the Internet, as well as **Vannevar Bush,** the so-called godfather of the information age, who helped set up ARPAnet. Requiring a greater degree of technical know-how to use than any previous form of communication, the Internet is clearly a triumph of the **Technopoly Conspiracy.**

∿ ✿ ⊙

Jesus Christ

♍ ✖ ❇ ⚲ ⊙

Jim Jones

🐾

Jonestown Massacre

🐾

KGB

✍ 🐾 △ ✿

Knights Templar

♍ ✖ ❇ ⚲

Yoshio Kodama

✝

Maharishi Mahesh Yogi

India-born guru of the World Plan Executive Council and its **New Age** yoga discipline, Transcendental Meditation. The yogi, who had his fifteen minutes of fame in the sixties when the **Beatles** and the Rolling Stones cuddled up to him and his philosophy, has been re-born of late in the divine personhood of his former Lord of Immortality front man, **Deepak Chopra**.

Charles Manson

Marilyn Manson

Né Brian Warner, this goth-rock (now glam-rock) geek cleverly adopted the names of **Charles Manson** and **Marilyn Monroe** for his stage (and band) name, a mock-ironic Nietszche-esque ploy that has forever endeared him to America's cynical disgruntled youth. His album *Antichrist Superstar* scored big for his label, the controversial Interscope Records (onetime purveyor of the gangsta rap of Tupac Shakur and Snoop Doggy Dogg, Interscope is now a wing of liquor man Edgar **Bronfman**'s entertainment empire). In 1996, Manson was made a high priest in the **Church of Satan,** and his girlfriend, Rose McGowan (star of *Scream* and *Phantoms*), came from the same adults-who-have-sex-with-kids cult (**Children of God**) as River and Joaquin Phoenix.

Mind Control

Reverend Sun Myung Moon

New Age

The term "new age" was popularized in the mid-1980s to describe a nebulous, quasi-religious, wishy-washy, if at times palatably effective set of beliefs that was an outgrowth of the 1960s counter-culture and the 1970s "human potential movement." In the United States, the term alludes to the expectation that a new "spiritual" **Aquarian** age is dawning in which humans will realize their higher, more spiritual selves. New Age encom-

passes such notions as spiritualism, astrology, out-of-body experiences, reincarnation, and the occult disciplines, as well as unorthodox psychotherapeutic cures and pseudo-scientific applications of the "healing powers" of crystals and pyramids. Most New Age followers believe: 1) there are any number of routes to **God** or to spirituality and awakening, 2) there is no right or wrong, and 3) might makes right, all reasons that give Fundamentalists and the Vatican pause, and even lead some to claim the New Age as being **Satanic.**
〜 ☉

New Right

Having evolved in the mid-1970s out of the Old Right (those from the Barry Goldwater presidential campaign of 1964), the New Right, founded by the **Gang of Four,** solidified a broader base of public support for their Fundamentalist neoconservative anti-Communist big-business agenda, having built coalitions based on hot emotional issues like abortion and gun control. The New Right catered to the religious right and its Fundamentalist televangelist leaders, and it eventually gave birth to **Pat Robertson**'s **Christian Coalition.**
† ▩

> Ladies and Gentlemen, if you have a friend who says he does not believe in conspiracy, look him straight in the eye and tell them that they are ignorant. "I love you brother, I love you sister, but you are stupid."
>
> —**Texe Marrs, Austin, Texas, evangelist**

Nike

CEO and cofounder Phil Knight soon hopes to have a planet clothed and soled solely in Swoosh (or the Swooshstika, as Nike's ubiquitous logo is known among its harshest critics). Nike stole Michael Jordan away from Adidas, thanks to the influence of Nike advisor and gym rat Sonny Vaccaro, who some conspiranoiacs accuse of being **Mafia** friendly, though there's never been any proof of such slams. After Brazil's loss in the finals of the 1998 World Cup, in which Brazilian megastar (and Nike shill) Ronaldo apparently suffered a pregame seizure and then played ineffectively, soccer fans around the world accused Nike of forcing Brazil's coach—and his sick star—to play anyway. Nike was the footwear of choice for the thirty-nine suicides of **Heaven's Gate** cultists.

Ordo Templi Orientis

❊

John Whiteside Parsons

A jet-propulsion scientist, Parsons contributed to the design of the **Pentagon** and helped lay the groundwork for the California Institute of Technology's Jet Propulsion Lab. He was also high priest of the Riverside, California, lodge of the **Ordo Templi Orientis** and a devotee of occult superstar **Aleister Crowley.** In 1945, Parsons and his occult buddy **L. Ron Hubbard** cooperated on Crowley's sorcerous **Babylon Working** project.

> If a people permit exploitation and regimentation in any name, they deserve their slavery.
>
> —**John Whiteside Parsons,**
> **occultist and buddy of Scientology founder L. Ron Hubbard**

Project Grill Flame

A joint **CIA–U.S. Army** exploration into the possibilities of nonlethal warfare—in this case, psychic remote viewing. Grill Flame recruited **Scientologists,** the **Stanford Research Institute,** and veteran **Mind Control** psychiatrist **Dr. Louis Joylon West** to oversee GIs who experimented with out-of-body experiences, i.e., the grunts and their scientist bosses who were trying to use ESP and other extrasensory means in order to spy on **Communists** and anyone else deemed a threat to national security.

Psychedelic Rangers

♒

Muammar Qaddafi

🏛 ☺

239

Scientology

🦎 〰️ ☉

> So it is that thousands of plots in favor of the established order
> tangle and clash almost everywhere, as the overlap of secret net-
> works and secret issues or activities grows ever more dense
> along with their rapid integration into every sector of economics,
> politics and culture. . . . All these professional conspirators are
> spying on each other without really knowing why. . . . Who is ob-
> serving whom? On whose behalf, apparently? And actually? The
> real influences remain hidden, and the ultimate aims can only be
> seen with great difficulty and almost never understood.
>
> —Guy Debord, *Comments on the Society of the Spectacle*, 1992

The Sovereign Order of the Solar Temple

This **Masonic**-style **Templar**-esque late-twentieth-century cult,
led by Grand Master Luc Jouret (a Belgian **New Age**y homeopathic
doctor) and Joseph di Mambro (a wealthy businessman), proclaimed themselves Knights of **Christ** and earned their earthly
wages laundering funds through the infamous **BCCI**. Their ritual
murder-suicides of 1994 to 1997, in which seventy-four temple
members, including Jouret and di Mambro, were found dead (most
burned) in Switzerland, Canada, and the French Alps, were meant
to transport sect members to a new life on the star Sirius.

Tavistock Institute

〜 ▦ 🌐

Temple of Set

A **Satanic** religious group founded in 1975 by **U.S. Army** psychological operative and occult enthusiast Michael Aquino, after he had
a falling-out with Anton LaVey and his **Church of Satan.** The temple revolves around Set, the dark Egyptian deity. LaVey's daughter is
now a member of Set, and Aquino has twice been investigated by
authorities in relation to a 1987 child-molestation scandal at the
U.S. Army's former base at the Presidio in San Francisco, though
he was never charged.

☉

★ † ♟ **Unification Church**

† ⛪ † **World Anti-Communist League**

🦀 **World Vision**

† ⛪ **Yakuza**

241

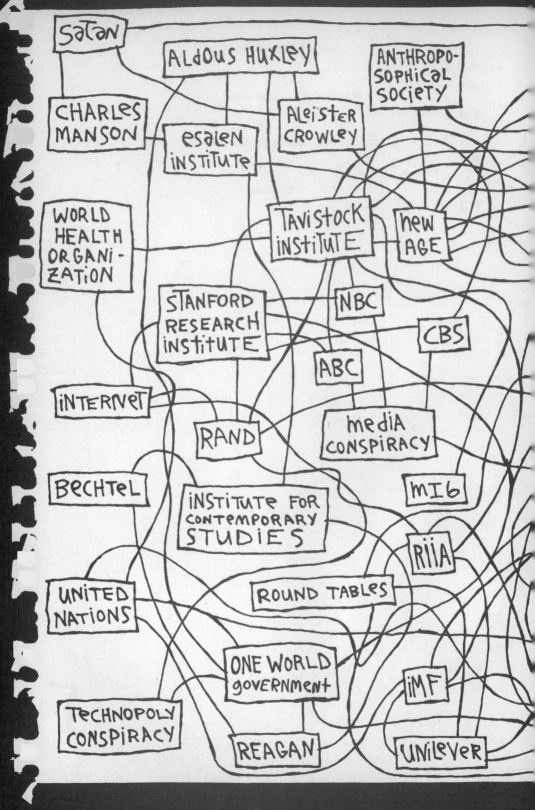

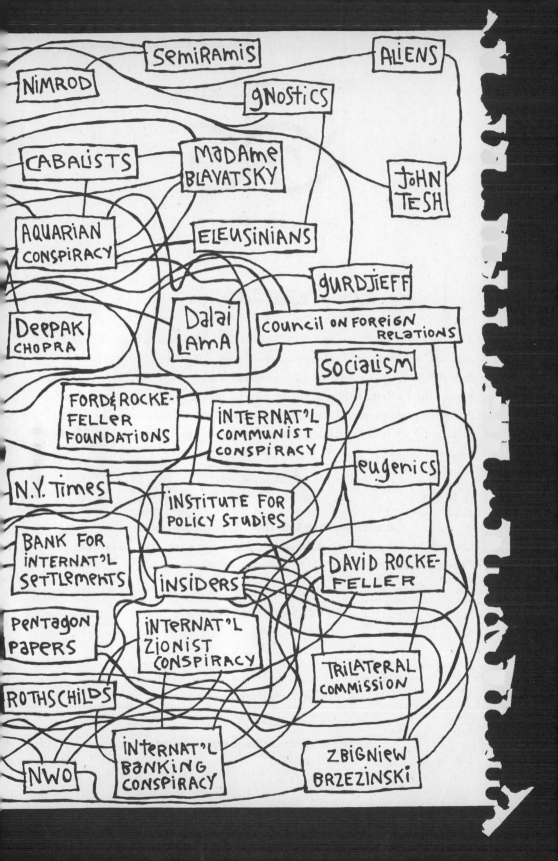

Conspiracy

The rise of the New Age (the so-called approach of an Aquarian Age of enlightenment) seems to have coincided with the New Age—friendly growth of various institutes and think tanks, like Tavistock and Esalen. Or is it all merely so much media-driven drivel? Another massive distraction dreamed up by the Insiders to keep our minds off what truly matters, i.e., paying closer attention to what's *really* going on?

Aliens

♍ ✖ ❋ ⸸ ☉

American Broadcasting Corporation (ABC)

Owned by **Disney/Cap Cities,** this TV network is a co-owner of **Voter News Service.**

▩

Anthroposophical Society

✡

Aquarian Conspiracy

♍

Bank for International Settlements

⸸ ★ ⛰ ⊕

Bechtel

This San Francisco–based **Transnational** superpower chemical corporation specializes in the construction and engineering of chemical and nuclear-plant start-ups. It also protects and designs nuclear, petrochemical, and aviation facilities, from the Alaska Pipeline, Hoover Dam, and San Francisco's underground-railway BART system to the Britain-to-France Chunnel and a nuclear-storage complex in Russia. During the mid-1980s, Bechtel developed a lucrative business association with **Saddam Hussein,** supplying his military machine with plenty of **Biochemical Warfare** "dual-use" technology (dual use meaning not the big, big stuff—tanks, airplanes, missiles—but the little things in war—ammunition, spare parts, defense electronics—that are used to build all those bigger goodies). Just prior to the **Gulf War,** Bechtel teamed up with the foreign chemical giant ASEA Brown-Boveri to construct a billion-dollar chemical plant outside Baghdad. The plant, known as Petrochemical Complex II, needed only a wee bit of tweaking from the Iraqis and—voilà!—they soon had themselves a mustard gas—

Romans 3:300

The Club of Rome: A subversive cabal of "future planners" from all over (Switzerland, Japan, the United States, etc.), assembled in 1968 and founded by Aurelio Peccei for the purpose of creating a **One World Government**—a union of Anglo-American insiders and the old nobility of western Europe.

The 300 Club: In 1909, Germany's Jewish foreign minister, Walther Rathenau, let slip that "300 men, all of whom know each other, guide the economic destinies of the Continent." Similarly, former Egyptian president Gamal Abdel Nasser claimed that "300 Zionists, each of whom knows all the others, govern the fate of the European continent." Both statements are taken as proof by some that an actual evil world-controlling 300 Club exists.

The Committee of 300: This ultra-elite group (who also call themselves the Olympians), styled after the **Illuminati,** the mystery cults, and the Cathars, now operate via the **Tavistock Institute, NATO,** the **Bilderbergers,** and the Club of Rome. The committee seeks a welfare planet subservient to its control.

producing factory. An **Institute of Contemporary Studies** bene-factor, ICS member, and **Reagan**'s former secretary of state, George Shultz was once Bechtel's president, and another ICS member and Reagan's former secretary of defense, Caspar Weinberger, served as Bechtel's general counsel. No doubt the presence of Shultz and Weinberger did no amount of harm in helping secure Bechtel's early 1980s sale of AWAC planes to Saudi Arabia. ☺

Madame Helena Blavatsky

✡ ⚔ ᘒ

Zbigniew Brzezinski

✍ ☺ 🌐

Cabalists

✖ ✡

Deepak Chopra

ᘒ

Columbia Broadcasting System (CBS)

The network-TV subsidiary of **Westinghouse** and yet another employer of **Henry Kissinger,** CBS is co-owner of the **Voter News Service** (the company responsible for counting the votes during each presidential election). CBS's pioneering president, William Paley, eagerly cooperated with the **CIA** and its **Mighty Wurlitzer** propaganda machine. ▦

> Our job is to give people not what they want, but what we decide they ought to have.
>
> **—Richard Salant, former president of CBS News**

Council on Foreign Relations

♍ ✍ ☺ 🌐

Aleister Crowley

♒ ᘒ

Dalai Lama

♱ ✝ ⮔ ☉

Eleusinians

✖ ✳ 〰

Esalen Institute

Cultlike California self-improvement retreat for **New Age** yuppies, founded in 1962 by Michael Murphy and Richard Price, with the help of **Aldous Huxley. ICS** head Lawry Chickering is friends with Murphy. A leader in the "human potential movement," Esalen encouraged meditation combined with self-motivation. **Charles Manson** visited the institute days before the Tate-LaBianca murders, and Robert DeGrimston, founder of the Process, is rumored to have lectured there.

Eugenics

✡ ♱ ✧

Ford and Rockefeller Foundations

✍ ▨ ⊕

Gnostics

♍ ✖ ♱

G. I. Gurdjieff

By day a mild-mannered fashion designer and traveling carpet salesman but since boyhood a freak for the occult—as evidenced by his teenage initiation into the Community of Truth Seekers, a group who believed that in the world's beginning there'd been but a single world religion. Gurdjieff spent ten years in Tibet as the young **Dalai Lama**'s tutor and his schools of today espouse a **New Age**y self-awareness through intense de- and reconditioning. Joseph Stalin, future totalitarian dictator of the USSR, was another student of Gurdjieff's. Gurdjieff inspired the quasi-Reichian Bhagwan Shree Rajneesh cultists of Oregon.

Aldous Huxley

✍ 🐦 〰

247

Insiders

✍ △ ⊕

Institute for Policy Studies (IPS)

Founded by James Warburg and funded by the **Rothschild** dynasty, the IPS was incorporated in 1963 by two **Tavistock Institute** graduates and its objective, some say, was simple: Create a New Left movement in the United States (fueled by British **Socialist** and **Eugenics** enthusiast Bertrand Russell). The IPS backed such diverse and seemingly anti-Establishment groups as the Black Panthers, the Weathermen, and the **Pentagon Papers** whistle-blower Daniel Ellsberg. ∾

Institute of Contemporary Studies (ICS)

This San Francisco—based neoconservative think tank was founded in 1972 by **Reagan** cronies Edwin Meese, Caspar Weinberger, and H. Monroe Browne. ICS propaganda includes a study of expansions in entitlement programs and their "dragging" impact on the economy and a book on the many forms of Communist coercion. Lawry Chickering, a sixties radical turned neoconservative, is now the tank's director and he pals around with **Esalen** founder Michael Murphy.

International Banking Conspiracy

♍ ✖ ✿ ★ ✍ ⩗ ⌫ ⌇ ⚲ ⊕

International Communist Conspiracy

♍ ❋ ✡ ✍ △ ☺ ✿

International Monetary Fund

★ ⊕

International Zionist Conspiracy

♍ ✖ ❋ ✿ ✍ ▩ ⊕

Internet

⌇ ✿ ☉

Charles Manson

🐾 ⌇

Media Conspiracy

♍ ✿ ⩗ △ ✿

MI6

✡ ⌫ ▩

National Broadcasting Company (NBC)

Founded in 1926 by David Sarnoff as a division of the **Radio Corporation of America**, NBC is now owned by the **Military-Industrial Complex** giant, **General Electric**, and home to **Council on Foreign Relations** member and mush-mouthed *Nightly News* anchorman Tom Brokaw.

New Age

☞ ☉

New World Order

♍ ✳ ✍ ☺ ⊕

The New York Times

New York City's most powerful daily newspaper, the *Times* was started by Jews and its late publisher Arthur Hayes Sulzberger knowingly employed many a **CIA** spook, most of whom worked with the Agency's **Mighty Wurlitzer** propaganda machine.
✺

Nimrod

✖ ✳ ✧

One World Government

♍ ✧ ✍ ⊕

The Pentagon Papers

▱

RAND

✍ △ ✿ ☉

Ronald Reagan

🐾 ⚬ ☺ ✺

David Rockefeller

✍ ⊕

The Rothschilds

♍ ✧ ★ ✍

The Round Tables

In 1891, **Cecil Rhodes** and Alfred, Lord Milner created these **Illuminati**-inspired secret society "think tanks" as a means for British movers and shakers (hoity-toity colonialists and merchant barons from business, royalty, and the government) to promote the financial, cultural, and sociopolitical interests of the English-speaking world. These hidden advisors, sometimes referred to as the Oxford Group or the Cliveden Set, were funded by Rhodes and fellow **Insiders** and **International Bankers** like the **House of Morgan,** the **Rockefellers,** and the **Rothschilds** and were the forerunners to the **RIIA** and the **CFR.** Its members were supposedly chosen based on the principles of the secretive Scottish Rite **Freemasons** and have included George Bernard Shaw and **Hitler**'s finance minister Hjalmar Schacht.

Royal Institute of International Affairs

✍

Satan

♍ ✖

Semiramis

✖

Socialism

✳ ✡ ✍

Stanford Research Institute (SRI)

Founded in 1946 and said by some conspiranoiacs to be yet another **Tavistock Institute** creation, this Silicon Valley think tank has been an enthusiastic research partner in the field of **Mind Control,** at times joining with the **CIA** (for its **MK-ULTRA LSD** project) and the **U.S. Army** (for its **Project Grill Flame** psychic remote viewing out-of-body perception projects—experiments that relied, to a great extent, on the participation of higher-level members of **Scientology**). In the 1950s, the company helped Walt **Disney** decide on Anaheim as his Disneyland site. SRI worked with the U.S. Army on ARPAnet (on what eventually became the **Internet**) and has also been hard at work on **Biochemical Warfare** analysis and in the "future sciences" and on developing methods for best realizing a **One World Government** and a **New World Order** (as evidenced by its legendary 1974 technical paper that a few conspiranoiacs claim served as the basis for Marilyn Ferguson's 1980 **New Age** tome *The*

Aquarian Conspiracy). Other conspiranoiacs claim that SRI orchestrated the plague of recent gang wars as a way to shock society and cause waves of social upheaval, which would then require more policing of all citizens. SRI has provided studies for **Bechtel, Hewlett-Packard,** and **TRW,** among many other **Military-Industrial Complex** corporations. *Men Are from Mars, Women Are from Venus* author John Gray began leading his male-female relationship seminars while working at SRI as a computer programmer.

✿

Tavistock Institute

Technopoly Conspiracy

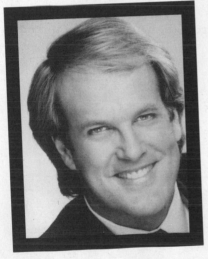

John Tesh

Perpetrator of **New Age** Muzak and the ex-host of *E.T.* (*Entertainment Tonight*). According to folks at the *Globe,* Tesh is actually an **Alien.**

☉

Trilateral Commission

Unilever

Established in 1930, this Dutch-British soap conglomerate has its hands in chemicals, agribusiness, detergents, and many other products, from Lipton and Vaseline to Pepsodent and Q-Tips. One of the top three advertisers in the United States (along with **Procter & Gamble** and Philip Morris), its board of director membership intersects with **Royal Dutch/Shell.** In 1983, Unilever director and **Zionist** Sir Harold Lever met with London's Ditchley Group (an offshoot of the **RIIA** and the **Round Tables**) and hatched the idea that the United States join the **Bank for International Settlements** and that the International Monetary Fund's powers be broadened wide enough to influence U.S.—

251

not just third world—banks. Both steps were later embraced by the **Reagan** administration, moving America one step closer to a **One World Government** under the control of the **UN** and the **Insiders**. ⊕

United Nations

♍ ✿ ✍ ⊕

World Health Organization (WHO)

Between 1966 and 1977, nearly 100 million central Africans (plus 14,000 Haitians working in central Africa and a large number of Brazilians) were injected with a smallpox vaccine in a program sponsored by WHO, leading to the distinct albeit media- and science-establishment-blackballed possibility of a connection— either intentional or unintentional—between the vaccine and the outbreak of HIV and **AIDS.** If it was intentional, it may have been a virus designed for **Biochemical Warfare** purposes; if unintentional, perhaps the vaccine was contaminated by some unknown organism. ✿

Official Memorandum

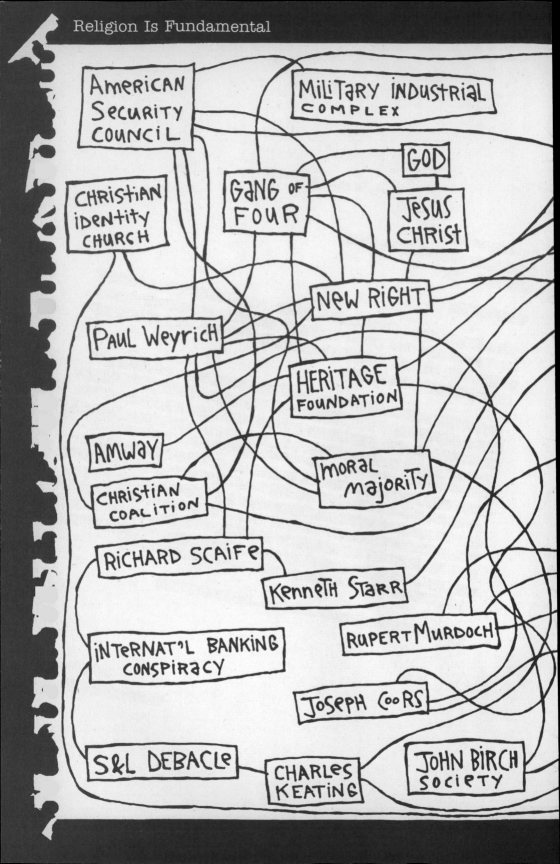

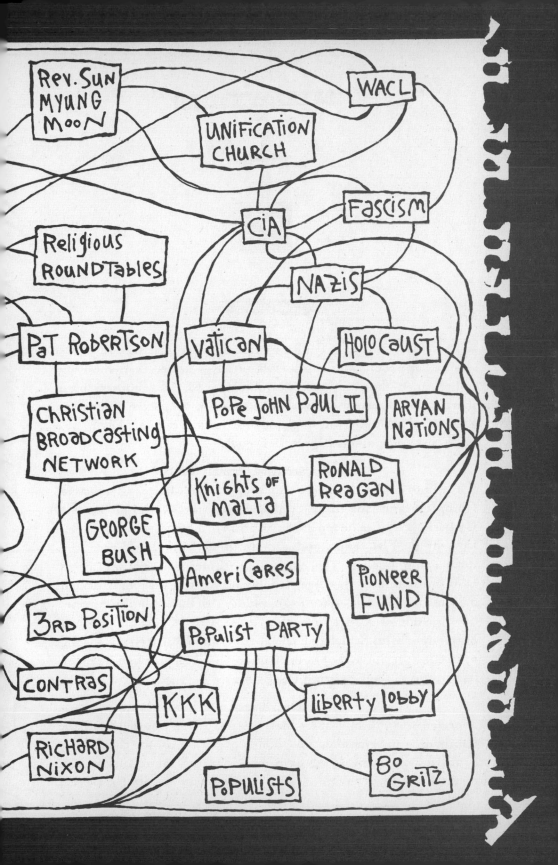

In this case, Religion Is Fundamental and often Fascistic. In RIF, it seems that people who consider themselves holier-than-thou and righter-than-thou naturally gravitate toward one another, often share a certain misguided zeal (like those in the Aryan Nations or Kenneth Starr), and will stop just short of a presidential coup or a Holocaust—or not—to achieve their goals.

American Security Council (ASC)

Sometimes called the heart and soul of the **Military-Industrial Complex** (and not to be confused with the **National Security Council,** a legitimate federal institution), the ASC was founded in 1955 by ex–**FBI** agents and with funding from **Lockheed,** Motorola, and Boeing. The council continues to wage war against **Communism** and **New Age**y secular humanism with an onslaught of films, books, and other propaganda. ASC's half-million members include ex–**CIA** agents, the Conservative Caucus, the **Moral Majority,** Phyllis Schlafly's Eagle Forum, and **Paul Weyrich**'s Committee for the Survival of a Free Congress—all forerunners or member groups of the **Christian Coalition.**

AmeriCares

Founded in 1979 by Robert Macauley, a pal of **George Bush** and family, this international do-gooder organization for third world countries was discovered to have been sneaking "humanitarian aid" to the **Contras** in the mid-1980s, while taking money from other

Contra-friendly companies and groups like **Pat Robertson**'s **Christian Broadcasting Network, Reverend Sun Myung Moon**'s **Unification Church,** and the **Knights of Malta.** Father Bruce Ritter, the former director of New York's Covenant House who resigned amid allegations that he'd sexually molested some of the nonprofit's young male runaways, served as vice president of AmeriCares; **Zbigniew Brzezinski** served as an honorary board chairman; and J. Peter Grace, Jr., chairman of the onetime **Nazi**-friendly W. R. Grace and Co. and himself a Knight of Malta, served as an advisory committee chairman.

Amway

For nearly forty years, this Michigan-based direct-sales distributor (short for American Way Association) has hawked more than four hundred types of home- and personal-care products in over seventy-five countries. Amway also sells Coca-Cola and the Rand McNally Atlas. In 1991, its chief rival, **Procter & Gamble,** won a $75,000 case against Amway for spreading rumors linking P&G to satanism. Five years later P&G again took Amway cofounder Jay Van Andel and his company to court for the exact same transgression (only updated)—P&G said that Amway used its Amvox E-mail system to spread yet more P&G-is-**Satan** rumors (a case later dismissed). Van Andel sits on the board of trustees at the **Heritage Foundation.** Denouncers of homosexuality, godlessness, and affirmative action, these hucksters of "soap and hope" (House majority whip Tom DeLay is a former Amway man) have also fought off (and won) charges of fraud by the Canadian government and a U.S. federal pyramid-scheme investigation.

Aryan Nations

✡

George Bush

〰️ △ ✐ ☞ ☺ ✿ ⊕

Christian Broadcasting Network (CBN)

Still a part of **Pat Robertson**'s media empire, though the network is not as mighty after it sold off the Family Channel to **Rupert Murdoch**'s News Corp. in 1997 for $1.9 billion. Founded in 1960 by televangelist, **Christian Coalition** founder, and failed 1988 Republican presidential candidate Pat Robertson, the CBN is a multimillion-dollar media outlet with an audience of 16 million, reaching 67 million homes. CBN devoted itself to Fundamentalist recruiting and proselytizing, and in the 1980s the network gave the **Knights of Malta** close to $2 million for its Central America operations (ostensibly the Knights were doing charitable humanitarian-aid work down there, carried out by the Knights-friendly folks at **AmeriCares**).

🕱

Christian Identity Church

✡

> Do not let your left hand know what your right hand is doing.
>
> —Matthew 6:3

Christian Coalition

☙

CIA

♍ ★ ⚒ ✝ 🏠 🐗 ♒ △ 🔲 ☙ ☺ 🕱 🌐 ☉

Contras

🔲 ☺

Joseph Coors

A pro-apartheid anti-choice Fundamentalist beer baron, Coors floated the initial $250,000 to get **Paul Weyrich**'s **Heritage Foundation** think tank off the ground. Coors was also a major source of funds for the **Contras**.

Fascism

♍ ❄ ⚜ ✝ 🏠 ☙ ☺

Gang of Four

✝ ☙

God

♍ ✖ ❄ ☉

Bo Gritz

Heritage Foundation

This archconservative D.C. "lobbying group" was funded into existence by Fundamentalist beer baron **Joseph Coors** (who floated $250,000 to get the foundation off the ground) and Catholic New Right organizer **Paul Weyrich**. A haven for overeducated reactionaries like Dinesh D'Souza (author of Jerry Falwell's biography and *Illiberal Education*) and Roger Pearson (a publisher of books claiming the genetic superiority of whites, and who served as a principal organizer of a 1978 anti-Semitic conference of the **World Anti-Communist League**), Heritage floods Congress and the media with its right-wing ideological agenda (which is quite the same as that of the **Trilateralists** and the **Transnationals**). Devout Fundamentalist and **Amway** cofounder Jay Van Andel also sits on its board of trustees, and other board members include rabid **Clinton** hater **Richard Scaife** and George **Bush**'s son Jeb.

Holocaust

✡ ✝ ★ ✧

International Banking Conspiracy

♏ ✖ ✡ ★ ✍ 〰 ∅ ☞ 〜 ⊕

Jesus Christ

♏ ✖ ❋ ☞ ☉

John Birch Society

△

Charles Keating

Smug Fundamentalist crook whose mismanagement as head of San Diego's thrift, Lincoln Savings & Loan, led to the **Savings & Loan Debacle**. A **Moral Majoritarian** and avid antiporn crusader (he amassed a huge portfolio of porn, argued for the people in the case of

259

The People v. Larry Flynt, and was **Nixon**'s appointee to the Federal Commission on Obscenity and Pornography), in 1991 Keating was sent to prison on charges of fraud, racketeering, and conspiracy (though the latter two charges were later reversed).

Knights of Malta

✖ ♨ ☺

Ku Klux Klan

✳ △

Liberty Lobby

△

Military-Industrial Complex

♍ ★ ✝ △ ☺ ✿ ▨

Reverend Sun Myung Moon

✝ ♨ ↝ ▨

Moral Majority

Jerry Falwell's Fundamentalist sect, which was instrumental in the 1980 election of **Reagan** as president and guided into being by **New Right Religious Round Table** reactionaries like **Paul Weyrich** and Richard Viguerie.

Rupert Murdoch

Australian-now-American media despot and panderer to the lowest common denominator, Murdoch owns the News Corporation, which owns (or has owned) HarperCollins, *The Times* of London, *The National Enquirer,* New York Knicks, Fox TV, *New York* magazine, Sky TV, and the 20th-Century Fox film corporation. Ted Turner once referred to him as "that **Nazi**." Murdoch recently absorbed Fundamentalist televangelist **Pat Robertson**'s Family Channel network into his antifamily empire (of Fox TV's unending series of *World's Scariest Car Chases, Murders, Animals Attacks, Disasters,* etc.), a purchase that only seems like an unlikely marriage. In 1997, Murdoch joined the board of the Cato Institute, the libertarian think tank that claims global warming is a figment of our imagination. In 1998, **Pope John Paul II** bestowed a papal knighthood on Murdoch, who is only the third non-Catholic to be inducted into the **Vatican**'s pontifical order (the others were Bob Hope and Walt **Disney**'s brother, Roy). In that same year, his longtime friend and advisor, the bald ex-felon Michael Milken, reportedly brokered his purchase of the L.A. Dodgers, and earlier that year Murdoch also laid out a whopping $1 billion bid for England's premier soccer club, Manchester United. ▩

Nazis

♍ ★ ✝ ⛰ 👣 ☼

New Right

👓 ▩

Richard Nixon

✝ ⛰ △ ▱ ☺ ☼

Pioneer Fund

⚑ ✝

Pope John Paul II

★ ☼

> The media lies and lies for money. The government lies and lies for power.
>
> —**U.S. bumper sticker**

Populist Party

Willis Carto's 1980s neo-Nativist racialist hodgepodge of **Klansmen, Christian Identity** freaks, Militia enthusiasts, and other bigoted anarchists who hate paying taxes, hate the feds, and hate all nonwhites. Its 1992 presidential candidate was ex–Green Beret and Almost Heaven founder **Bo Gritz.**

Conspiranoia! TV

The X-Files, The Prisoner, Lazarus, Nowhere Man, The Pretender, Dark Skies, V, Millennium, Twin Peaks, The Night Stalker, In Search of . . .

Populists

U.S. political party formed in 1891, primarily to represent agrarian interests and advocate the free coinage of silver and government control of monopolies. Venerable historian Richard Hofstadter blames the Populists for having laid the foundation for today's conspiracy theories—which are most often sympathetic toward white American-born Protestant farmers and laborers. The Populists spread the notion that the little guys were getting screwed over by Wall Street's **International Bankers** and their tight-fisted lending policies.

Ronald Reagan

🐾 ∾ ☺ ▦

Religious Round Tables

Taking a page from **Cecil Rhodes** and his **Insiders' Round Table** societies, in 1979 the **New Right** formed their own informal cabal of Fundamentalist activists who were "dedicated to the moral rebirth of America." Howard Phillips, Jesse Helms, and **Paul Weyrich** set up a series of seminars aimed at politicizing Fundamentalist preachers—a fusion of **God** and politics.

Marion "Pat" Robertson

In 1997, this Fundamentalist televangelist and 1988 presidential wanna-be sold his Family Channel cable station (part of Robertson's **Christian Broadcasting Network**) to News Corp.'s antifamily media tycoon **Rupert Murdoch** for $1.9 billion. Robertson founded the **Christian Coalition** in 1988 and still hosts *The 700 Club* on TV. In Pat's own words, "in America today, the people who have come into [our] institutions are primarily termites. They are into destroying institutions that have been built by Christians. . . . The termites are in charge now, and that is not the way it ought to be. The time has come for a godly fumigation."

Savings & Loan Debacle

✐

Richard Mellon Scaife

Spoiled Pittsburgh heir to the **Mellon** fortune (other notorious Mellon relatives being **Harry Anslinger** and **William Mellon**

Hitchcock). To say he hates **Clinton** would be a gross understatement. A recovered drunk prone to temper tantrums, Scaife has poured his money into anti-Clinton groups and projects such as Fundamentalist **Paul Weyrich**'s Free Congress Research and Education Foundation, the archconservative Accuracy in Media group, the Landmark Legal Foundation (who advised Paula Jones and whose lawyers now represent Monica Lewinsky tape-betrayor Linda Tripp), and Pepperdine University, where "life regent" Scaife founded the School of Public Policy and a chair awaits for independent counsel **Kenneth Starr** as the school's first dean.

Kenneth Starr

Hardly the "independent" counsel his title suggests, prosecutor Starr, who managed to have President **Bill Clinton** impeached but not thrown out of office, has plenty of Fundamentalist supporters and schmoozes only, it seems, with people out to nail Clinton. He's a member of the Federalist Society of right-wing jurists; he's lectured at **Pat Robertson**'s Regent University; and he's pals with publisher Alfred Regnery, whose book company favors anything salaciously damning regarding Bubba. Starr also has a dean's seat waiting for him at Pepperdine University—courtesy of Clinton hater **Richard Scaife,** who also threw money at the Landmark Legal Foundation, which initially gave advice to Paula Jones and with whom Starr had once worked and where Starr's fellow federalist lawyer James Moody also worked (Moody, it turns out, represented Monica Lewinsky's confessor, Linda Tripp).

The Third Position

The theory that right-wing and left-wing, Republican and Democrat, **Fascist** and radical, Jew and Christian are indistinguishable and are colluding, conspiring, and cooperating against the rest of us—as proof, one need look no further than **Rupert Murdoch**'s recent purchase of **Pat Robertson**'s Family Channel, or that the anti-Establishment Black Panthers received funding from the seemingly pro-Establishment **Ford Foundation,** or that the . . .
⌖

Unification Church

★ ✝ ∞

Vatican

♍ ✖ ✳ ♌ ⛰ ☺ ☉

Paul Weyrich

One of the **Gang of Four** who founded the Fundamentalist **New Right,** a cofounder of the **Heritage Foundation,** and later the founder of the Free Congress Research and Education Foundation, which received $720,000 from **Clinton**-hater **Richard Scaife** in 1995. A bit of a hatemonger himself, Weyrich was an associate of the **John Birch Society** and used to write a column for one of its weekly publications, *Review of the News.*

World Anti-Communist League

✝ ⛰ ↪

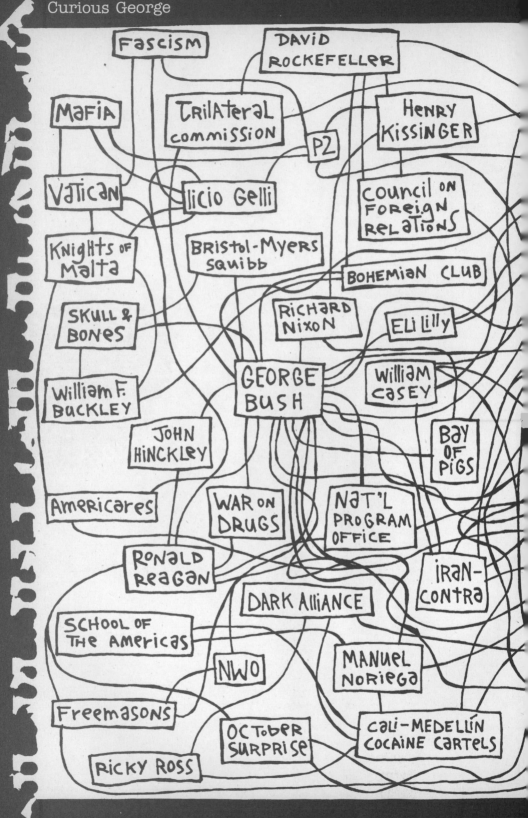

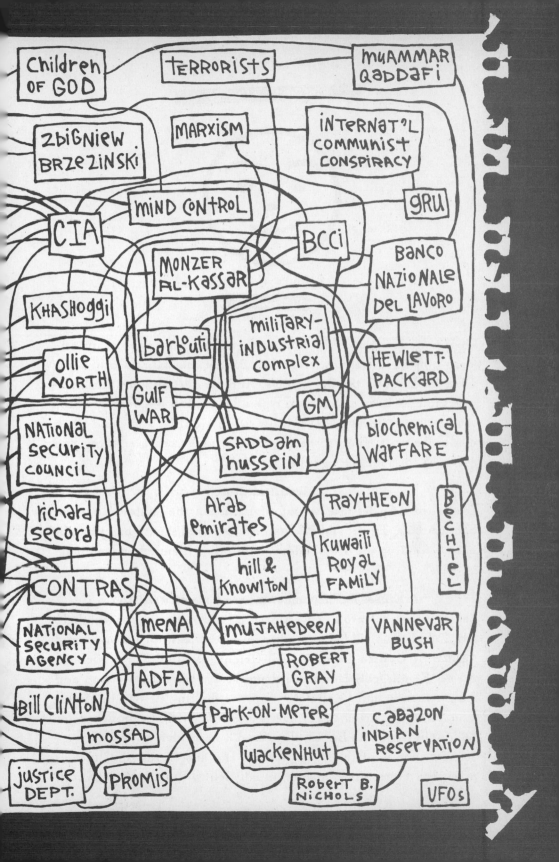

Conspiracy

George Bush reigns as the éminence grise of conspiranoia, insinuating himself into almost every dark corner, be it Iran-Contra, the CIA, Eli Lilly, or the Bay of Pigs. And no dilettante he, Bush appears to have been a hands-on type of conspirator—contrary to the media's never-investigated refrain of what did he know and when did he know it. Indeed, he seems to have known everything and everyone for a long, long time.

Arab Emirates

Fearful of a Soviet takeover of Afghanistan, the Arab emirates of Saudi Arabia, Egypt, and Pakistan orchestrated the Afghan jihad by naïvely funding the **Mujahedeen** (and other Islamic Fundamentalist sects).

Arkansas Development Finance Authority (ADFA)

Set up during **Clinton**'s governorship (and at his urging) with help from Webb Hubbell (who received an ADFA loan for his work) and headed by **Contra**-friendly FOB (friend of Bill's) Larry Nichols, the ADFA allegedly laundered drugs and money that went to and from Arkansas and Central America via the tiny airstrip in **Mena**. The ADFA was a client of Hillary's law firm. Nichols, though, later fell out of favor with Bubba, then sued him for defamation of character, and out of that lawsuit came the allegations of Clinton's marital indiscretions, which eventually led to Paula Jones's lawsuit, which led to **Kenneth Starr,** which led to Monica Lewinsky, which led to Clinton's impeachment.

Banco Nazionale del Lavoro (BNL)

Up until the early 1990s, this Italian commercial bank with an Atlanta, Georgia, branch helped funnel huge loans to Iraq, enabling **Saddam Hussein** to import products essential to his war machine, products that came from clients like those of BNL's international advisory board member **Henry Kissinger**'s company, Kissinger Associates, **General Motors,** and **Hewlett-Packard.** At one point, BNL's management was infiltrated by arms-dealing **Fascist Licio Gelli**'s **Masonic P2** lodge.

Bank of Credit and Commerce International

✏ ᔆᵇ

Ihsan Barbouti

Saddam Hussein's main arms dealer and chief secret-projects coordinator, Barbouti owned two companies in the United States and one in Germany. He designed **Muammar Qaddafi**'s chemical-weapons plant in Rabat, Libya, and brokered various **CIA**-Hussein and U.S. **Military-Industrial Complex** arms deals involving Hussein, such as the funneling of "agricultural loan guarantees" (actually **Biochemical Warfare** weapons) to Hussein from the U.S. Department of Agriculture. Barbouti often dealt with and ran arms for **Richard Secord** (the former CIA **Air America** pilot and Iraqgate figure affiliated with **Oliver North**) under the auspices of **Wackenhut Securities.**

Bay of Pigs

△

Bechtel

∞

Biochemical Warfare

The development of deadly compounds, viruses, and gases (like sarin, mustard gas, botulism, and ebola) involving the **Pentagon,** the **CIA,** and pharmaceutical companies and universities. During **WWII,** Japan's Manchuria-based **Unit 731** performed biological warfare experiments on POWs, and from 1953 to 1968 the **National Cancer Institute** contracted **UC-Berkeley** for various forms of biochemical warfare research. In 1969, **Nixon** officially put an end (maybe) to such U.S. research, but in Russia the **Biopreparat,** now privatized, carries on the bio-chemical warfare research and development that it had been set up to do under the old Soviet regime (and the **KGB**).

✧

Bohemian Club

✖ ⛰ 〰

Bristol-Myers Squibb

America's worldwide pusher of synthetic drugs, baby formula, beauty products, and household cleaners, from Bufferin and Excedrin to Clairol, Drano, and Enfamil infant formula, which has earned B-MS the enmity of many a mom: Boycotted for the way it's pushed its baby formula on poor mothers, in 1998 Bristol-Myers settled a class-action lawsuit (with two other companies) after being accused of price-fixing their Enfamil formula (though they were not found guilty). During **WWII,** Bristol-Myers supplied penicillin and morphine to the troops. In the 1990s, the company developed the AIDS drug DDI, one of the **AIDS** cocktails. CEO Richard Gelb and his brother, company president Bruce Gelb, are both staunch Republicans and close friends of **George Bush**'s. Bruce left Bristol-Myers in 1989 to head the U.S. Information Agency and later served as ambassador to Belgium during the Bush administration. The Gelbs' parents founded Clairol, and both boys attended the exclusive Phillips Academy with Bush and later Yale as well (where Bush and Richard graduated in the same class, 1948—leading to the likelihood that Dick Gelb was a member of the **Skull & Bones** secret society).

✧

Zbigniew Brzezinski

✍ ❀ ⊕

William F. Buckley

The "patron saint of conservatives," this ultraconservative Sunday gasbag (as Calvin Trillin has so named D.C.'s TV pundits) and Yale grad is a **Skull & Bones** member, as well as a **Knight of Malta.**

Buckley also willingly participated in the **CIA**'s **Mighty Wurlitzer** propaganda campaign.

▨

George Bush

〰️ △ ▱ ↷ ⚲ ✿ ⊕

Vannevar Bush

Cofounder of **Raytheon** and organizer of the **Manhattan Project,** Bush (1890–1974) conceived the National Science Foundation and the **Pentagon**'s ARPAnet project and has been hailed by many as "the godfather of the information age." His 1945 *Atlantic Monthly* essay, "As We May Think," sowed the seeds for what eventually became the World Wide Web. During **WWII,** Bush designed code-breaking machines for the supersecret project that later evolved into the **National Security Agency.**

✿

Cabazon Indian Reservation

Deemed a separate nation by the U.S. government and therefore one that does not come under the jurisdiction of federal regulations or firearms laws. According to convicted drug felon Michael Riconosciuto, one of Octopus journalist Danny Casolaro's main informants, this patch of California desert has been the site of covert antigravitation experiments and the manufacturing of fuel-air explosives, poison gases, and other **Biochemical Warfare** weapons. A client of **Wackenhut Securities,** Cabazon and Wackenhut jointly operated a front company, the Meridian Arms Corporation. UFOs have often been sighted near the reservation, and Cabazon's and Wackenhut's matériel was intended to be exported to the **Contras.**

⊙

Cali-Medellín Cocaine Cartels

▱

William Casey

★ ♨ ▱ ▨

271

Children of God

↷

Bill Clinton

△ ✎ ⊕

Contras

✎ ⌖

Council on Foreign Relations

♍ ✐ ∾ ⊕

The Dark Alliance

✎

Accidents? Suicides?

On September 14, 1982, Alfred Hitchcock's favorite leading lady, the former Hollywood movie star Princess Grace Kelly of Monaco, died in a car "accident." Some conspiranoiacs claim that her husband, Prince Rainier, got greedy and began skimming a little too much money off the top of all the **Golden Triangle**-to-Europe heroin money flowing through the open Corsican-**Mafia**-friendly borders of his little principality—so the **P2** lodge ordered the hit on the prince's wife (despite her having been accepted into the **Knights of Malta** shortly before her death).

River Phoenix, child member of the **Children of God** cult. In a 1991 interview in *Details,* Phoenix hinted at the group's pedophilic tendencies, admitting that he'd had intercourse at age four and was having sex regularly with other Children of God kids at ten—statements that ran counter to the policy of the Children's leader, David Berg, of not talking to the media. Two years later, on the night of the Argentinian raid on a Children of God compound, Phoenix, at Johnny Depp's Viper Club, died within minutes of a poisonous drug overdose—perhaps silenced, some conspiranoiacs speculate, by Berg for having hinted at his cult's child-prostitution activities.

Pope John Paul I, the former patriarch of Venice who took to the papacy in 1978, only to die thirty-three days later of a reported heart attack. In actuality, the Smiling Pope, as the media had dubbed him, was probably poisoned (though it's impossible to confirm, since no autopsy was performed). Worse than the fact that he advocated birth control and took a softer line on abortion, divorce, and homo-

Eli Lilly & Co.

♈ ♒ ☉

Fascism

♍ ✳ ⚔ ✝ ⛪ ☙ ⚱

Freemasons

♍ ✳ ✡ ⚔ △

Licio Gelli

⛪ ▨

sexuality was that JPI wanted to scale down the **Vatican**'s vast financial holdings and expose his fellow clergymen's long-standing ties to the **P2** lodge and the **Mafia** and to assorted Italian **Freemasons**—all of which made him plenty of enemies fast.

Freelance journalist Danny Casolaro was on the verge of a breakthrough in his investigation into the "Octopus" of **Iran-Contra** when, after meeting with an ex-**CIA** spook and **Bush Justice Department** official on August 10, 1991, he was found dead the next morning in the bathtub of his Martinsburg, West Virginia, hotel room. Never found were his notes, his manuscript, or a suicide note.

In July 1993, **Clinton** counsel and Whitewater financial advisor Vince Foster, the alleged liaison for **Mena-Contra** drugs-and-guns smuggling operations of the 1980s, was found shot to death in a park outside D.C. The death was ruled a suicide, a fact bitterly disputed by Clinton-hater **Richard Scaife**.

On April 3, 1996, the T-43 airplane carrying **Bill Clinton**'s commerce secretary Ron Brown and thirty-four others crashed over Croatia during a trade mission. But according to Richard Scaife–funded muckrakers, Brown was killed by a bullet to the head—well before the plane itself crashed. (Brown, a longtime FOB and the former head of the Democratic National Committee, was about to be indicted for alleged improper fund-raising tactics and had too much insider dirt on the president and was too much of a potential liability to let live—what with the 1996 presidential campaign heating up.)

General Motors (GM)

U.S. auto industry leader, number one in cars and trucks (Buick, Cadillac, Saturn, and Chevy) and the world's largest industrial corporation. GM solidified its position in the defense industry with its acquisition of **Howard Hughes**'s Hughes Electronic Corporation. A major member of the **Military-Industrial Complex**, GM was one of **Henry Kissinger**'s clients when he ran his own company, Kissinger Associates.

Robert Keith Gray

Chairman and CEO of D.C.'s ultrapowerful **Hill & Knowlton** public-relations firm, this native Nebraskan cofounded the controversial George Town Club (infamous as a site of the late 1970s

Trifecta World

The **Freemasons** have a three-step method on how to attain world domination and bring about the **New World Order:** 1) ritual sacrifices—murdering innocent victims using ancient patterns and techniques. Jack the Ripper, for instance, murdered in a manner almost identical to that of the killers who cut up Hiram Abiff, King Solomon's master Mason and temple builder. The **Manson** Family murder of Sharon Tate recalls a Masonic ritual of appeasing the moon goddess. And David "Son of Sam" Berkowitz's 1978 shootings were highly ritualized, as are most of today's serial killers (which doesn't necessarily make all serial killers Freemasons, just Masonic in style and so, perhaps, influenced by the ancient craft. 2) destruction of the imperfect world and the creation of a perfect New World Order (or, as it says on the U.S. seal, Novus Ordo Seclorum, the "Dawn of a New Age"), which was partly accomplished with the atomic bomb, first tested at the trinity site which is located on the 33rd degree of latitude—there are 33 degrees of Freemasonry; **Christ** died at age 33, et cetera. 3) the Killing of the King, achieved in 1963 with the assassination of **John F. Kennedy** (head of Camelot), killed in Dallas, which is also located at 33 degrees latitude and along the Trinity River and near a triple underpass. In 1977, Elvis Presley, the King, died in Memphis, Tennessee—nine years (3×3) after the assassination of **Martin Luther King, Jr.,** in the same city.

Koreagate scandal in which South Korean businessman Tong Sun Park bribed various U.S. congressmen). Outed in Susan Trento's 1992 book, *The Power House*, since the mid-1980s Gray has been dogged by conspiranoiac allegations that link him to **CIA** spook **Ed Wilson.** (One of Wilson's former business partners later claimed that he, Wilson, and Gray had "directed sexual blackmail operations" out of the George Town Club, though no one has been able to prove any of these charges.)

GRU

The former Soviet Union's military intelligence unit. During the 1980s, the GRU was part of the **Bush-North Iran-Contra** effort to illegally provide weapons to Iran (against Iraq) and the **Contras** (against the Sandinistas). But the GRU, through their witting double agent **Monzer Al-Kassar** and the unwitting **CIA** agents **Richard Secord** and **John Singlaub,** got rich off all the money Bush and North were throwing around. Ironically, the GRU made enough swag off these sales alone to provide even more and better arms to their Sandinista compadres (loading up on Western weapons—doubly ironic), as well as to the IRA, the hard-line Basque **Terrorists** of Spain, and the Japanese Red Army.

> If just 10 percent of what the so-called crazies were saying was true, I was working for an evil agency.
>
> —**Secretary of Energy Hazel O'Leary, 1993**

Gulf War

George Bush's 1991 invasion of the Middle East, a war whose ostensible purpose was to retaliate against **Saddam Hussein**'s 1990 invasion of Kuwait and drive his troops out but played out more like the slaughter of tens of thousands as video game. The war was partly the result of a P.R. blitz orchestrated by the Kuwaiti royals and their D.C. lobbyists, **Hill & Knowlton. Military-Industrial Complex** conspirator **Raytheon** shot to fame during the Gulf War for its smart piece of weaponry, the SCUD-busting Patriot missile. Another component of the American victory may have been the **PROMIS** software used by the Iraqis.

Hewlett-Packard

A top-ten PC maker and a **Military-Industrial Complex** giant. HP exploited the U.S. "dual-use" clause (which was legal) in order to circumvent the 1980s embargo on Iraq and supply **Saddam Hussein** with auxiliary and secondary weapons.

Hill & Knowlton

Known as the Beltway's top spin doctors for political candidates and other clients (such as the tobacco industry, **Du Pont,** and **IBM**), H&K is the world's largest public-relations and lobbying firm. In 1989, the firm was hired by Covenant House to work damage control for the New York City safe house after its director, Father Bruce Ritter, allegedly molested several of Covenant's young boys—no surprise, in a way, given that some conspiranoiacs accuse H&K's homosexual CEO, **Robert Keith Gray,** of having once been involved in a 1980s **CIA** operation that used male call boys and drugs as a way to lobby congressmen (though such allegations have never been proven). Former National Public Radio president, **Peace Corps** regional director, and staunch anti-Communist liberal Frank Mankiewicz (who was also a onetime Hollywood producer and is the son of *Citizen Kane* screenwriter Herman Mankiewicz, and a

French Twist

In a move that's pissed off many an academic (and military buff) and an action that's only added to his reputation as a bit of an outlandish (if fey) intellectual kook, French postmodern theorist Jean Baudrillard went so far as to write a whole book declaring that (much like those who say we never landed on the moon) . . . *The Gulf War Did Not Take Place.* Part of his argument has to do with what he persuasively calls "the hyperrealist logic of the deterrence of the real," meaning (one thinks) that if it's live on CNN it's basically metaphorical—i.e., it *ain't really* happening, and therefore, the world being on a "delusional course" anyway, Baudrillard wrote elsewhere, "we must adopt a delusional standpoint towards the world."

buddy of conspiranoiac filmmaker Oliver Stone) oversaw H&K's Citizens for a Free Kuwait propaganda campaign that led to the **Gulf War.**

Paranoids have all the facts.

—Oliver Stone, *The New York Times* (1992)

John Hinckley, Jr.

Saddam Hussein

The Iraqi dictator who built up his army for a war against Iran, with the help of the **CIA, Henry Kissinger,** and the U.S. **Military-Industrial Complex.** Later, Hussein used these very same American-made weapons and know-how in the **Gulf War.**

International Communist Conspiracy

Iran-Contra Affair

The notorious late 1980s scandal that tarnished President **Reagan**'s political image (and legacy). In 1986, Reagan was forced to confirm reports that the United States had illegally sold weapons to Iran in exchange for the release of the American hostages being held in Lebanon. The profits from these sales had been channeled to the **Contra** rebels, the **CIA**-backed "freedom fighters" who were battling Nicaragua's left-wing government. The Iran-Contra operation was a joint CIA–**National Security Council** venture, in which both CIA director **William Casey** and NSC staffer **Oliver North** played parts. (North orchestrated the logistics of the deal.) Members of the CIA–defense industry cabal known as the **Secret Team** were also involved, including **Richard Secord,** Ted Shackley, Ed Wilson, Iranian-born arms dealer Al Hakim, **John Singlaub,** and Casey himself. As vice president, **George Bush** reportedly promoted the Iran-Contra drugs-for-arms deal.

277

Justice Department

△

Monzer Al-Kassar

A freelance Syrian drug smuggler and **CIA** arms dealer, Al-Kassar served as **Richard Secord**'s gunrunner to the **Contras.** The lover of Syrian president Hafez Al-Assad's niece, Al-Kassar's Middle East drug exploits, carried out with the blessing of the "off-the-shelf" **CIA** unit protecting him, may have led, some theorize, to the 1988 bombing of Pan Am flight 103. He helped the *Achille Lauro* **Terrorists** escape, and he dealt weapons to the Libyans, to Irish **Marxists,** to the Hezbollah, to Basque Terrorists, to anyone who'd pay, really. He also worked as the PLO's banker and transferred much of their money to the **BCCI**—all the while, however, Al-Kassar's true allegiance was to his own greedy self and to the **GRU,** the Soviet Union's military intelligence unit, to whom he funneled weapons and the profits from his drug sales.

Adnan Khashoggi

✝

Henry Kissinger

✝ 🐀 ⊕

Knights of Malta

✕ 🏠 ⚐

Kuwaiti Royal Family

Guilty of slant drilling against Iraq (the Kuwaitis were pretending to drill for crude oil on their own land when, in fact, they were actually angling their pipes into Iraqi land). Their deep pockets and **Hill & Knowlton**'s shrewd lobbying efforts created a front group called the Citizens for a Free Kuwait. The Citizens, supposedly innocent Kuwaiti common folk and their children, were really nothing more than skilled actors (and royal family relatives). Under the shrewd guidance of H&K, though, they played the U.S. Congress and the public like a harp, showering listeners with false tales of Iraqi abuses and atrocities in order to goad the United States into a war with Iraq and **Saddam Hussein.** Until a few years ago Kuwait (i.e., the Kuwaiti royal family) was the major shareholder in British Petroleum and a 14 percent owner of **Daimler-Benz.**

Mafia

♍ ❋ ⛰ 〰 △ ✐ ▦

Marxism

✡ ✍

Mena

✐

Military-Industrial Complex

♍ ★ ✝ △ ⚑ ✿ ▦

Mind Control

👁 〰 👁 ✿ ☉

Mossad

Israel's equivalent of America's **CIA** and **FBI,** the Ha-Mossad le-Modiin ule-Tafkidim Meyuhadim (the Institute for Intelligence and Special Tasks) was formed April 1, 1951, by David Ben-Gurion with the help of the **MI6** (British intelligence). Aka the Institute, the Mossad conducts external espionage and performs covert operations abroad. Agent Amiram Nir supposedly worked with former Panama dictator **Manuel Noriega** and his U.S.-to-**Cali-Medellín Cocaine Cartels** drug-smuggling operation. In Arkansas, the Mossad is said to have found out about Vince Foster's payoff role in the drugs-and-guns-and-money **Mena** operation, and so the Israelis blackmailed Foster for information on other FOBs (Friends of **Bill Clinton**'s—who by this time had made it to the White House). One of the Mossad's training courses bears the **Bernays**ian title "The Lie as Art."

Mujahadeen

✐

National Program Office

Created in 1982—outside of and in violation of the U.S. Constitution—by President **Reagan** and **Oliver North,** this secret federal agency established a line of succession for the presidency in the event of a nuclear invasion. Run by then vice president **George Bush,** it designated that if all seventeen legal successors to the executive position were dead or unavailable, the next in line to take over would be a series of nonelected officials. This agency spent more than $8 billion on flawed communications equipment.

National Security Agency

Aka Never Say Anything, this ultrasecret, nearly untouchable U.S. intelligence agency (the largest of all intelligence agencies and immune to congressional review—unlike the **CIA**) within the Department of Defense was established by President **Truman** in 1952 to intercept any communications thought by it to be of national security interest and is responsible for all cryptographic and communications intelligence and security. **Lockheed-Martin, IBM,** and **TRW** are three of the NSA's biggest contractors-cooperators—having developed various spy satellites, encryption devices, and computer systems for the agency. There's also a convenient crossover of NSA employees to Lockheed-Martin, IBM, TRW, **Wackenhut Securities,** and E-Systems (another key surveillance-system company). The NSA, headquartered at Fort Meade, Maryland, runs the **Echelon** global surveillance system. IBM's first computers were developed thanks to funding from the NSA (whose budget dwarfs the CIA's), and communications giants like **AT&T** have willingly cooperated with the agency, allowing the NSA to listen in on people's conversations and other communications. During the 1960s, for instance, as part of Operation Shamrock, the NSA routinely read American citizens' telegrams and eavesdropped on their phone calls. The NSA also took part in the (ab)use of **PROMIS.** Lately, the NSA has taken a keen interest in biometrics, a kind of cousin to **Cybernetics** that often involves the implantation of microchips in humans.
✧ ⊕

National Security Council (NSC)

More secretive even than the **CIA,** the NSC was established through the National Security Act of 1947 by President **Harry Truman** to serve as a direct line of communication between the White House and the newly formed CIA. Statutory members of the NSC are the president, the vice president, and the secretaries of state and defense. The military advisor to the NSC is the chairman of the joint chiefs of staff and the intelligence advisor is the director of central intelligence. The NSC's staff of analysts is directed by the assistant to the president for national security affairs (or the national security advisor). Many of the fundamental tenets of the NSC are outlined in National Security Paper 68 (NSC 68), a document approved in April 1950 by the president. Written in response to the August 1949 detonation of the first Soviet atomic bomb, the paper outlined "the necessity for just suppression" and depicted the **Cold War** in ideological terms, describing the Soviet Union as "inescapably militant" and "possessed by a worldwide revolutionary movement." It also revised earlier analysis and, over **Council on Foreign Relations** member George Kennan's reservations, concluded that the Soviets possessed the means to militarily overrun Western Europe and directly challenge U.S. security. It recommended a massive military buildup and increased foreign aid. During the 1950s, the council basically exempted **Multinational** oil companies from the reach of U.S. law in order to make sure that world currency would flow into the coffers of the big American-owned oil companies. In the 1980s, the NSC played a major role in the **Iran-Contra** scheme, having been dragged into the illegal guns-and-drugs mess by **Reagan**'s NSC advisor Robert McFarlane and McFarlane's hump, **Oliver North**.

New World Order

♏ ☀ ✍ ∞ ☺ ⊕

Robert Booth Nichols

Freelance journalist Danny Casolaro's father figure and main source of information. A drug trafficker and money launderer, Nichols ran a munitions company affiliated with the **Cabazon Indian Reservation** and **Wackenhut Securities** and was a onetime employee of the powerful Japanese **Yakuza** warlord Harold Okimoto. Nichols was the subject of an **FBI** investigation, in which a bureau wiretap caught Nichols and a division president of **MCA** discussing a possibly very hostile takeover of the Universal Pictures film company. Days before Casolaro's "suicide," Nichols threatened the journalist's life, after Casolaro discovered that Nichols had at one time offered to talk to the **Justice Department** about his relationship with Gambino **Mafia** godfather

John Gotti. A friend of actor Steven Seagal's (a **Dalai Lama** insider who liked to brag about a pre-Hollywood past in which he was a **CIA** operative and **Yakuza** bag boy).

Richard Nixon

✝ ⛪ △ ▱ ⚰ ☼

Manuel Noriega

▱

Oliver North

Using his position as **National Security Council** deputy, this ex–U.S. Marine orchestrated the logistics of the late-1980s **Iran-Contra** affair, selling weapons to Iran at very inflated prices, then using those profits to buy arms for the Nicaraguan **Contra** "freedom fighters." Before his ignominious stint at the NSC, North was tutored by veterans of the **Secret Team** and also worked at **FEMA,** where he helped set up the **National Program Office.** North famously invoked the Fifth Amendment during the congressional hearings on his role in the mess.

October Surprise

This was the secret agreement between President **Reagan** and the Ayatollah Khomeini, the Islamic Fundamentalist leader (1900–1989) who overthrew the Shah of Iran (Reza Pahlavi) in 1979 and took just

Surprise! You're Dead!

Virtually every person intimate with the details of the supposed **Reagan**-Khomeini hostages deal died soon after news of the arrangement leaked out. Iranian foreign minister Sadegh Ghotzbadeh was executed (supposedly for plotting the overthrow of the Ayatollah); arms dealer Cyrus Hashemi died two days after being given news of his having cancer; Reagan's 1980 campaign manager and **CIA** director **William Casey** developed brain cancer two days after the **Iran-Contra** hearings began and died not long afterward—without ever uttering another word; CIA Beirut station chief William Buckley was kidnapped and died at the hands of Islamic Fundamentalists; fund-raiser Carl "Spitz" Channel died after a hit-and-run; and Amiram Nir, the **Mossad**'s answer to **Oliver North,** was killed in an airplane crash.

under one hundred Americans hostage from the U.S. embassy in Tehran. In 1980, per Earl Brian's suitcase-full-of-cash request, the Ayatollah kindly agreed *not* to release the hostages until *after* the 1980 U.S. presidential election, virtually guaranteeing **Reagan**'s win over **Jimmy Carter.** As agreed, the Ayatollah freed the American hostages on January 20, 1981, the day after Reagan's inauguration.

P2

※ ▲ ▓

Park-O-Meter Inc.

According to Danny Casolaro source and convicted drug felon Michael Riconosciuto, this Arkansas company, tied to **Clinton** friend and **Justice Department** official Webster Hubbell, was merely a front for **Biochemical Warfare** research and manufacturing (possibly to be used by the **Contras** in Nicaragua).

PROMIS

Initially, this 1982 Prosecutor's Management Information System software program, designed by Inslaw, a computer-software company, was to help U.S. prosecutors keep track of complex investigations. Instead, once Inslaw installed the system in the U.S. attorney's office (then headed by Attorney General Edwin Meese), the **Justice Department** refused to pay Inslaw their $10 million. This forced Inslaw to declare bankruptcy, allowing the Justice Department to seize PROMIS for its own. The J.D. then gave PROMIS to Hadron, a firm owned by Earl Brian, who was a good friend of Meese's (some say it was in return for Brian's help in negotiating the **October Surprise**). Brian, former head of UPI and himself convicted of bank fraud and conspiracy in 1996, said he knew nothing about PROMIS. Meese's wife, coincidentally, happened to be one of Hadron's investors. According to convicted drug felon and self-proclaimed programming genius Michael Riconosciuto, the **CIA** hired Riconosciuto to inject PROMIS with an electronic back-door access, a kind of Trojan Horse addendum unbeknownst to the eighty-eight countries (like Iran, Iraq, South Korea, et cetera) that bought the program, which later allowed the CIA and the **NSA** to monitor the buyer country's military and intelligence files. (The **Mossad** and **Robert**

Maxwell's Pergamon Press also got ahold of the redesigned software and sold it, too.) After the United States devastated Iraq's army in the **Gulf War,** the Iraqis (and many others) wondered if maybe it was the rigged PROMIS software they'd bought that ensured the Americans of such an obscenely easy victory.

Muammar Qaddafi

⌂ ⌘

Raytheon

A **Military-Industrial Complex** demigod, Raytheon owns E-Systems (the countersurveillance technology company now in charge of the **HAARP** project, after Raytheon bought **APTI** from **ARCO** in 1994). Raytheon also developed the SCUD-busting Patriot missile, the anthropomorphically idolized smart weapon used in the **Gulf War.**

✿

Ronald Reagan

☞ ∾ ✝ ⚐ ▦

Ricky "Freeway Rick" Ross

▱

School of the Americas

▱

Richard Secord

▱

Skull & Bones

⚐ ⋀⋀⋀

Terrorism

✳ ★ ⌂

Trilateral Commission

♍ ✍ ∾ ⊕

UFOs

⚐ ⊙

Vatican

♍ ✖ ✳ ⚐ ⌂ ✝ ⊙

Wackenhut Securities

A private security and surveillance agency, founded in 1954 by ex-**FBI** man George Wackenhut and based in Coral Gables, Florida. Wackenhut has since branched out into prison management and other clandestine activities, and now has more than 30,000 armed employees and offices throughout the United States and in dozens of foreign countries. Its clients include **Westinghouse,** the Alaska Oil Pipeline, the Hanford nuclear waste facility, the Savannah River plutonium plant, and the **Cabazon Indian Reservation.** Wackenhut's board members have included right-wingers culled from the **CIA,** FBI, Secret Service, and marines, and its employee roster, too, is jammed with ex—government operatives (until his death in 1987, their outside legal counsel was CIA director **William Casey**). In return, the Hut gets much of its business from the agencies and companies of the **Military-Industrial Complex.** Wackenhut also maintains a millions-long list of "derogatory types."
⊙

War on Drugs

〰〰 ✏

285

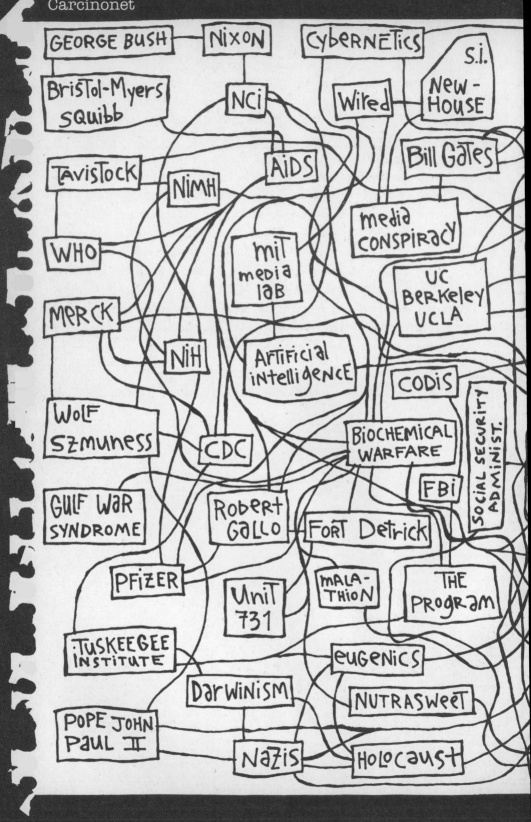

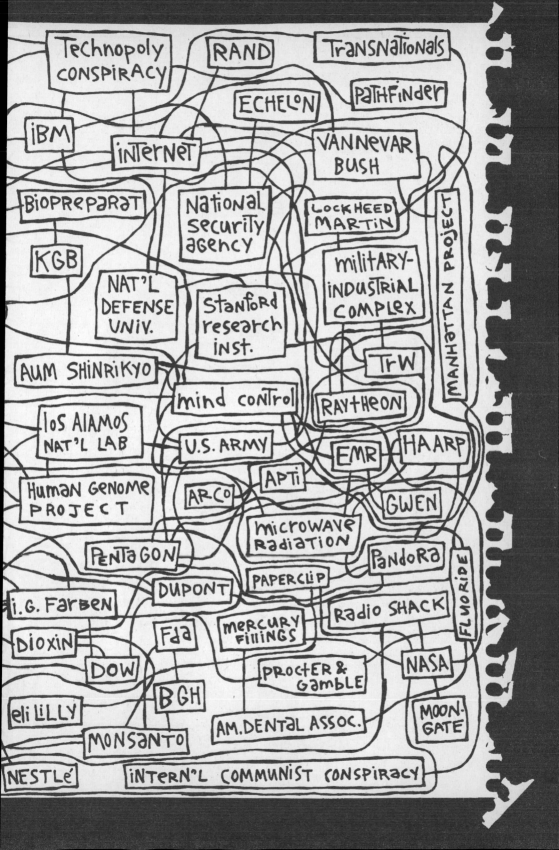

Conspiracy

AIDS and the Internet. Mind Control and disease. Somehow it all makes sense, they all go together, they all link up.

AIDS

Deadly "plague" that first appeared in 1981, usually transmitted through sexual contact or contaminated blood. According to Dr. Alan Cantwell, author of *Queer Blood*, AIDS and HIV blossomed possibly as a result of a U.S. government experiment: In 1978, the **National Institutes of Health** and the **CDC** inoculated more than 1,000 nonmonogamous gay men with an experimental vaccine (designed by **Merck** and Abbott Labs, among other pharmaceutical companies) designed to stamp out hepatitis B. By 1984, 64 percent of those vaccinated had developed AIDS. According to German scientist Jakob Segal, AIDS grew out of the **U.S. Army** Biological Warfare research at **Fort Detrick** (where scientists merged the visna sheep virus with the human T-cell leukemia virus) as an act of **Eugenics** designed to eradicate gay men and Africans.

American Dental Association (ADA)

Founded in 1859, this professional society of dentists advocates the use of **Fluoride** as an effective ingredient against tooth decay and approves the use of **Mercury** as fillings for cavities.

APTI

Acronym for **ARCO** Powers Technologies, Inc. Until recently, APTI was a subsidiary of the **Military-Industrial Complex** defense-industry giant ARCO. Contracted by the **Pentagon** to build the **HAARP** project and manage it, ARCO sold APTI to E-Systems in 1994.

ARCO

Military-Industrial Complex defense-industry behemoth; initial owners-contractors of the Alaska-based **HAARP** project, via its subsidiary **APTI**. ARCO is the largest producer of oil on the state's lucrative, recently opened North Slope, and its former CEO, Lodwrick Cook, is a personal friend of **Bill Clinton**'s (who in 1996 overturned the twenty-three-year-old ban on the export of North Slope crude). Alaska's citizens refer to their governor, Tony Knowles, as the governor of ARCO.

Artificial Intelligence (AI)

The simulation of intelligent behavior in computers or the insertion of computers into the neural network of humans—either way, the melding of human and robot. AI research is hottest at MIT''s **Media Lab,** where professor Neil Gershenfeld gushed to *New York* magazine that, in thirty years, "We will edit the human genome to grow this stuff [computer chips] out of us."

> The ultimate scenario is to develop a complete genetic code for the computer that would function as a virus does, but instead of producing more virus, it would assemble a fully operational computer inside a cell.
>
> —Genex Corporation geneticist (1990s)

Aum Shinrikyo

✝ ❧

Biochemical Warfare

☺

Biopreparat

A secretive **Biochemical Warfare** web of at least forty facilities spread across the former Soviet Union (the USSR's answer to **Fort Detrick**) and known among its own scientists as the System. Now a privatized group, the System was set up in 1973 (one year after the USSR signed the Biological & Toxin Weapons Convention Agreement banning the development, use, and stockpiling of biological weapons—and four years after **Nixon** had suppposedly shut down the United States's biowarfare program) to cure known diseases and create new ones (such as variants on viruses like anthrax and botulism and the gas sarin). Before the collapse of the USSR, the Biopreparat often answered to the wishes of the **KGB**. Scientists from Shoko Asahara's **Aum Shinrikyo** cult apparently dealt with Biopreparat researchers and purchased their sarin gas from them via the KGB.

Bovine Growth Hormone

A synthetic hormone, manufactured by **Eli Lilly & Co.**, Upjohn, and American Cyanamid, BGH is designed to increase milk production in dairy cows, but it is rumored to cause health problems in cattle, problems that in turn are treated with antibiotics, leaving an antibiotic residue in the milk sold to humans—causing some to wonder if it might have something to do with mad cow disease or chronic fatigue syndrome.

This Is Your Brain on Marlboros

In June 1995, Los Angeles conspiranoiac congressman Henry Waxman revealed several secret documents from tobacco giant Philip Morris that unveiled the extent of the company's nicotine research. According to Waxman's Morris papers:

- in one 1969–1972 study, Morris scientists administered electric shock to college students to see if they smoked more cigarettes under stressful conditions.
- in 1977, Morris and an unnamed university hospital agreed to inject nicotine into people in order to measure their brain waves.

Bristol-Myers Squibb

☺

George Bush

〰 △ ✐ ↝ ⚲ ☺ ⊕

Vannevar Bush

☺

Centers for Disease Control (CDC)

Formerly overseen by **AIDS** "discoverer" **Dr. Robert Gallo,** this federal agency was founded in 1946 as the Communicable Disease Center (the name was changed in 1993) and has its headquarters and main laboratories in Atlanta, Georgia. Currently, the CDC is "studying" chronic fatigue syndrome (the Epstein-Barr virus more commonly known as the Yuppie disease), **AIDS,** and other diseases. In 1978, in a project overseen by Soviet-trained Polish epidemiologist (and Jew) **Wolf Szmuness,** the **National Institutes of Health,** and the CDC, more than 1,000 nonmonogamous gay men were inoculated with an experimental vaccine (designed by Abbott Labs and **Merck,** among other pharmaceutical companies) designed to stamp out hepatitis B. By 1984, 64 percent of those vaccinated had developed AIDS. Between 1985 and 1989, the CDC was responsible for most of the shipments of lethal American-produced **Biochemical Warfare** agents that were sold to Iraq.

CODIS

Shorthand for the **FBI**'s combined DNA Index System, a nationwide databank of DNA profiles now used by federal, state, and local law-enforcement agencies to help solve crimes in which DNA evidence (taken from the junk DNA inside the human genome) tends to turn up (usually in sex-assault cases).
⊙

Cybernetics

Think of Arnold Schwarzenegger's *Terminator* character and you pretty much have the idea and the goal of most cybernetics research, which is the development of robots and other self-thinking machines—some all metal, some half-metal, half-human. As far back as 1964, **CIA** director Richard Helms

291

gushed (to the **Warren Commission,** no less) that "cybernetics can be used in the molding of a child's character, the inculcation of knowledge and techniques, the amassing of experience, the establishment of social behavior patterns . . . all functions which can be summarized as control of the growth processes of the individual."

Darwinism

Dioxin

More commonly known as Agent Orange, this supertoxic defoliant was used in the **Vietnam War** and produced by **Dow Chemical** and also manufactured by **Monsanto.** During the Vietnam War, the U.S. military sprayed millions of gallons of the stuff over Southeast Asia (often over its own troops—knowingly), subjecting U.S. soldiers to the poisonous hydrocarbon. Many children whose parents

Humans as Horticulture

Colorado Republican state senator Charles Duke thinks maybe someone's been sticking microchips in American babies—so as to monitor and control their behavior come adulthood.

In 1998, British cybernetics professor Kevin Warwick, at his own request, had a computer chip implanted in his left biceps—to have his movements monitored by a computer, which would also automatically turn on lights, tell Warwick he had E-mail, et cetera.

In 1992, the Colorado State judicial system came out with a report called "Vision 2020," which urged the state's courts to implement electronic monitoring devices, or, as it specified in its report, ". . . use genetic engineering, chemicals and chip implants to change human behavior."

The robotic **Oklahoma City Bombing** "suspect" Timothy McVeigh says that while he was in the **U.S. Army,** which is nothing more than an arm of the **NWO** anyway, his superiors embedded a computer chip in his ass in order to control him (then) and try to keep tabs on him (later).

The **New World Order** conspirators, say the Brit-wary among us, pull Prince Charles's strings by means of a royal butt computer-chip implant.

were exposed have developed severe birth defects and genetic disorders, ranging from spina bifida to leukemia. Banned as an herbicide since 1979, dioxin compounds have nonetheless turned up near many industrial-waste sites and in parts of the Great Lakes.

Dow Chemical

Dow, the nation's largest chemical corporation behind **Du Pont**, introduced Saran Wrap in 1953 and later produced the **Dioxin** used by the U.S. Air Force in its napalm strikes during the **Vietnam War**. Dow also supplied **Saddam Hussein** with many **Biochemical Warfare** ingredients and products prior to the **Gulf War.** In 1992, Dow Corning grudgingly ceased production of its silicone breast implants, partially due to the longtime concern over the safety of implants.

Du Pont

⚕ 〰〰
〰〰

Echelon

The **NSA**'s global surveillance system, so powerful an electronic net that it's capable of intercepting any and all phone, fax, and modem signals. Initially forged in 1948, and known back then as the UKUSA Agreement (an alliance of the United States, Great Britain, Canada, Australia, and New Zealand), it was set up for the gathering of signal intelligence (or, SIGINT, in spy speak). Eventually, UKUSA evolved into Echelon.

Electromagnetic Radiation (EMR)

☢

The type of energy emitted by all those huge electrical power lines and transponders (many of which act as the umbilical cord to the companies tied to the **Military-Industrial Complex**). EMR critics say that behind every power line lies a hotbed of cancer statistics. The big industry people who own those EMR lines (your local utility megaconglomerate) deny such charges and come back with studies of their own (using their scientists and/or funded by their big bucks) that refute the statistics of their critics. In New Mexico, the Taos hum could be low-intensity EMR, courtesy of the EMR brain-control technology and **Mi-**

crowave **Radiation** research being done at nearby **Los Alamos National Laboratory.** Or maybe the hum's origins stem from yet more EMR work going on three hours farther south at the Los Alamos Lab in Albuquerque. According to *The New Yorker* writer Paul Brodeur in his book *The Zapping of America*, "all the talk about death rays and charged particle beams has been little more than an elaborate smokescreen designed to hide the fact that the U.S. is developing a directed energy weapon that uses a high-powered microwave pulse."
⊙

Eli Lilly & Co.

☞ 〰 ☺

Eugenics

✡ ⚶ ∞

FBI

♍ ✳ ✝ ☞ 〰 △ ⊕ ⊙

FDA

☞

Fluoride

✍ ☞

Fort Detrick

Founded in 1943, when it went by the equally benign name of Camp Detrick, this is the site of America's nascent **Biochemical Warfare** program. It was known until 1969 as the Army Biological Warfare Laboratory, then renamed the **National Cancer Institute**'s Frederick Cancer Research Facility. Now just Fort Detrick, at one time the toxins and other noxious agents developed here were tested on the general population. (From 1950 to 1969, the government performed more than three hundred open-air germ tests in San Francisco—in one 1950 run-through, an innocent bystander died as a result of a U.S. Navy flunkie spraying the rare serratia bacteria all over the city.) It was from here that a team of Fort Detrick scientists trekked down to Africa in the 1970s, returning with the heretofore unknown agent that eventually came to be known as

HIV. And if HIV wasn't synthesized at Fort Detrick, some ask, then why did the **National Institutes of Health** have the fort's army scientists look into a cure for **AIDS**? Scientists at the fort are now doing a much more sophisticated type of germ-warfare research for the **CIA** (such as developing designer viruses that can kill one specifically targeted individual and no one else). Much of the expertise in biological warfare at Detrick came from Japanese military doctor Shiro Ishii and his teammates from **Unit 731**. Fort Detrick is just a beaker's throw away from the brand-new Institute of Human Virology at the University of Maryland, headed by AIDS "pioneer" **Robert Gallo**.

Robert Gallo

Now director of the brand-new Institute of Human Virology (at the University of Maryland), Gallo was the alleged "discoverer" of the Human Immunodeficiency Virus (HIV) in 1984. The former head of the U.S. **AIDS** program, Gallo was a longtime research scientist at the **National Cancer Institute** and participated in a 1962–1976 inoculation project that involved the infection of monkeys with the first known immunosuppressive virus, part of the same class of viruses that now includes HIV.

Bill Gates

✳ ▨ ⊕

Gulf War Syndrome

Debilitating disease afflicting U.S. military veterans of the **Gulf War** and possibly caused by a lethal combo of chemicals given to troops before going off to storm **Saddam Hussein**'s desert, chemicals that were supposed to protect them from insects and nerve gases—chemicals developed by the **CDC**, the **NIH**, and American pharmaceutical companies. It symptoms are eerily reminiscent of the effects of Agent Orange.

The Russian and U.S. governments fill the air with low-frequency sound waves meant to control us.

—Steve Carlton, *Sports Illustrated*, April 1994

GWEN

Begun in the 1980s, this web of Ground Wave Emergency Network towers spans the length of the United States. Some of the towers reach as high as 300 feet in the air and as far as 330 feet into the ground and broadcast short pulses of **Electromagnetic Radiation** (EMR) in the form of very low frequency (VLF) messages. Part of **Federal Emergency Management Agency**'s Continuity of Government program and a kind of EMR precursor to **HAARP**.

⊕

HAARP (High-Frequency Active Auroral Research Program)

The **Pentagon**'s $30 million transmitter experiment high up in the Arctic (200 miles outside Anchorage, Alaska) and cosponsored by the U.S. Navy and Air Force, in which 180 72-foot-high towers will fry the Earth's ionosphere, making it the world's largest high-frequency phased-array transmitter (bigger than its predecessor cousin, the VLA—Very Large Array—outside the White Sands missile range in southern New Mexico, not very far from **Roswell**). According to the Pentagon, HAARP's no more sinister than an advanced communications and surveillance project. Critics (from rational environmentalists to nutty **UFO**-phobics) fear the worst: that it's the prototype of many future superheaters capable of beaming invisible smart rays at missiles, satellites, even the gray matter inside the heads of enemies, agitators, and subversives; that its rays will fuck up pacemakers, cause earthquakes and citywide power blackouts, knock the Earth's atmosphere totally out of whack, scramble people's brains, be used as a "final weapon" in an end-time scenario battle between Earthlings and **Aliens,** change and maybe even control the weather and so disrupt the sensitive guidance and communications systems of missiles, satellites, aircraft, and other sky-high objects that they'll rain down from the heavens like cats and dogs. Some of the naysayers' complaints sound pretty farfetched, but half the possible implications of the above laundry list of HAARP-caused chaos were outlined in a patent filed by Texas physicist Bernard Eastlund, a patent owned by ARCO Powers Technologies, Inc. **(APTI),** until recently a subsidiary of the **Military-**

Industrial Complex defense-industry giant **ARCO,** the company originally contracted by the Department of Defense (the Pentagon) to make HAARP sing. But it doesn't stop there. In 1994, ARCO unloaded APTI to another branch of the Military-Industrial Complex, E-Systems, experts in countersurveillance technology, whose parent company is **Raytheon**—one of the world's defense industry monoliths that shot to fame during the **Gulf War** for *their* smart piece of weaponry, the SCUD-busting Patriot missile. In the list of references for Eastlund's superweapon patent, the Texan cited two profiles of Nikola Tesla, the Croatian-born inventor who claimed to have developed a "death beam" capable of melting airplane motors from hundreds of feet away.

⊙

Holocaust

✡ ☪ ★ ☦

Human Genome Project

This ongoing scientific endeavor, initially set up in 1987 under the auspices of the **NIH,** hopes to pinpoint and identify every one of the 80,000 genes in human DNA. Soon after its startup, however, independent entrepreneur and former NIH researcher J. Craig Venter, with private backing, announced that he would have a map before the government did. It's also rumored that the U.S. government keeps a genetic record of all its citizens in secret DNA banks— a not-so-farfetched notion, considering that all information gathered by the HGP is being entered into the GenBank database at **Los Alamos National Laboratory.**

⊙

IBM

✝ ⊕

I.G. Farben

★

International Communist Conspiracy

♍ ☀ ✡ ✍ △ ∾ ☺

Internet

꙰ ꙮ ☉

KGB

🖋 🐃 △ ꙰

Lockheed-Martin

† △

Los Alamos National Laboratory

In the **Manhattan Project** days, LANL was run jointly by the **University of California** and the **U.S. Army,** and it was here that the first atomic bomb was developed. Now run by the Department of Energy and the University of California, LANL is the site of much nuclear and **Biochemical Warfare** research. A main SDI contractor, other LANL researchers are hard at work on **Microwave Radiation** experiments and **EMR Mind Control** technology (in a project overseen by U.S. Army vet John Alexander, who also happens to have a degree in thanatology and who may be a member of the **Aviary**). LANL is also rumored to be the site to which the downed **Aliens** of the **Roswell** spacecraft were brought (and dissected by **FBI** operatives), frozen, and then put into storage. All the information gathered from the **Human Genome Project** is being entered into LANL's GenBank database.
☉

Malathion

One of a series of poisons known as organophosphates, this carcinogenic nerve gas was accidentally discovered by **I.G. Farben**

Conspiranet

www.paranoia.com/~fraterk/conspire.html
www.gate.net/~asia/
www.weberman.com
www.webcom.com/~conspire/ufolink.html
www.nwlink.com/~ufocntr/index.html
NameBase
CIABASE
www.conspire.com
www.calweb.com
www.crl.com
www.disinform.com

chemist Gerhard Schrader in 1936. Approved by the **FDA** in the 1970s for pesticide use, the U.S. Department of Agriculture began spraying the deadly agent over huge swaths of Southern California, ostensibly to wipe out the Mediterranean fruit fly.

Manhattan Project

Massachusetts Institute of Technology (MIT) Media Lab

Cofounded in 1985 by cyber guru (and *Wired* columnist) Nicholas Negroponte, who believes that computers will, in time, be implanted in our bodies, the lab hopes to "invent and creatively exploit new media for human well-being and individual satisfaction." Aside from its research in interactivity and virtual reality, it's the lab's work in **Artificial Intelligence** that gives one pause—for example, one researcher recently completed the first phase of an AI project called BodyNet, in which the human body (by the end of phase three) will be hardwired with a computer network. Or take the comment of one lab professor, who predicts that in thirty years bioengineers "will edit the human genome to grow this stuff [computer chips] out of us." Yikes! Its corporate sponsors and investors include **Media** and **Transnational** conspirators like Sony, **Nike,** and **Bill Gates**'s Microsoft.

Media Conspiracy

Merck

This West Point, Pennsylvania, pharmaceutical Goliath manufactures chemicals, veterinarian and food products, and consumer brands like Calgon and Mylanta, and in the late 1970s Merck made the experimental hepatitis B vaccine (along with the **NIH** and the **CDC**) for **Wolf Szmuness.** During **WWII,** Merck's director, George Merck, oversaw the United States's germ-weapons research program. Merck's board of director membership intersects with **IBM, GM,** and AT&T.

Mercury Fillings

Those little bits of metal that dentists use to fill the cavities in your teeth might actually be contributors to chronic fatigue syndrome and/or transmittors of crucial radio signals between **NASA** and **Aliens.**

Microwave Radiation Transmission (MRT)

Not the innocent kitchen appliance you've been led to believe, say Wavies, victims of microwave brainwashing. Wavies claim that the little devices (as well as many other, far larger unseen microwave-energy sources, like **HAARP** and the **GWEN** towers) are being used by either the government or **Aliens** as a way to get into people's heads, i.e., **Mind Control.**

⊙

Military-Industrial Complex

♍ ★ ♱ △ ⚲ ☺ ▩

Mind Control

🐚 〰 ↝ ☺ ⊙

Monsanto

★

Moongate

According to conspiranoiac **UFO**logist Richard Hoagland, who once worked as a science advisor to **CBS** News, **NASA**'s 1976 photos of the Cydonia region of Mars show relics of an ancient intelligent **Alien** civilization. Similarly, conspiranoiac William L. Brian II, in his 1982 book *Moongate: Suppressed Findings of the U.S. Space Program,* says NASA has covered up knowledge of lunar life for years. Brian (and others) believes in the "Alternative 3" scenario, which claims that the yearly disappearance of thousands of humans, well, those folks haven't just moved to California, they've been zombified and put to work up on the dark side of the moon building secret lunar bases under the supervision of Earth scientists, preparing the moon for the resettling of the world's soon-to-be-evacuated elite (when the apocalypse hits or when the Aliens invade, whichever comes first).

⊕ ⊙

★ ☉

National Cancer Institute

The largest of seventeen biomedical research institutes and centers that comprise the **National Institutes of Health,** located just outside Washington, D.C., in Bethesda, Maryland, the NCI coordinates national and comprehensive research programs on cancer cause, prevention, detection, diagnosis, and treatment. From 1962 to 1976, NCI ran a massive experimental virus inoculation program (overseen by **AIDS** "pioneer" **Robert Gallo**). It was once home to various and sundry biowarriors (or were they **Biochemical Warfare** warriors?) involved in the Viral Cancer Program launched in 1971 (as part of **Nixon**'s early 1970s War on Cancer campaign) and designed to organize experiments in the hopes of finding carcinogenic viruses. There's plenty of crossover of employees and research goals between the NCI and the **CDC.**

National Defense University (NDU)

Having unwittingly scooped itself with the development of the **Internet,** the **Pentagon** (whose ARPAnet program birthed the Internet), which of course views information as both a weapon and a target, hopes that their university's new Information Resources Management College, at the school's Washington, D.C., "campus," will function as a kind of West Point for cybercombat and help them stay abreast of all the other phreaks screaming down the information *autobahn*—specifically, the Info College wants to exploit the retarded Lao-tzu *Art of War* mentality so many businesspeople have been duped into thinking is the key to success. Using virtual-reality scenarios and computer simulations, officials from the Environmental Protection Agency and the **FBI** get wireless with CEO wanna-bes from Boeing, **IBM,** Oracle, and GTE.

National Institute of Mental Health

🐾 ☉

National Institutes of Health (NIH)

The NIH, part of the Public Health Service, originated as the Laboratory of Bacteriology in 1887. The NIH conducts and supports biomedical research into the causes, prevention, and

301

cure of diseases. In the 1950s and 1960s, the NIH proffered "full support and protection" to the **CIA** during its **MK-ULTRA** program and later participated in **Wolf Szmuness**'s hepatitis B inoculations.
☉

National Security Agency

☺ ⊕

Nazis

♏ ★ ✝ 🏛 🐃 ⚱

Nestlé

The world's leading food company, this Swiss colossus makes everything from Lean Cuisine and Quik to Friskies dog food. Often referred to as "the most **Multinational** of the multinationals," Nestlé also manufactures pharmaceuticals and cosmetics, such as L'Oreal. It's also the world's largest maker of infant formula and, despite repeated boycotts, continues to force-feed its "free sample" formula to third world mothers. Like a scene out of a **New World Order** nightmare, Nestlé initially gives its formula away to indigent mothers, who try it, then find out that they and their newborns are hooked and their breast milk has dried up, so moms and babies have

Nuclear USRDA

In 1946, researchers at Vanderbilt University gave hundreds of pregnant women a "vitamin cocktail," a little pill that contained radioactive iron.

In the late 1940s, nearly two dozen unsuspecting hospital patients throughout the country were injected with plutonium and subjected to "metabolism tests," as part of the Atomic Energy Commission's curiosity about the longterm effects of radioactivity.

In the 1950s, the Atomic Energy Commission and the **National Institutes of Health** lured twenty-four boys from Boston's Fernald School into joining a science club, which was really a ruse for the government's dietary experiments, one of which included giving the boys radioactive oatmeal as part of their recommended daily allowance.

little choice but to pay for more Nestlé's, which is great for Nestlé but bad for most infants, as the formula requires water and the water in most underdeveloped nations is contaminated—causing malnutrition, sickness, disease, and about one million bottle-related deaths a year. Nestlé's president, Helmut Maucher (who also heads up the European **Round Table**), happens to be chairman of the **International Chamber of Commerce,** one of the groups lobbying for passage of the **Multilateral Agreement on Investments.**
⊕

Si Newhouse

The Newhouse family's publishing conglomerate, Advance Publications includes *Parade* (the Sunday newspaper insert), Condé Nast magazines (*Details, Vanity Fair, The New Yorker, GQ, Allure, Glamour,* et cetera), the Street & Smith sports digests, and various newspapers throughout the country (New Orleans's *Times-Picayune* and Cleveland's *Plain Dealer*), plus the recently acquired **Wired.** And until it was bought by the German publishing behemoth and onetime reported **Nazi** accommodators Bertelsmann AG, Advance also owned all of Random House Inc. (Alfred A. Knopf, Ballantine, Vintage, and Fodor's travel guides). The Jewish Newhouse bigwigs, CEO Si, brother Donald, and their cousin Jonathan, have also been dabbling in cable TV (with **Time Warner**) and on the **Internet** (with CondéNet).
卐

Richard Nixon

✝ ⛪ △ ▱ ⚰ ☺

NutraSweet

Initially developed by G. D. Searle (now owned by **Monsanto**), this food additive (aka aspartame) may or may not promote headaches, allergic reactions, seizures, memory loss, and brain tumors. As a DNA derivative, the **Pentagon** once lumped it in with a list of possible **Biochemical Warfare** weapons.

Pandora

The **Pentagon**'s 1965–1970 research project set up under the auspices of ARPA (the Advanced Research Project Agency) to develop top-secret military uses for **Microwave Radiation**

303

technology. Many Pandora scientists were **Paperclip** recruits. **Lockheed** was a major Pandora contractor. One report stated that "the potential for exerting a degree of control on human behavior by low level microwave radiation seems to exist and [it is] urged that the effects of microwaves be studied by possible weapons applications."

Paperclip

★ 🐾

Pathfinder

Despite all those cool photos of the red planet, naysayers insist that this Mars landing was no more real than the **Apollo** *11*'s 1969 moon landing, and that is was a fraud perpetrated by the Jet Propulsion Lab and **NASA** to boost interest in the big-brother **Internet** (home of mars.com). After all, Pathfinder "landed" on Mars on the suspiciously convenient date of July 4—opening day of the crappy **Alien** invasion flick, *Independence Day*.

☉

NASA Flew to Mars for Rocks? Sure.

—From a headline, *The New York Times* (July 20, 1997)

The Door Revolving

In 1981, **Ronald Reagan** appointed his old chum Arthur Hayes as his new FDA commissioner (Hayes had worked at **Fort Detrick** during its early **WWII Biochemical Warfare** days). In that same year, despite many reports showing aspartame (the key to **NutraSweet**), produced by G. D. Searle, as a possible cause of brain damage in children, having negative effects on short-term memory, and being possibly carcinogenic, Hayes approved aspartame as acceptable for human consumption. In 1985, Hayes left the FDA to shill for Burton-Marsteller, the public-relations firm for G. D. Searle.

Pentagon

The pentagram-shaped headquarters of the U.S. military and the **Department of Defense** (DOD), located in Virginia. Its construction was overseen by **John McCloy,** the so-called godfather of the American Establishment. This is the federal agency principally involved in **AIDS** research. In 1969, Dr. Donald M. MacArthur told a congressional hearing on **Biochemical Warfare** that biowarfare experts were close to developing a genetically engineered "super germ"—one the human immune system would be virtually powerless against.

⊙

Pfizer

This pharmaceutical giant, at one time the research home of ex-**CDC** director and **AIDS** "discoverer" **Dr. Robert Gallo,** was contracted from 1961 to 1971 by the **National Cancer Institute** to concoct a huge variety of viruses. Pfizer also worked with the **U.S. Army** to secretly grow "unspecified . . . biological agents" for the Viral Cancer Program. Now it manufactures Viagra, the male-impotence drug—another pill approved by the **FDA** (and the **Vatican**), perhaps too quickly, given that sixteen men who've used the little blue wonder pill since its mid-1998 debut have died (though most appeared to have had cardiovascular disease).

Skin Deep

Before being shut down in 1974, University of Pennsylvania School of Medicine dermatologist Albert Kligman, who created the skin cream Retin A, conducted two decades' worth of experiments on hundreds of "volunteers," mostly African-American prisoners from Holmesburg penitentiary outside Philadelphia. Kligman's clients included the **U.S. Army, Pfizer,** Johnson & Johnson, Helena Rubenstein, and R.J. Reynolds tobacco, and the studies ranged from the testing of various toothpastes, shampoos, and deodorants to trials that involved the smearing of dioxin on prisoners' faces and giving them **MK-ULTRA**-linked mind-altering drugs.

Pope John Paul II

★ ✝

Procter & Gamble

★

The Program

🦅 🗒

Conspiracy theory is a way of processing information, a way of making links in the combined sense of discovering as well as creating. . . . Conspiracy theory is about interpretation and analysis. . . . Conspiracy theory challenges secrecy with information. . . . Conspiracy theory is a way to think globally and act locally. . . . Conspiracy theory knows that . . . everything has to be interpreted.

—Jodi Dean, *Aliens in America: Conspiracy Cultures from Outerspace to Cyberspace*, 1998

Radio Shack

Subsidiary of the Texas-based Tandy Corporation and demanders of extremely personal info (**Social Security** number, please? Home phone number?) just for a pack of batteries—all part of a ruse, some say, to recruit unsuspecting citizens to the moon to finish construction of those lunar bases. Other Shackheads claim their Tandy-subsidiary products are beacons for **NASA** transmittals (between NASA and the **Aliens**).

⊙

RAND

✍ △ 〰 ⊙

Raytheon

☺

Social Security Administration (SSA)

An elaborate Ponzi scheme con game—investment swindle bilking U.S. citizens of 15 percent of their paychecks—money then used to fund a **One World Government** run by the **International Bankers.** The SSA relies on the use of Social Security numbers to track taxpayers—a personal identification number that, by law, is supposed to be used ONLY for tax purposes, but banks and stores like **Radio Shack** try to cajole it out of their customers at every opportunity.

Stanford Research Institute

॰ॐ॰

Wolf Szmuness

A Polish Jew (1919–1982) who fled to the USSR after the **Nazis** wiped out his entire family. Szmuness received his medical degree from the Soviets and later worked in Poland, where he became close friends with the future CEO of the **Vatican, Pope John Paul II.** In 1978, Szmuness oversaw the inoculation of 1,000 nonmonogamous gay men in New York City with a hepatitis B vaccine. In 1980, the **CDC,** much thrilled by Szmuness's New York vaccine program, expanded the trial to nonmonogamous gay men in San Francisco, Los Angeles, Denver, St. Louis, and Chicago—and soon **AIDS** was sprouting up not just in Manhattan but nationwide.

Universal Product Code

Aka the International Bar Code, this two-inch bit of vertical lines on every new product you buy is used as a tracking device, which They say is to monitor the sale of items—but just as conceivable is that They use the UPC to track the every move of every citizen. How else to explain those "cashless society" proposals floating through the corporate boardrooms and legislative warrens, in which the powers-that-be want tiny microchips implanted into people's hands, making it just that much easier and more efficient for any UPC laser to scan a person automatically and credit or debit one's bank account or check one's medical records or criminal history or mental profile?

Technopoly Conspiracy

♍ 〰 ⊕

Thompson Ramo Woolridge (TRW)

Former credit-check giant and still key member of the **Military-Industrial Complex,** TRW supplies many other defense-industry companies with supersophisticated electronic technologies (an automated fingerprint-matching device, systems work on missiles and satellites, et cetera). Until it sold its Information System and Services unit for $1 billion in 1996, TRW maintained a database on the credit histories of virtually all U.S. citizens (including bank accounts, **Social Security** numbers, credit-card histories, phone statements, et cetera). A critical link in the **NWO,** TRW developed the supersensitive Rhyolite satellites in the early 1970s that were used by the **NSA** to spy on the USSR, and TRW is the company whose black vault code room was infiltrated by American potheads Christopher Boyce and Andrew Dalton Lee, the two dopes who tried to sell TRW's NSA codes and other secrets to the Russians (shenanigans dramatized in the 1985 film *The Falcon and the Snowman*).

Transnationals

♍ ✝ ⊕

Tuskegee Syphilis Study

The now-infamous forty-year-long (1932–1972) medical study and nontreatment of more than four hundred poor, syphilis-infected black men conducted by the U.S. Public Health Service (and later the **CDC**) at Alabama's Tuskegee Institute—ostensibly to see what the long-term effects of syphilis were. Racist, definitely, but it also

Pass the Viagra

SCUM, the Society of Cutting Up Men, whose most famous member (pardon the pun) was Andy Warhol's failed **Assassin** of 1968 Valerie Solanas, has been accused by some as being responsible for polluting the water supplies of the world's most virile cities (Los Angeles and London) with huge phallocidic quantities of estrogen, the female sex hormone, thereby lowering the sperm count of men everywhere.

smacked of social **Darwinism** and **Eugenics,** and not until 1997 did the U.S. government finally issue an apology to the study's few remaining survivors.

Unit 731

Aka the Ishii Corps, during **WWII,** in a remote area of Japanese-controlled Manchuria, a Japanese military doctor by the name of Shiro Ishii conducted a series of abominable **Biochemical Warfare** experiments on thousands of POWs (first Russians, Chinese, and Koreans, later British and Americans), subjecting them to plague, anthrax, botulism, and other viruses and bacteria. After the war ended, U.S. war hero General Douglas MacArthur spared Ishii and his comrades a war-crimes hearing in exchange for their know-how, which they gladly jumped at, lending their expertise to the United States's burgeoning germ-weapons research at Camp **Detrick** in Maryland.

University of California

〰

U.S. Army

★ 🦬 △ ☉

Wired

San Francisco—based magazine for propellerheads and other computer and Web nerds, now owned by **Si Newhouse** (of Condé Nast). **MIT Media Lab** cofounder Nicholas Negroponte was its charter columnist and loudest proponent of computer culture.

World Health Organization

∾

New Wired Order

In the early 1970s, **Nixon** crony John Ehrlichman suggested, in a confidential report, that the government stick a radio in every U.S. home, the better to brainwash little preschoolers to the ways of **New World Order** citizenship, and besides, the devices could also be used as part of a "wired nation"—a way to localize the country's police forces and medical records in one convenient databank.

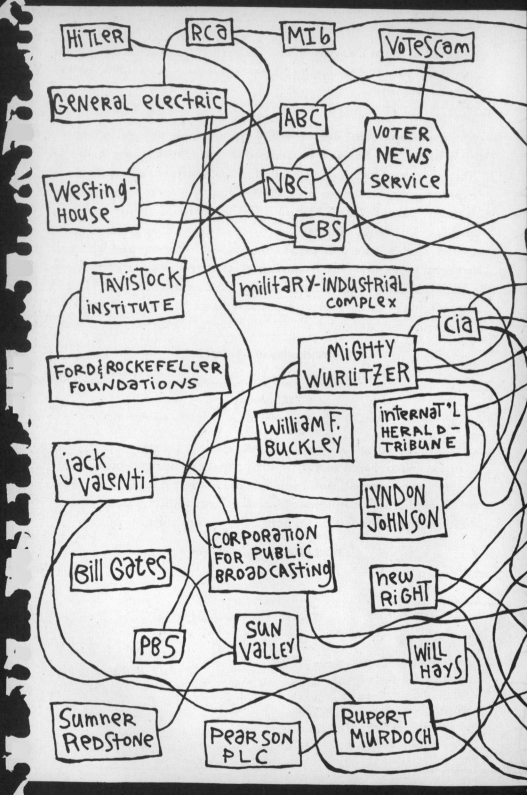

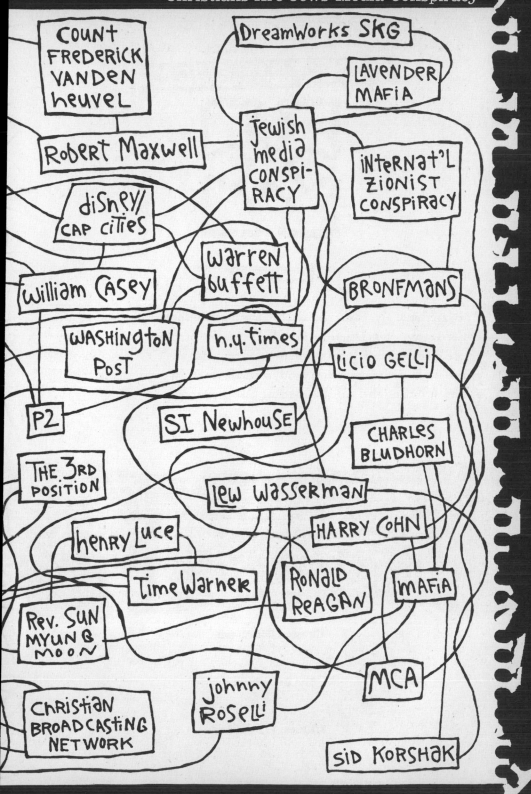

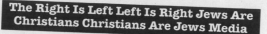

The Right Is Left Left Is Right Jews Are Christians Christians Are Jews Media

Conspiracy

The media only care about the media—whether it is liberal or conservative, Christian-controlled, Jew-controlled, or atheist-controlled. It's all infotainment (sports, music, TV, film, magazines) and disinformation and misinformation and propaganda aimed at telling the public anything but the truth.

ABC

〜

There have been some odd communions of the mind between the far left and the far right in viewing the world as one vast and varied conspiracy, and those communions have exponentially increased the ability of looneys of various stripes to get their nonsense into print.

—**Michael Kelly,** *Columbia Journalism Review,* 1993

Charles Bludhorn

🏠

The Bronfmans

✡ △ ☙

William F. Buckley

☺

Warren Buffett

✍

William Casey

★ ⛰ ▱ ☺

CBS

∽

Christian Broadcasting Network

☦

CIA

♍ ★ ✍ ✝ ⛰ 🐾 ⌇ △ ▱ ➵ ☦ ☺ 🌐 ☉

Harry Cohn

△

Corporation for Public Broadcasting (CPB)

Chief funder of **PBS** and most of the country's public TV stations, the CPB was proposed by the Carnegie Commission and created in 1967 by President **Lyndon Johnson**, who stated that "television regulation is built upon informal alliances and nonpublic agreements between members of Congress, members of interest groups, and members of the federal bureaucracy." Its charter members included the chairman of the Atomic Energy Commission (later known as the Nuclear Regulatory Commission) and bigwigs from **IBM**, **GE**, and **Time Inc.**, plus future Hollywood ratings czar **Jack Valenti** and **Insider** John D. **Rockefeller** III. Most of CPB's start-up money came from the **Ford Foundation**, whose president also happened to be the head of Shell Oil.

Disney/Cap Cities

✡

Radio Conspiranoia!

World-Wide Christian Radio, *Voice of Prophecy*, *For the People*, *Intelligence Report*, Sun Radio Network, *Radio Free America*, Pacifica Radio Network (KPFA, KPFK, WBAI), and Art Bell.

DreamWorks SKG

✡

Ford and Rockefeller Foundations

✏ ∾ 🌐

Bill Gates

✳ ☼ 🌐

Licio Gelli

🏛 ☺

General Electric (GE)

This U.S. aerospace corporation, founded as an electric energy firm in 1892, is a major member of the **Military-Industrial Complex,** manufacturing everything from jet engines to light bulbs and Hotpoint ranges, as well as having its hands in nuclear energy. GE also owns **NBC** television. Initially financed by the **Morgan** banking dynasty, GE is now the highest-valued company in the United States. CEO and chairman Jack Welch attends the **World Economic Forum** and is a member of the **Council on Foreign Relations.**

Will Hays

A former U.S. postmaster general for Warren Harding and part of Harding's supercorrupt administration, home of the Teapot Dome scandal (Hays had disposed of $260,000 of Teapot Dome money to various Republican buddies). In 1922, Hollywood's studio moguls hired Hays, aka the Gargoyle, to clean up its films, and, by exten-

Accidentally on Purpose

From 1946 until 1965, **General Electric** ran the Hanford nuclear waste facility (in Washington State). During those years, the government released massive amounts of radioactive iodine into the air from the facility, ultimately more than three times the amount that was leaked at Three Mile Island and about ten times greater than the leak at Chernobyl. Why? To see how far downwind the radioactive cloud could be traced.

sion, its public image. In 1930, Hays and his office (aka the Legion of Decency) authored the highly moralistic Production Code, which lasted until 1968 and which prohibited scenes of adultery, nudity, and kissing (among other no-nos) and served as the precursor to **Jack Valenti**'s ratings system. In 1933, during the IATSE strike against the Hollywood studios, the Hays Office hired mobman **Johnny Roselli** as "a labor negotiator."

Adolf Hitler

ʃ ★ †

International Herald-Tribune
Joint publication of *The New York Times* and *The Washington Post*—both of which are owned by Jewish families.

International Zionist Conspiracy
♍ ✖ ✺ ✿ ✍ ∾ ⊕

Jewish Media Conspiracy
✡

Lyndon Baines Johnson
△

Sidney Korshak
Not the *Night Stalker* guy but a **Mob**-connected Hollywood lawyer from Chicago (hometown of **Sam Giancana** and Frank Nitti) who acted as a "consultant" between many Hollywood stars and the Las Vegas hotel casinos (Debbie Reynolds, Dean Martin, and Barbra Streisand were among his clients). According to law-enforcement officials in 1976, Korshak was "the most important link between organized crime and legitimate business." Tight with **Lew Wasserman**, Korshak had a real knack—and value to all of the studio heads—for settling virtually every Hollywood labor dispute from the 1960s through the 1980s.

Lavender Mafia
✡

Henry Luce
〰 △

Mafia

♏ ✳ 🏔 〰 △ ▱ ☺

Robert Maxwell

✡

M16

✡ ▱ ∾

The Mighty Wurlitzer

〰 △

Military-Industrial Complex

♏ ★ ✝ △ 🕯 ☺ ☼

Reverend Sun Myung Moon

✝ 🏔 ∾ 🕯

Rupert Murdoch

🕯

Music Corporation of America (MCA)

Jules Stein's onetime Chicago-based talent agency (which came about at the height of Al Capone's Windy City reign), MCA went Hollywood in 1937 and was joined there by **Lew Wasserman** in 1938, who expanded the company's operations and transformed it into a film and music conglomerate so all-encompassing that it came to be known as the Octopus. Wasserman was named president in 1946. In 1952, the Screen Actors Guild, under the presidency of

Hollywood Conspiranoia!

The Assassination Bureau, The Godfather, The Godfather II, The Dogs of War, Being There, Executive Action, The Matarese Circle, The Manchurian Candidate, The Parallax View, Three Days of the Condor, Enemy of the State, Capricorn One, Conspiracy Theory, JFK, The UFO Incident, The Conversation, Seven Days in May, Slacker, Panther, The President's Analyst, Nixon, All the President's Men, Shadow Conspiracy, Pi, Blow Out, The Boys from Brazil, Z, Marathon Man, The Odessa File.

former MCA client **Ronald Reagan,** granted MCA a waiver that allowed the agency to also act as producers—in effect, okaying them as a studio *and* an agency (despite a certain conflict of interest). Now owned by Seagram's and Edgar **Bronfman,** Jr.

National Broadcasting Corporation (NBC)

Founded in 1926 by David Sarnoff as a division of the Radio Corporation of America, NBC is presently one of the four major television networks in the United States. NBC is owned by **General Electric.**

▨ ∾

New Right

↝ ⸸

The New York Times

∾

Si Newhouse

✿

P2

❋ 🏔 ☺

Pearson PLC

This British publishing and media empire, lorded over by Sir Dennis Stevenson, owns a portion of BSkyB, the satellite TV network held by **Rupert Murdoch**'s News Corporation, and also owns half of *The Economist* and all of the Penguin Group, whose subsidiary is Dutton Books.

Public Broadcasting Service (PBS)

Home of the Teletubbies, *Sesame Street,* and Mister Rogers and often derided by conservatives as a purveyor of liberal claptrap. (Fundamentalist **Moral Majority** minister Jerry Falwell's cronies, for example, have warned that the purple Teletubby Tinky Winky, who sports a purselike magic bag and a triangular antenna, is actually a gay icon, and is "damaging to the moral lives of children.") Hardly all that liberal or gay, PBS seems to be much more careful not to bite the hands that feed it: PBS's corporate backers include Mobil Oil (*Masterpiece Theatre*), the agribusiness octopus Archer Daniels Midland (the price-fixing pol-buying funder of the *Newshour with Jim Lehrer*), and **GM** subsidiary Ken *Civil War* Burns.

Radio Corporation of America (RCA)

Put together in 1919 by **GE, Westinghouse**, the **House of Morgan**, and **United Fruit Company** as a British intelligence center. During **WWII, MI6** officer Sir William Stephenson (code-named Intrepid) listened in on U.S. companies from his midtown New York head-quarters (at 30 **Rockefeller** Center), in the hopes of identifying American businesses that might still be in cahoots with the **Nazis**. Eventually, all three of the major TV networks—**NBC, ABC**, and **CBS**—were spun off from RCA.

Ronald Reagan

🐎 🐍 ⚰ 😊

Sumner Redstone

Chairman and CEO of Viacom, Inc., the huge New York City—based media conglomerate, of which Redstone owns 67 percent. Viacom's entertainment companies include Paramount Pictures, Spelling Entertainment Group (*Beverly Hills 90210*), the Blockbuster music and video chains, the Discovery Zone theme parks, Simon & Schuster book publishers, and cable channels like Comedy Central, the Sci-Fi channel, MTV, VH-1, USA, and Showtime. In 1998, the National Conference of Christians and Jews gave Redstone its humanitarian-of-the-year award—presented to him by Barry Diller, a Jew and a good friend of **Lavender Mafia** mogul David Geffen.

Conspiranoia! Syllabus Lit 101

Libra by Don DeLillo, *The Crying of Lot 49* by Thomas Pynchon, *Harlot's Ghost* by Norman Mailer, *Mumbo Jumbo* by Ishmael Reed, *Brave New World* by Aldous Huxley, *1984* by George Orwell, *Masters of Atlantis* by Charles Portis, *Another Roadside Attraction* by Tom Robbins.

Johnny Roselli

△

Sun Valley Retreat

Überfinancier Herb Allen's invitation-only (and until just recently, boys-only) Idaho summer camp, called a "Disneyland for billionaires," for media and communications moguls. Begun in 1982, it's not as private or dark as the **Bohemian Club,** but just as many deals are made here, such as the initial get-together (via **Warren Buffett**) between the heads of Disney, Inc., and Cap Cities/ABC that eventually led to the creation of **Disney/Cap Cities.**

Tavistock Institute

☞ ∽ ⊕

The Third Position

⚱

Time Warner

〰〰 △

Jack Valenti

Often referred to as Hollywood's "little general," since 1966 the diminutive Valenti, a onetime special advisor to **Lyndon Johnson** (LBJ appointed Valenti to the inaugural board of directors of the **Corporation for Public Broadcasting**), has been president of the Motion Picture Association of America, the film industry's self-censoring organization and former stomping grounds of Hollywood's original censor, **Will Hays.** Valenti took the ratings-czar

Sun Valley Attendees

Tom Brokaw, Diane Sawyer, Michael Eisner, **Warren Buffett, Bill Gates,** Barry Diller, **Rupert Murdoch,** David Stern (NBA commissioner), **Sumner Redstone** (Viacom CEO), and Jeff Berg (CEO of International Creative Management).

job after being convinced to do so by **Lew Wasserman.** As one studio head once said, "The MPAA wagged to Lew's desires."

Count Frederick Vanden Heuvel

An **MI6** agent during and after **WWII,** in 1948 the count partnered with Czechoslovakian-born (and future British publishing magnate) **Robert Maxwell** to form Pergamon Press—initially a front for intelligence-gathering on ex-**Nazis.** Some speculate that Katrina Vanden Heuvel, a member of the **Council on Foreign Relations** and editor of *The Nation,* the leftist weekly journal sympathetic to **Jews** and **Communists,** is a distant relative of the count.

Voter News Service

Conceived in 1964, this privately held company, formerly known as News Election Service, counts the votes during presidential elections and is America's only source for election results. It is owned by **ABC, NBC,** and **CBS** in conjunction with the Associated Press and United Press International.

Votescam

The belief that the **CIA** created the **Voter News Service** in order to control the media and control how the public votes, using the election service's easily rigged computers to do so.

The Washington Post

〰️ △

Lew Wasserman

One of the most feared and respected men in Hollywood, and still one of its most powerful (even though he's semiretired and in his eighties). Former president of MCA (the **Music Corporation of America**), which, under his stewardship, grew from a talent agency into a major Hollywood film studio. Earlier, while Wasserman was still an MCA agent, he served as personal advisor to struggling actor **Ronald Reagan.** When Reagan later took over as president of the Screen Actors Guild (SAG), Wasserman persuaded his old client to obtain an unusual waiver, one that freed MCA from the acting union's prohibition against agents simultaneously serving as producers. (In return, Reagan extracted a deal guaranteeing TV residuals for actors.) His friends include Motion Picture Association of

America ratings czar **Jack Valenti** and Hollywood lawyer and labor-dispute "fixer" **Sidney Korshak.** Wasserman also ran Universal Pictures during the 1980s and of late has become a mentor of sorts to new MCA owner, Edgar **Bronfman,** Jr.

Westinghouse

Once a supporter of the now-defunct Fascist **American Liberty League,** this Pittsburgh-based industrial behemoth, when it's not building or managing nuclear reactors and nuclear power plants or figuring out better information and home-security systems, oversees any one of its family of media subsidiaries: **CBS** Radio, CBS Television (*Late Night with David Letterman, 60 Minutes*), Infinity Broadcasting, Telenoticias (a leading Latin American cable and satellite network), or Group W Satellite Communications. **Wackenhut Securities** guards a good number of its nuclear facilities.

Blackout

According to the Code, a Brooklyn, New York–based activist group co-founded by Tupac Shakur, virtually every creative artist of color (from Jimmie Hendrix and Bob Marley to Shakur and Biggie Smalls) have been or are under constant **FBI, CIA, DEA,** and **ATF** surveillance. The Code also says that "the record industry is owned and managed by racist, sexist white men who are driven to realize maximum profit by any means necessary. Therefore, as with Tupac, Biggie, and all of the subsequent young artists, they steal . . . sign and exploit . . . set up fronts as black-owned labels and production companies . . . edit and select material that promotes violence and deprecating video images of women . . . and collaborate with police to frame and arrest young artists who resist to conform to the norm."

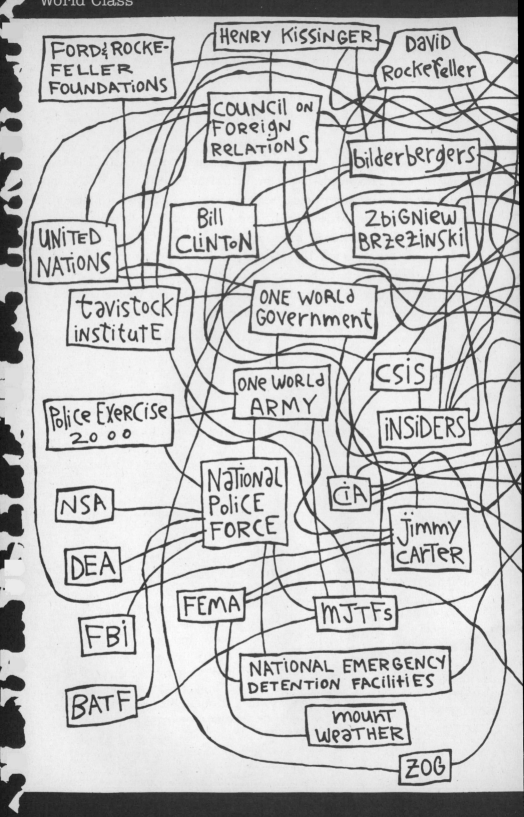

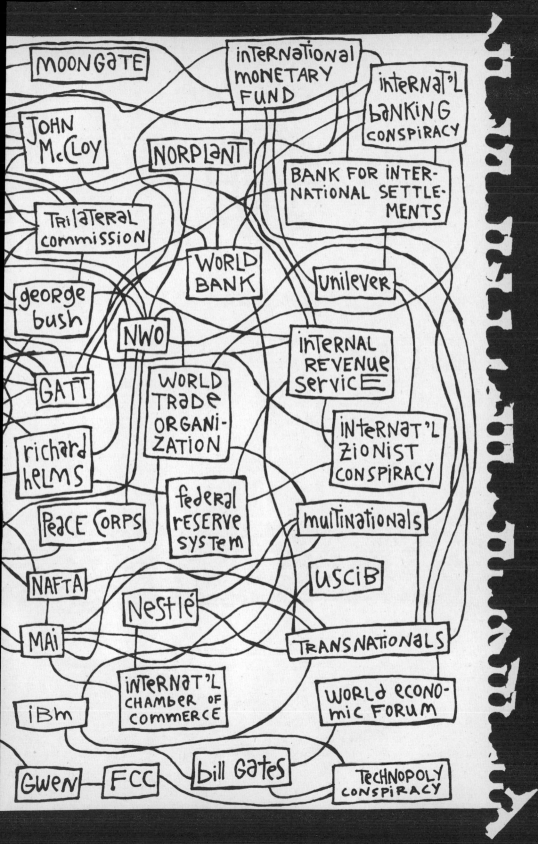

Conspiracy

"World" refers to the Transnational corporations that run the globe—and their backroom organizations, clubs, institutes, think tanks, commissions, and retreats that they—and only they—belong to, and how U.S. leaders kowtow to the demands of these Transnationals (as evidenced by the imminent one world military and one world economy). "Class" refers to the socioeconomic separation between the world's population and that of the CEOs and COOs who collude with and control the Transnationals.

> Quis custodiet ipsos custodes?—Who will observe the observers?
>
> —Sir Arthur Stanley Eddington, quoting Juvenal,
> *The Philosophy of Physical Science* (1958)

Bank for International Settlements

♟ ★ ⛰ 〰

Bilderbergers

✖ ✍

Zbigniew Brzezinski

✍ 〰 ☺

Bureau of Alcohol, Tobacco and Firearms (BATF)

Established in 1972 by the Treasury Department, the BATF enforces federal laws relating to alcohol, tobacco, and firearms and explosives and since 1982 has been responsible for investigating commercial arson. The BATF has had disastrous run-ins with the Militia, notably its 1992 assault on Randy Weaver and his family at Ruby Ridge, Idaho, and also oversaw the 1993 raid on David Koresh's Branch Davidian compound in Waco, Texas, in which four ATF agents and more than eighty Branch Davidians were killed. Both events have inspired resentment and distrust among antigovernment armed Militia groups (as well as leftist ACLU types) and are thought to have led to the 1995 bombing of an Oklahoma City federal building. Part of the proposed **National Police Force.**

George Bush

〰️ △ ✐ ⌖ ♦ ☺ ☼

Jimmy Carter

The aw-shucks Georgia governor handpicked for the U.S. presidency by both the **Council on Foreign Relations** and the **Trilateral Commission.** At their weekend meeting in 1972, the **Bilderbergers** tagged Carter as the 1976 presidential candidate and even supplied him with the list of names who would fill his cabinet. Charter Trilateralist **Zbigniew Brzezinski** was his national security advisor. Carter himself was a Bilderberger, a Trilateralist, and a member of the Council on Foreign Relations. The **Federal Emergency Management Agency** was established during his presidency. Carter had ties to the **BCCI**, the primary money-laundering institution for drug dealers and terrorists worldwide.

Center for Strategic and International Studies (CSIS)

✍

CIA

♏ ★ ✍ ♰ ♨ ☞ 〰️ △ ✐ ⌖ ♦ ☺ ▦ ☉

Bill Clinton

△ ✐ ☺

Council on Foreign Relations

♏ ✍ ∽ ☺

DEA

〰

FBI

♏ ✳ ✝ 🐬 〰 △ ☼ ☉

Federal Communications Commission (FCC)

According to the Militia of Montana, the FCC maintains 150 emergency towers that emit a steady stream of deadly ionospheric radio waves (emissions allegedly responsible for China's rash of earthquakes in the 1970s and the midwest floods of the late 1980s and early 1990s) in the hopes of hastening damage to the world's food crops. The ensuing famine would then create chaos and a power vacuum, laying the groundwork for a **One World Government** and a **NWO** police force.

Federal Emergency Management Agency (FEMA)

Established during the **Carter** administration, primarily as a natural-disaster relief agency and secondarily as a civil defense arm, FEMA was remade by **Reagan** officials (notably **Oliver North**) into a postnuclear-attack contain-and-control bureaucracy. FEMA devised an overarching postapocalyptic readiness plan that included the rounding-up of subversives into national detention centers (the **National Emergency Detention Facilities**), suspension of the U.S. Constitution, war-game exercises (REX 84 ALPHA), declaration of martial law (carried out by State Defense Forces), and construction of an underground command center (FEMA's subterranean bunker in Olney, Maryland). The ominous black choppers have been sighted near FEMA's detention facilities, and some suspect FEMA scripted the 1992 Los Angeles riots as a way to gauge the public's response to gang revolt.

Federal Reserve System

♏ ✡ ✍

Ford and Rockefeller Foundations

✍ 〰 ▦

Bill Gates

❋ ✧ ▦

> When you have problems, there are two approaches. One is to
> try to solve the problem. The other is to find somebody to blame
> for it so you don't have to go to all the trouble of solving the
> problem. . . . That is why there are so many totally nutty con-
> spiracy theories floating around.
>
> —**Robert Anton Wilson,** *Covert Action,* **1998**

General Agreement on Tariffs and Trade (GATT)

Since 1947, this multilateral pact, part of a de facto **One World
Government**—along with the **IMF,** the **World Bank,** the G-7 nations, and the **Transnational Corporations**—has tried to reduce
trade barriers and foster an international exchange of goods. Set up
by members of the **Trilateral Commission,** the **Council on Foreign Relations,** and the **Bilderbergers,** GATT and NAFTA basically have the same goal (benefiting the same folks): Give the
Transnationals easy access to everyone everywhere and usher in the
New World Order. Now known as the **World Trade Organization,**
GATT's about to be one-upped by the **Multilateral Agreement on
Investment.**

GWEN

✧

Richard Helms

✍ 🐾

IBM

✝ ✧

Insiders

✍ △ 〰

327

Internal Revenue Service (IRS)

United States tax-collection agency designed by the **International Bankers** and exploited by the **Trilateralists,** who use the IRS as a tool to tax citizens to death, destroy the U.S. economy, and absorb it into the **New World Order.** A glorified collection agent for the **Federal Reserve,** truly paranoid anti-Semites swear that the IRS is a private Jewish-run corporation and, along with the Federal Reserve and the graduated income tax, is part of the **Zionist Occupied Government.**

International Banking Conspiracy

♏ ✖ ✡ ★ ✍ 〰 ⌦ ☞ ∾ 🕯

International Chamber of Commerce (ICC)

Billing itself as "the world business organization," the ICC has played a major role in the push for the **Multilateral Agreement on Investment**—and hopes, should the MAI eventually become a reality, that it will use the ICC's Court of Arbitration to settle disputes. ICC members include such **Transnationals** as **Dow, GM,** Novartis, and British Petroleum, and the ICC's chairman just happens to be **Nestlé**'s president, Helmut Maucher (who also heads up the European **Round Table**), and its secretary general is, why, looky here, Maria Livanos Cattaui, who developed the Davos, Switzerland, **World Economic Forum.**

International Monetary Fund

★ ∾

International Zionist Conspiracy

♏ ✖ ✳ ✡ ✍ ∾ 🁢

Henry Kissinger

✝ 🐀 ☺

John McCloy

✍

The evidence is now quite strong that we have been invaded by aliens and abductees are subject to their abilities. They have not made formal contact because they did not want to. They have remained secret because they want to. They have been engaging in a systematic physical exploitation of humans because of a specific agenda that advances their designs. Humans do not figure into the equation as partners.

—**David Jacobs, Temple University history professor,**
"UFOs at Fifty: Some Personal Observations," 1997

Moongate

✿ ☉

Mount Weather

Also known as the Western Virginia Office of Controlled Conflict Operations, this mysterious underground military base is carved into a mountain near the town of Bluemont, Virginia, forty-six miles from Washington, D.C. Virtually a self-contained facility, Mount Weather has about a dozen buildings bristling with antennae and microwave relay systems, an on-site sewage-treatment plant, enough water to last some two hundred people more than a month, and a control tower and a helicopter pad near its entry gate. Designed as the self-sustaining underground command center for the **Federal Emergency Management Agency** (FEMA), Mount Weather acts as a hub for approximately one hundred other federal relocation centers, most of which are concentrated in Pennsylvania, West Virginia, Virginia, Maryland, and North Carolina. Together this network of underground facilities constitutes the backbone of America's "Continuity of Government" program. In the event of a nuclear war, declaration of martial law, or other national emergency, the president, his cabinet, and the rest of the executive branch would be "relocated" to Mount Weather.

Multi-Jurisdictional Task Forces (MJTFs)

Basically a national police force, the MJTFs are paramilitary domestic invasion squads that conduct massive military-style raids (most often with the excuse of battling the **War on**

329

Drugs) and are comprised of as many as a dozen different federal, state, and city law-enforcement agencies—the DEA, **FBI, BATF,** National Guard, state patrol, and county and city sheriffs and police. Part of the blame (or foresightedness) for their existence must go to former **LAPD** chief Daryl Gates, who founded the country's first SWAT team back in the midsixties. Responsible for such seemingly unconstitutional assaults on civilians as Operation Redi-Rock, a 1994 blockwide raid in Chapel Hill, North Carolina, in which black people were selectively stopped and searched by gun-toting men in ninja hoods and fatigues, the war games of the MJTFs appear to be but a warm-up, some warn, to a **UN**-sponsored **New World Order/One World Government.** MJTFs were used in the alleged **Tavistock-SRI**-sponsored L.A. riots.

> Other centuries have only dabbled in conspiracy like amateurs. It is our century which has established conspiracy as a system of thought and a method of action.
>
> —Serge Moscovici, "The Conspiracy Mentality" (1987)

Multilateral Agreement on Investment (MAI)

If you've never heard of it, that's because the **Transnationalist Insiders** don't want you to. Deemed by its critics as "**NAFTA** on steroids," this secretive international trade treaty, if it ever passes, would effectively gut labor unions and environmental and consumer protections, as well as undermine health care, human rights, education, and community development. Since 1995, the leading industrialized countries of the Organization for the Economic Cooperation and Development (aka the "rich nation's club") have been hunkered down in Paris putting together this plan. The MAI would grant Transnationals a kind of international statehood, guaranteeing, its member countries hope—er, sorry, its member **Multinationals**—"national treatment" of all foreign-based corporations. And that's merely one of the MAI's many outrageously scary demands.

Multinationals

♍ ✝ △

National Emergency Detention Facilities

These twenty-three national 32,000-to-44,000-person-capacity detention sites were authorized by President **Reagan** for use during a national crisis. Florida's Camp Krone, for example, used in the 1980s to impound thousands of Haitian refugees, is one such facility.

National Police Force

The coming link-up of the **BATF** (Bureau of Alcohol, Tobacco and Firearms), the DEA (Drug Enforcement Administration), the **CIA**, the **FBI**, the **NSA** (National Security Agency), and state and local police, organized by the federal government at the behest of the **UN**, according to those who dread the coming **NWO**. The **NWO**'s leading members in turn only do what the **Insiders** tell them to do—which is work toward the establishment of a **One World Government**.

National Security Agency

☺ ✿

Nestlé

✿

New World Order

♍ ✳ ✍ ∿ ☺

Norplant

Approved by the **FDA** in 1991, Norplant was initially developed by New York's Population Council. Once inserted under a woman's skin, this long-lasting contraceptive (consisting of six matchstick-size flexible tubes containing a synthetic progesterone hormone) lasts for about five years. Norplant testing on women began in 1972 in several developing countries, including Bangladesh, Brazil, Haiti, and Indonesia. Domestically, legislation has been introduced to make Norplant a condition for receipt of public assistance. The **U.S. Agency for International Development** (USAID) provided much of the $20 million in testing expenses. Some feel that the Western introduction of Norplant into third world countries fits right in with the goals of the **Insiders**, the **IMF**, and the **World Bank**, and is but one slippery step closer to a **New World Order**.

Plane Crashes?

On December 8, 1972, United Airlines flight 553 crashes just outside Chicago, killing 43 of its 61 passengers, one of whom was **E. Howard Hunt**'s wife, Dorothy, rumored to have been close to blabbing about that "whole **Bay of Pigs** thing."

The downing of Korean Airlines flight 007 might have been the result of Company tampering. When a Soviet fighter jet shot down the plane on September 1, 1983, killing all 269 aboard, it may not have been the simple act of naked Soviet aggression the U.S. government and western media said it was. According to one conspiranoiac, the **CIA,** with the **Reagan** administration's influence and blessing, coerced the plane's pilot to steer his civilian craft into sensitive Soviet air space, hoping that this would set off the Soviet defense system (thereby allowing the CIA to study it). Unfortunately, it backfired—but only partially, since right after the shoot-down, approval for Reagan's stalled proposal for the new MX missile was passed by Congress. Another theory has it that the civilian plane was gunned down by the Soviet fighter jet in order to permanently silence U.S. congressman Larry McDonald (of Georgia), the real target of the attack. McDonald, it turns out, had long harangued the **Insiders** and the members of the **International Banking Conspiracy** and was on the verge of blowing open their connections to Moscow and all those plans for a **New World Order**.

Some theories have it that when army major Charles McKee and four **CIA** agents (who'd possibly just negotiated an arms-for-hostages-and-drugs deal, as part of the **Iran-Contra** web) found out that an "off-the-shelf" CIA unit was protecting **Monzer Al-Kassar**'s unauthorized Middle East drug runs, on December 24, 1988, the five unwittingly boarded Al-Kassar's usual drug-run flight, Pan Am 103 in Frankfurt. The New York–bound 747, returning from Lebanon, exploded over Lockerbie, Scotland, killing 259 people.

On July 17, 1996, TWA flight 800 went down off Long Island on its way to Paris, killing all 230 people onboard. The National Transportation Safety Board blamed the crash on an explosion in the center fuel tank, but Elaine Scarry, in the venerable *New York Review of Books* no less, has speculated that it may have been **Electromagnetic Radiation** that brought down the 747.

North American Free Trade Agreement (NAFTA)

The attempt to eliminate all trade barriers in North America and create a common market among the United States, Canada, and Mexico. Negotiations for NAFTA began in 1990 and went into effect on January 1, 1994. Under its provisions, all barriers to trade in goods and services from the Yukon to Yucatán are to be phased out over fifteen years. As conspiranoiac critic Noam Chomsky says, "It's not free, it's not about trade, and it's not based on an agreement."

One World Army

The coming army of the imminent **One World Government**'s **New World Order** but still a not-yet-recognizable (or even yet totally assembled) **Transnational** military organization that would combine the defense forces of the United States's **National Police Force** (**FBI, BATF,** et al.) and those of other world governments, and that would carry out the orders of the **UN,** which in turn would answer to the demands of the **Insiders**.

One World Government

♏ ✡ ✍ ∾

Peace Corps

Sent forth into the third world in 1961 by **JFK** as his "goodwill ambassadors," only to be exploited by the **CIA** as an excellent cover job. The Peace Corps's mission used to mean improvement of a host country's agricultural and health-related conditions and lifting up its poor and disadvantaged. Today, the third world oddly includes the Czech and Slovak Federal Republics, Poland, and Hungary. A training ground for future **New World Order** drones, the corps drills its third world subjects in the little Fortune 500, Forbes-friendly things such as speaking English like a corporate bureaucrat, focusing on business skills, and getting into lockstep with the Western-style political and socioeconomic ideology. All of which are main ingredients for a seat at the NWO table. The corps was expelled by Bolivia and Peru in the 1970s for its alleged sterilization of peasant women without their knowledge.

Police Exercise 2000

333

Worldwide military-personnel war games hosted by the state of Alaska in 1992. The 1991 Brandt Commission referred to the

Police Exercise 2000 maneuvers as a possible future world government with "supranational authority" and an "international police [force] to enforce the edicts of the new world order."

David Rockefeller

✍ ∞

Tavistock Institute

⌖ ∞ ▦

Technopoly Conspiracy

♍ ∞ ✧

Transnationals

♍ ✝ ✧

Trilateral Commission

♍ ✍ ∞ ☺

Unilever

∞

United Nations

♍ ✡ ✍ ∞

U.S. Council for International Business (USCIB)

Founded in 1945 "to promote an open system of world trade, investment and finance," the USCIB not only hopes the **MAI** passes (since it helped put the MAI together), it hopes that the MAI will eliminate, according to one USCIB official, "many of the restrictions which make it too costly for U.S. firms to access foreign markets." USCIB member firms include Chevron, **Du Pont**, Coca-Cola, **GE, GM, Ford,** and McDonald's.

World Bank

This Washington, D.C.—based world lending institution was founded in 1945, purportedly to dole out long-term loans to "developing" countries. Instead, it strongarms the third world into sociopolitically disastrous austerity and privatization programs, basically acting as bill collector for the **Transnational Corporations.** Headed by Robert McNamara from 1968 to 1981, the World Bank is now under the aegis of former **International Banker** James

Wolfensohn (a member of the **Bilderbergers** and the **Council on Foreign Relations,** the onetime CEO of the **J. Henry Schröder Banking Corporation,** and a **CBS** director) and it often plays a kind of good cop—bad cop routine with the **IMF** when dealing with cash-strapped countries. Its 1950s support of hydroelectric dams inflicted huge environmental damage (and created virtually no profits), and in Indonesia, World Bank—funded projects have led to the forcible displacement of millions of Javanese peasants, the deaths of hundreds of thousands in East Timor, and the razing of millions of acres of rain forest.

World Economic Forum

✍ ✝

World Trade Organization (WTO)

Born on January 1, 1995, right after the **GATT** global free-trade agreement in 1994, the WTO has the power to remove obstacles to trade. Participating governments have also granted it the power to judge whether another country's economic laws are barriers to open trade or not.

Zionist Occupied Government

✡

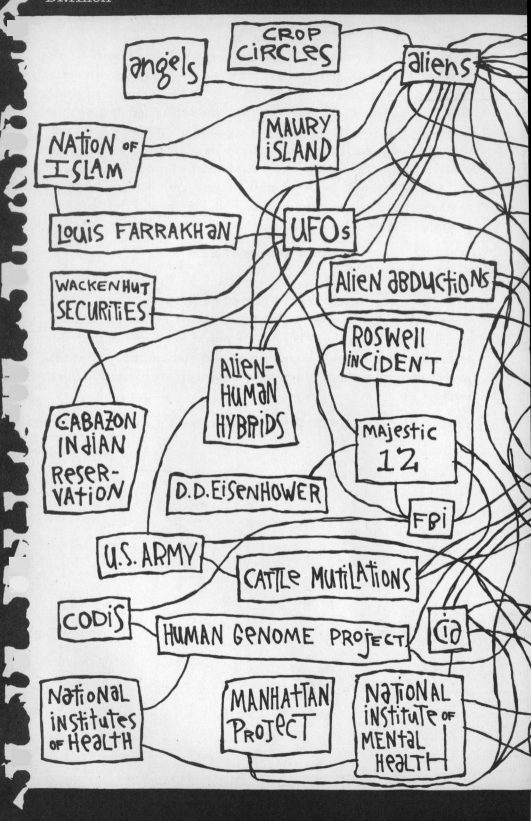

The DNAlien

Conspiracy

The Aliens are coming! The Aliens are coming! No, wait. They're already here!

The absence of evidence is not evidence of absence.

—Participant at the 1992 MIT conference on alien abductions

Alien Abductions

Unproven phenomenon of humans being kidnapped by **Aliens** and sometimes experimenting upon them in sadistic ways. Some abductees say that their otherworldly captors are snatching humans in order to monitor our reactions to things like nuclear fallout. Abductees (and **UFO**logists in general) received a generous shot of respectability in 1994 when Harvard psychiatry professor John Mack published *Abduction,* his study of the phenomenon (Mack, say some conspiranoiacs, had once served on cult leader Werner Erhard's EST board).

Alien-Human Hybrids

The claim, among certain abductees and their advocates, that the **Aliens** are using us for interbreeding; or that they're hybridizing us with cows—citing the odd and disturbing fact that cow plasma has been approved by the **U.S. Army** for emergency battlefield transfusions.

Aliens

♍ ✗ ☀ ⚸ ♒

Angels

In bestselling paranormal author Whitley Strieber's universe, **Aliens** are actually angels descending upon us with spiritual messages, while Swiss psychiatrist Carl Jung long ago referred to **UFOs** as "technological angels."

Area 51

Aka Dreamland and S-4, this secretive military enclosure is guarded by **Wackenhut Securities** and located on a swath of desert in Nevada (just north of Sin City) and has long been used by the U.S. Air Force to test out experimental planes and other new aircraft. Area 51 is now world famous as a hot spot for spying **UFOs** and **Aliens,** who are rumored to be living and working in a vast subterranean Alien village, or maybe they're being kept in air force—built bases down the road from State Route 375, aka the Extraterrestrial Highway. Black choppers, those unmarked black-on-black helicopters frequently spotted near **Cattle Mutilations,** UFO sightings, and **Alien Abductions,** and reputedly a form of transport for the infamous **Men in Black,** have also been spotted near Area 51.

> *I believe there is a machinery of mass manipulation behind the UFO phenomenon.* It aims at social and political goals by diverting attention from some human problems and by providing a potential release for tensions caused by others. The contactees are a part of that machinery. *They are helping to create a new form of belief.*
>
> —Jacques Vallee, *Messengers of Deception* (1979)

The Aviary

A disinformation unit within the U.S. Air Force, dispatched to **UFO** contactees, conventions, and enthusiasts (and sometimes working from within UFO groups like MUFON and NICAP) with the purpose of discrediting serious UFO/**Alien** research—paradoxically, the Aviary does so by often touting the most outlandish of UFO/Alien stories. Aviary agents go by appropriately birdlike code names—Falcon, Condor, Bluejay, and Morning

339

Dove—and are also said to be comprised of **Scientologists** and agents from the **FBI** and **CIA**.

Babylon Working

A bizarre rite first dreamed up by occult master **Aleister Crowley** and later enacted by his protégés and fellow occult enthusiasts **L. Ron Hubbard** and **John Whiteside Parsons.** The Working's goal was to unlock a kind of interdimensional portal and establish contact with the Supreme Beings who lie on the other side and maybe even bring them over to our universe. In 1947, Hubbard and Parsons reenacted Crowley's Working, perhaps succeeding in ushering in the Old Ones and the Spirit Guides (while ushering out Crowley, who died that year) and perhaps even bringing with them **UFOs, Aliens,** Bigfoot (the mythical big hairy creature of the world's forests), the goatsucking Chupacabra of Puerto Rico, and the Loch Ness Monster, the mythical serpentine Scottish lake—dwelling creature. After all, 1947 was the year all these beings first officially showed up on the planet.

Black Lodge

ʄ

Brotherhood of the Snake

A prehistoric serpent-loving cult dating back to 3400 B.C. Some theorize that they were originally founded in order to free earthlings from the "custodians"—i.e., the **Aliens.** Unfortunately, the Alien-custodians impersonated their way into, and to the top of, the brotherhood, and today these unearthly agents go from secret society to secret society, manipulating current events.

Cabazon Indian Reservation

☺

Cattle Mutilations

A bizarre western-U.S. phenomenon of dead cows that have been mysteriously cut into with scarily surgical precision and whose carcasses are often totally devoid of blood. Some **Alien Abductees** say that it's the **Aliens** who're mutilating bovines—in order to assess the effects of nuclear fallout on the Earth's food chain. Black choppers have often been reported seen near these sites.

CIA

♍ ★ ⚶ ✝ 🏠 🐾 ♒ △ ▱ ☙ ⚱ 😊 🔲 🌐

CODIS

✸

Crop Circles

Mysterious Mayan- or Incan- or Aztec-style designs cut into the crops and fields of farmers worldwide—some say the circles are either the after-landing and after-takeoff impressions left by **Alien** spaceships or they're the huge beacons left by earthbound Aliens as messages to their **UFO** mother ships.

Dagobert II

✖

Dalai Lama

⚱ ✝ ☙ ♾

Dwight D. Eisenhower

🏠

Electromagnetic Radiation

✸

Louis Farrakhan

△

FBI

♍ ✳ ✝ 🐾 ♒ △ ✸ 🌐

God

♍ ✖ ✳ ⚱

HAARP

✸

Heaven's Gate

☙

L. Ron Hubbard

♒ ☙

Human Genome Project

☼

Internet

∾ ∿ ☼

Jesus Christ

♍ ✖ ✳ ∾ ⸸

Los Alamos National Laboratory

☼

Majestic-12 (MJ-12)

A nineteen-person cabal comprised of military brass, intelligence agents, and academics (like its most infamous reputed member, **Manhattan Project** physicist and **Bohemian Club**ster Ed Teller, the "father of the hydrogen bomb"), assembled by the U.S. Air Force, who gathered together to cover up the 1947 **Roswell Incident.** The "for your eyes only" briefing they prepared for President **Eisenhower** described the discovery at the New Mexico crash site of four EBEs ("extraterrestrial biological entities"). Two of the **Aliens** were found deceased, the other two were subdued and spirited off (with help from the **FBI**) to the lab at **Los Alamos** for testing. More recently, MJ-12 has been suspected of tampering with the **Human Genome Project,** in hopes that the project might reveal new possibilities for **Biochemical Warfare.**

Manhattan Project

🦎 ☼

It is really going to be interesting to see when the official mainstream, the small percentage of elites that determine what we are supposed to think is real, wake up to the fact that the consensus view of reality is gone.

—John Mack, Harvard psychiatrist and author of *Abduction*, 1996

Maury Island

This island in the Puget Sound in Washington was the site of a supposed dumping of metallic waste by a **UFO** on June 21, 1947 (thirteen days before the **Roswell Incident**), qualifying it as the modern
world's first "authenticated" UFO sighting. Supposedly caught on
film by Harold Dahl, who reported his experience to former **OSS**
agent, Fred Lee Crisman.

Men in Black

Merovingians

Microwave Radiation Transmission

Mind Control

Moongate

NASA

Nation of Islam

National Institute of Mental Health

National Institutes of Health

New Age

Pathfinder

Pentagon

Radio Shack

✸

RAND Corporation

✍ △ ∞ ✸

> The aliens who are here now are just the forerunners for a much larger group, and that group's arrival is expected within the next four years. The government hopes to avoid worldwide panic by preparing us through advertising and entertainment media for our encounter with alien beings.

—Karla Turner, *Into the Fringe: A True Story of Alien Abduction*, 1992

The Roswell Incident

The government claims that the infamous July 2, 1947, saucer crash in the New Mexican desert (right after the **Maury Island** sighting) was just an experimental weather balloon (complete with dummies) that fell to Earth that day. **UFO**logists maintain that an **Alien** spaceship mistakenly landed in Roswell with at least one injured little green guy on board. The U.S. Air Force then allegedly dispatched a secret unit to the site hours after the crash, a group known as **Majestic-12,** who, with help from the **FBI,** stole the spaceship and spirited away the dead and injured Aliens north to **Los Alamos National Laboratory.** There, the FBI dissected the Aliens and shipped off their saucer to

Project Sign/Grudge/Blue Book

A U.S. Air Force program begun in 1947—right after the **Roswell Incident**—to investigate **UFO**s. The government's thinking, back then, was that UFOs were more likely **Communist** invaders than extraterrestrial visitors. By the early 1950s, however, the project (now code-named Blue Book) had morphed into a Gaslight-style propaganda campaign to discredit UFOs as **Aliens** and underreport the number of sightings in general.

a secret hangar at Ohio's Wright-Patterson Air Force Base. Roswell is also the birthplace of Demi Moore, star of supernatural films like *Ghost* and *The Seventh Sign*—coincidence? Or genetics?

Scientology

☞ ⋙ ⋘ ∾

Search for Extraterrestrial Intelligence (SETI)

Originally funded by **NASA**, SETI scientists continue to bombard and monitor the cosmos with and for various radio transmissions, hoping to contact other life forms (**Aliens**). Abandoned financially by **NASA** several years ago, SETI now receives much of its funding from Intel cofounder Gordon Moore, David Packard of **Hewlett-Packard,** and Microsoft cofounder and oddball billionaire Paul Allen. Harvard, too, home to **Alien Abduction** professor John Mack, also has its own SETI program. Begun informally in 1960 by West Virginia scientist Dr. Frank Drake, SETI now operates as an international exchange with the name Project Phoenix, under the direction of Drake and Jill Tarter (who served as the model for Jodie Foster's character in *Contact*).

Temple of Set

∾

John Tesh

∾

> Do not discount what I and other abductees are reporting simply because your mind will not allow you to believe there is a connection between some members of our government and some of the aliens. Do not discount what I am reporting because you automatically lump all such information into your government conspiracy category. I am not a government agent disseminating disinformation. . . . I have to remain open to the idea, although it is *extremely* difficult for me, that our government may in fact be trading alien technology for genetic material, or at least is aware of what is being done to us and has chosen to look the other way.
>
> —Katharina Wilson, *The Alien Jigsaw*, 1993

UFOs

U.S. Army

Vatican

Wackenhut Securities

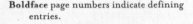

Index